HEDGE FUND ALPHA
A Framework for Generating
and Understanding Investment Performance

To Roman,

Best of luck with
your future investments,

John

HEDGE FUND ALPHA

A Framework for Generating and Understanding Investment Performance

Editor

JOHN M LONGO
Rutgers University, USA

World Scientific

NEW JERSEY · LONDON · SINGAPORE · BEIJING · SHANGHAI · HONG KONG · TAIPEI · CHENNAI

Published by

World Scientific Publishing Co. Pte. Ltd.

5 Toh Tuck Link, Singapore 596224

USA office: 27 Warren Street, Suite 401-402, Hackensack, NJ 07601

UK office: 57 Shelton Street, Covent Garden, London WC2H 9HE

British Library Cataloguing-in-Publication Data
A catalogue record for this book is available from the British Library.

ISBN-13 978-981-283-465-2
ISBN-10 981-283-465-6

Printed in Singapore by World Scientific Printers

To my son Tyler, the highlight of my life.

PREFACE

Ten years ago, there were relatively few books about the hedge fund industry. The dearth of prior material may be related to the notoriously secretive nature of hedge funds and to a much smaller asset base relative to the roughly $2 trillion that they control today. At present, there are quite a few good books on hedge funds, but they appear to be clustered around

a handful of subtopics. The topics mostly include interviews with successful hedge fund managers, general discussions of hedge fund strategies, and "how to start a hedge fund" books primarily intended for aspiring hedge funds managers. As someone who works in the hedge fund / investment management business and teaches an MBA class on the topic, I perceived a significant gap within the literature. Few books created a framework for generating superior risk adjusted returns, or **alpha**, and for growing the hedge fund management company in an intelligent manner. These topics are what most hedge fund professionals care greatly about.

The following questions came to my mind as I began to formulate the material for this book:

- How does hedge fund research differ from traditional "long only" research despite their common goal of achieving alpha?
- What is the best way of executing various hedge fund strategies in order to turn *expected* returns into real profits?
- What hedge fund strategies are best suited to earning alpha in emerging markets, arguably the most fertile investment frontier for the decades ahead?
- What is the typical lifecycle of a hedge fund strategy?

- What is an intelligent method for evolving from a single strategy fund to a multistrategy fund (or series of funds)?
- What is a rigorous approach for conducting due diligence on a hedge fund?
- Can understanding the psychological aspects of hedge fund managers help explain their actions and performance?
- "Hedge fund risk management" seems to be somewhat an oxymoron given many recent high profile failures, but is there any value that can be added to this topic?
- Is there a systematic approach for managing a successful fund of fund?
- What are the current trends and future outlook for the hedge fund industry?

These and other questions served as the basis for the chapters in this book. Although some of the topics may appear somewhat disjointed and the flow is not as smooth as I would like it to be, they all coalesce around two points: (a framework for) **generating** and **understanding alpha**. Hence the title of this book.

I felt I had the outline for a strong book, but faced a problem. How could I credibly talk about generating alpha in China, for example, if I could not read or speak (Mandarin) Chinese? I have been to China more than a dozen times in the past decade, totaling nearly six months of time, but felt that someone who knew the culture intimately and was fluent in Chinese could do a better job than me alone. That is when I decided to find outside authors and co-authors to write portions of this book.

I found additional inspiration in one of the best books, in my opinion, ever written on hedge funds entitled, *Hedge Funds: Investment and Portfolio Strategies for the Institutional Investor* by Lederman and Klein. Their book also utilized outside experts for selected chapters.

One reviewer on Amazon.com said of the Lederman and Klein book:

> "The list of books written on hedge funds is a short one, and this book is certainly the finest on the subject. The professionals who contributed their specialized knowledge are of the highest caliber, and better yet, many of them can

be reached for counsel... I found all of the information to be useable and valuable information with absolutely no filler."

Similarly, my goal also is to produce a high quality and practical book with no filler. The primary target audience of this book is those working in the (broadly defined) hedge fund industry, and those contemplating the launch of their own hedge fund. Others, such as securities analysts, regulators, academics, students, and investors, may also find significant value in the material. The chapters are largely self-contained, resulting in some repetition, but also increased convenience for those readers only interested in particular topics.

First, I would like to thank my co-authors of this book, Jorge Barreiro, Erman Civelek, Mitchell Eichen, Jeffrey Glattfelder, Ali Jaffery, Sanjeev Khullar, Yaxuan Qi, Saad Rathore, Irina Samoylova, Wei-Kang Shih, Ben Sopranzetti, and Stephen Spence. Without them this book would not be possible. Second, I would like to thank my colleagues at Rutgers Business School, The MDE Group, and DealMaven / FactSet for their support. DealMaven, acquired by FactSet in January 2008, provided a grant to Rutgers Business School in partial support of this work. I would also like to thank Sheshang Patel, Rahat Azim, and Lim Shujuan for valuable research and editing assistance. Special thanks to Lorraine Fedor for contributing the artwork used for the book cover. Last, but not least, I would like to thank my entire family for their love and support.

John. M. Longo, PhD, CFA
Rutgers Business School
Department of Finance & Economics
New Brunswick, NJ

CONTENTS

Part II: Understanding Performance

Appendices

Index

AUTHOR BIOGRAPHICAL SKETCHES

Jorge Barreiro

Jorge is an analyst in the CFC Strategic Finance Group at Duff & Phelps, a financial advisory and investment banking firm. A graduate of Rutgers Business School, with double majors in Finance and Economics, he was a member of the winning team in the 2008 New York Society of Securities Analysts (NYSSA) Investment Research Challenge. Jorge is fluent in the Portuguese language.

Erman Civelek, CFA, CFP®

Erman is a Vice President and Investment Strategist at The MDE Group, Inc. The MDE Group has been ranked as the fourth best independent registered investment advisor (RIA) in the U.S. by *Barron's* in 2006 and 2007. He is responsible for performing fundamental and technical analysis on investment managers and the financial markets. In his role he has developed his abilities in the areas of manager evaluation, performance/risk analysis, and asset allocation. Erman's expertise is focused on alternative asset class strategies and is applied through the development and maintenance of MDE's quantitative and qualitative manager due diligence process for evaluating investment managers. Erman graduated summa cum laude with a BA in Economics from Rutgers College where he was a member of Phi Beta Kappa, beginning in his junior year.

Mitchell Eichen, J.D., LL.M.

Mitch is the founder and CEO of The MDE Group, Inc. and he is responsible for the firm's strategic vision. The MDE Group has been ranked the fourth best independent registered investment advisor (RIA) in the U.S. by *Barron's* in 2006 and 2007. As Chief Wealth Strategist, Mitch also focuses his unique interdisciplinary knowledge of financial planning, income tax and estate tax law, and investments to develop innovative and creative ideas for clients. Mitch enjoys writing and lecturing on a variety of financial topics. He is also a member of the Financial Advisory Board to the Rutgers Graduate School of Business. Mitch has an LL.M. in Taxation from the New York University School of Law (Graduate Division) and a J.D. from Georgetown University Law Center. He graduated magna cum laude with a B.A. in economics from Rutgers College where he was a member of Phi Beta Kappa.

Jeffrey Glattfelder, CFA, CAIA

Jeff is currently a product manager for Citigroup's Global Wealth Management unit, focusing on funds of hedge funds. Jeff has over 20 years of experience in the financial services industry, including product development, quantitative research, portfolio management and institutional client service roles. Jeff is a Chartered Financial Analyst, Chartered Alternative Investment Analyst, and a member of the Alternative Investment Committee of the New York Society of Security Analysts.

Ali Jaffery

Ali is an analyst with Aeneas Capital Advisors, an emerging markets hedge fund. Prior to Aeneas, Ali worked as a commercial banker. He has spent several years in the Middle East and Pakistan and now resides in New York. Ali has a Bachelor of Science degree in Economics from the Lahore University of Management Sciences in Pakistan and an MBA from Rutgers Business School.

Sanjeev Khullar

Sanjeev Khullar is Managing Director at Auriga Partners LLC, a money management firm, and the Founder of TradeGames.com, a financial analytics company. Over the years, he has served as senior advisor to hedge funds and financial institutions, providing trading, risk and portfolio solutions to both buy and sell-side firms. His assignments have often been at Board level and have included valuing multi-billion dollar subprime / derivatives portfolios, developing pricing models for clearinghouses and energy traders, creating high-alpha strategies for hedge funds, assisting liquidators and investors with discovery stemming from the collapse of high-profile funds, and integrating BlackRock, APT, Barra and Intex into the largest trading desks in the world. He previously headed all derivatives trading for Nomura Capital's North America trading operations, with $500 billion notional in swaps, options, mortgage derivatives, and dollar and non-dollar exotics. Sanjeev has an MBA from Harvard Business School, an MS in Computer Science from UW-Madison, and a B.Tech. in Electrical Engineering from the Indian Institute of Technology- Kanpur.

John Longo, PhD, CFA

Dr. Longo is Clinical Associate Professor of Finance at the Rutgers Business School, Senior Vice President of Investment Strategy and Chairman of the seven-person Investment Committee for The MDE Group, Inc. The MDE Group has been ranked as the fourth best independent registered investment advisor (RIA) in the U.S. by *Barron's* in 2006 and 2007. He has lectured around the world on a variety of financial related topics and has served as a consultant for numerous financial and technology firms. He serves on the Editorial Board of *The Investment Professional*, the flagship publication of The New York Society of Security Analysts. Previously, he was a Vice President at Merrill Lynch & Co., Inc. He holds PhD, MBA, and BA degrees from Rutgers University.

Yaxuan Qi, PhD

Yaxuan Qi is Assistant Professor of Finance at the John Molson School of Business at the Concordia University, and a Junior Research Professor in Mathematical Finance at the Institut de finance mathematique de Montreal. She received her Ph.D. in 2007 from Rutgers Business School. She obtained a B.A in Economics from the Central University of Finance & Economics in Beijing in 1998, and a M.A. in Finance from the Renmin University of China in 2001. Her main research area is Portfolio Choice and Asset Pricing, with a growing interest in Law and Finance.

Saad Rathore

Mr. Rathore is the founder of Algorithmic Capital Markets (ACM) — a company he started while attending Rutgers University. Mr. Rathore's earliest career foray was at Tradescape Inc where he was an equities trader and helped the founder plan future business objectives in entrepreneurial settings. Tradescape was sold to E*Trade. Mr. Rathore proceeded to work at the Merrill Lynch Global Research department where he worked with a top ranked *Institutional Investor* team. Subsequently, Mr. Rathore worked as an equity / portfolio research analyst for Philippe Investment Management and at a large, highly successful hedge fund. In 2001, Mr. Rathore launched a short term automated equity fund using expert systems and started developing and researching execution algorithms. ACM set up a research department and a software unit to help analyze such strategies including risk management for short term and long term investment strategies. ACM also started developing execution algorithms and software for execution sensitive clients. ACM acts in the capacity of lead risk modeler and developer for partner firm, RiskResources Inc., which serves a combined capital base of approximately $30 billion.

Irina Samoylova

Irina Samoylova is an analyst at Goldman Sachs & Co. She graduated from the Rutgers Business School with a B.S. degree in Finance. Irina was born and raised in Russia where she received an Associate Degree in Business Management from Pyatigorsk State Linguistic University. Irina completed a comprehensive independent research project on hedge funds in Russia and Eastern Europe during her Senior year at Rutgers. She was named a member of Phi Theta Kappa and served as VP of Finance for one of its chapters, Alpha Pi Theta. Irina was also admitted to The Honor Society of the New Jersey Collegiate Business Administration Association.

Wei-Kang Shih

Wei-Kang Shih is a Ph.D Candidate in Finance & Economics at Rutgers Business School. Mr. Shih's research interests include asset pricing theory, financial accounting, hedge funds, and investment analysis. His current research focuses on the effect of earnings management and its implications on asset pricing. Prior to joining the Rutgers Business School, Mr. Shih worked for a venture capital firm in Taiwan.

Ben Sopranzetti, PhD

Professor Ben Sopranzetti, Associate Professor of Finance & Economics at the Rutgers Business School, is an internationally renowned expert in the area of Valuation, Financial Strategy, and Investor Psychology. His most recent research interests lie primarily in the areas of Investment Banking and Emerging Financial Markets, especially China. He has written several papers in the area of Banking and Real Estate. Professor Sopranzetti has deep ties to industry and places over thirty students a year on Wall Street. He serves on several corporate boards and is a highly-regarded consultant to several bulge-bracket Wall Street investment banks. He has published in the *Journal of Business*, *Journal of Finance*, and the *Journal of Financial and Quantitative Analysis* among others. Professor Sopranzetti is widely recognized as a master teacher, and is the recipient of eight awards for excellence in teaching.

Author Biographical Sketches

Stephen Spence, CFA, CAIA

Steve is the Director of Quantitative Analysis of Terrapin Asset Management, LLC, a fund of hedge funds based in New York City. Prior to joining Terrapin, Mr. Spence spent 16 years with Merrill Lynch, where he served as a Director in the Management Science Group. This group supported strategic decision-making in complex business situations through the use of quantitative modeling and analysis. Mr. Spence led initiatives to improve clients' investment returns by developing quantitative equity portfolios and performance measurement systems. Mr. Spence is a Chartered Financial Analyst and received an MS in Operations Research from Case Western Reserve University, an MBA from Rutgers University and a BS in Mathematics from Bucknell University.

PART I

GENERATING PERFORMANCE

1

INTRODUCTION

John M. Longo, PhD, CFA

Rutgers Business School & The MDE Group, Inc.

1.1 Hedge Fund History and Evolution

1.1.1 Hedge Fund Defined

There is no uniformly accepted definition of a hedge fund. Many hedge funds today have no true hedge at all, rather they increase risk through leverage, concentration, and by trading in illiquid assets. In this book, we define a hedge fund as a private investment vehicle that charges an incentive fee and (almost always) an asset based fee. This broad definition would also include private equity funds and real estate partnerships that are not generally considered hedge funds. However, we will note in Chapter 15, that a current and future trend is the convergence among many alternative investments and the firms that manage them.

1.1.2 The First Hedge Fund

It is generally reported that A. W. Jones set up the first hedge fund in 1949. Under our definition of hedge funds, there are others that preceded Jones. I had the great pleasure of leading a group of forty Rutgers Business School students on a trip to visit Warren Buffett at his Berkshire Hathaway offices in 2006. Buffett mentioned that he believed

3

Benjamin Graham operated the first hedge fund since Graham's partnership utilized long and short positions and charged an incentive fee. Graham's partnership, formed in 1926 with Jerome Newman, included a number of hedged and unhedged strategies, such as convertible arbitrage and distressed securities. Over time it evolved to an approach that was primarily net long with a Value bias, while Jones's partnership was more dynamic in its use of leverage and short selling.

There were likely to be several trading and commodity pools in operation before Graham-Newman, some of which are noted in the classic trading tome, *Reminiscences of a Stock Operator*. However, until detailed evidence of their operations comes to light, I would agree with Buffett's belief that Graham-Newman operated the first hedge fund.

1.1.3 Evolution of the Hedge Fund Market

1.1.3.1 Billion Dollar Paychecks Attract the "Best and Brightest"

Hedge funds gained a fair amount of notoriety in the 1960's, subsequent to an article on A. W. Jones by Loomis (1966). In my opinion, two significant events propelled the hedge fund industry to where it is today as one of the hottest areas of finance. First, George Soros' Quantum Fund reportedly earned more than $1 billion in a single day on September 16, 1992 by shorting the British Pound in advance of the United Kingdom's withdrawal from the European Exchange Rate Mechanism. Soros, dubbed as "The Man Who Broke the Bank of England," became a superstar in financial circles. Eventually, Soros himself did earn more than a billion dollars in a single year. Until that time, most Wall Street professionals did not realize that nine and ten figure paychecks for a single year were possible. Of course they were aware of the rise and fall of Michael Milken in the junk bond market, but virtually creating a new market (i.e. a somewhat liquid and broad high yield bond market) from scratch is beyond the realm of most financial professionals.

Amazingly, there are practically no requirements needed to start a hedge fund. If you can raise capital then you are essentially in business for the *short-term*. In the long run, your fund needs good absolute or risk adjusted returns in order to have a viable business. Hedge fund manager compensation in recent years has continued to skyrocket. **Table 1** lists the compensation of the ten highest paid hedge fund managers in 2007, according to *Alpha*. Incredibly, John Paulson earned a reported *$3.7 billion* in 2007, due in part to shorting subprime securities through leveraged derivatives.

Table 1: Highest Paid Hedge Fund Managers, 2007

Name	Firm	2007 Compensation
John Paulson	Paulson & Co.	$3.7 Billion
George Soros	Soros Fund Management	$2.9 Billion
James Simons	Renaissance Technologies Corp.	$2.8 Billion
Philip Falcone	Harbinger Capital Partners	$1.7 Billion
Kenneth Griffin	Citadel Investment Group	$1.5 Billion
Steven Cohen	SAC Capital Advisors	$0.9 Billion
Timothy Barakett	Atticus Capital	$0.8 Billion
Stephen Mandel, Jr.	Lone Pine Capital	$0.7 Billion
John Griffin	Blue Ridge Capital	$0.6 Billion
O. Andreas Halvorsen	Viking Global Investors	$0.5 Billion

Source: *Alpha*, April 2008

1.1.3.2 Hedge Funds Outperform During 2000–2002 Bear Market

The second key event that may have spurred the exponential growth of the hedge fund industry was the bear market in U.S. equities of 2000–2002. Hedge fund returns were nominally positive, while U.S. equities experienced double-digit losses for three consecutive years. These results are shown in **Table 2** below. Value stocks, once thought to provide strong downside protection in the event of a bear market, were also hammered in 2002, losing 15.5% of their capital.

Table 2: Hedge Fund and U.S. Stock Market Performance, 2000–2002

Year	CS Tremont HF Index	S&P 500	Russell 1000 Growth	Russell 1000 Value
2000	4.85%	-9.10%	-22.42%	7.01%
2001	4.42%	-11.90%	-20.42%	-5.59%
2002	3.04%	-22.10%	-27.88%	-15.52%

Source: CS Tremont, Morningstar Principia

Hedge funds were virtually the only asset class, with equity exposure, that appeared to keep investors' heads above water. Institutional investors with significant allocations to alternative investments, such as David Swenson of Yale, were viewed as brilliant and therefore had their investment philosophies followed by an increasing number of foundations, endowments, pension funds, and family offices.

1.1.3.3 Other Notable Hedge Fund Events

Other notable hedge fund related events include the spectacular blowups of Long Term Capital Management, expertly chronicled in Lowenstein (2001), and Amaranth Advisors. The failure of Long Term Capital leaves an enduring lesson to be learned for all investors. Namely, the smartest people on earth can lose virtually all of their investor's capital when untimely market movements are combined with excessive leverage and illiquid underlying financial assets. The Amaranth failure cast doubt on the superiority of the multistrategy approach, relative to a fund of funds strategy, and resulted in many hedge funds revisiting their risk management systems.

On February 9, 2007, Fortress Investments Group (FIG) became the first publicly traded hedge fund management company in the U.S. FIG started strong, closing its first day at $31.50 per share, up 67.6% from its $18.50 per share offering price. In late October 2008, FIG was trading at roughly $4.90 per share in the aftermath of the subprime fallout and unraveling of the credit bubble. Other publicly traded hedge fund management companies, such as Och-Ziff Capital Management Group

(OZM), have thus far experienced disappointing returns since their initial public offerings (IPOs).

The global bear market of 2008 is shaping up to be the worst year ever for hedge funds, with most broad indexes down close to 20% at the end of October. Clearly, many funds will have to shut down since they will not be able to cover their operating expenses due to a lack of incentive fees. In Chapter 15, we discuss trends in the hedge fund industry and hedge fund performance in 2008, and the fallout from Bernard Madoff's alleged Ponzi scheme, will surely accelerate these trends.

1.2 Types of Hedge Funds

There are dozens of hedge fund strategies and they often don't fall neatly into a single category. In several cases, there is overlap between two hedge fund categories. For example, many statistical arbitrage strategies are also market neutral. Below are some of the more common strategies utilized by hedge fund managers. By no means is the list exhaustive, but it is likely representative of the bulk of assets deployed in the hedge fund investment universe. Within each strategy, there are often sector specific or international versions that some database vendors will categorize as a separate investment category.

1.2.1. *Activist* funds typically purchase a sizeable (i.e. 5% or more) stake in a company and attempt to unlock shareholder value by spurring management or corporate strategy changes. In many respects they operate similar to private equity firms, with the obvious exception that they own a limited amount of shares in publicly traded companies. Carl Icahn was and remains one of the more notable activist investors, that were pejoratively termed "corporate raiders" a couple of decades ago.

1.2.2. *Capital Structure Arbitrage* is a more generalized version of the convertible bond arbitrage trade and is typically executed through the use of complex derivative instruments, such as a credit default swap. As with most arbitrage trades, either side of the position can be taken, but the typical transaction combination is to be long the bond (through a synthetic position, such as selling short a credit default swap) and short the common stock. The strategy performs well in most circumstances, but has difficulty when there is a divergence between stock and bond prices.

1.2.3. *Convertible Arbitrage* funds typically buy convertible bonds and sells short the common stock of the same company. The hedge fund earns the coupon from the bond and the proceeds from the short sales of the common stock, resulting in a "double carry." The trade is not risk free since dividends may be owed from shorting the common stock and significant losses can be incurred if the bond defaults and the hedge ratio was incorrectly calculated. Liquidity issues can also overwhelm the fundamentals, as evidenced by the drop in convertible bonds in the second half of 2008.

1.2.4. *Distressed / Credit* funds focus on companies that are at risk of default, are in default, or have recently emerged from default. Credit is a more general term for the investment in fixed income securities. For example, credit funds may purchase a pool of loans from a bank, such as Citi or Goldman Sachs, at deep discounts. Both strategies place a heavy emphasis on legal work, financial statement analysis and the identification of the "fulcrum" security, or the one which has the maximum voting leverage in the event of a financial reorganization.

1.2.5. *Event Driven* funds engage in trades based on a specific event such as: merger, special dividend payment, earnings announcement, analyst opinion upgrade, or credit downgrade. Once the event is resolved, favorably or unfavorably, the fund moves on to the next trade.

1.2.6. *Fixed Income Arbitrage* funds purchase fixed income securities that appear to be undervalued and sell short other fixed income securities, with similar risk, that appear to be overvalued. Leverage is nearly always used to increase both the risk and return of the trade. A typical example would be to purchase a basket of mortgage backed securities and sell short a portfolio of Treasury securities with a similar duration. The fund captures the spread (since Treasuries always sell at a premium to AAA rated mortgage backed securities) times the leverage factor, minus the cost of borrowed funds. The trade may backfire during times of market distress, as in the case of the late 2007 through 2008 time period.

1.2.7. *Global Macro* funds generally do not focus on individual securities, but rather emphasize positions in derivatives and index securities on a global basis. They are often unhedged and utilize leverage, making them one of the higher risk hedge fund categories.

1.2.8. *Long / Short* funds purchase securities perceived to be undervalued while simultaneously selling short those viewed as being overvalued. The long to short, or hedge ratio, variation is based on the manager's outlook for the returns of the broader market. The strategy is typically employed for equity related securities, but is flexible enough to apply to nearly any asset class. The bulk of hedge fund assets are in Long / Short Equity related strategies, making this category the main focus of the examples in this book.

1.2.9. *Managed Futures* funds trade in futures contracts, such as commodities, currencies, metals, or index futures. Some analysts call these funds "commodity trading advisors" (CTAs), but the "managed futures" term better signifies the broad array of instruments these funds can employ.

1.2.10. *Market Neutral* funds balance the market risk of both the long and short side of the portfolio. A common market neutral example is a long position in Ford and short position in General Motors. The term typically applies to equity oriented funds, but it could also apply to fixed income securities where the duration (i.e. effective maturity) of the fund's long and short positions are balanced.

1.2.11. *Merger Arbitrage* funds typically purchase a basket of stocks that is the target of a merger or acquisition. The offsetting trade usually involves a short position in the bidding firms. The main risk of the strategy is the loss incurred when a deal falls through, effectively forcing the hedge fund manager to absorb the loss of the takeover premium. Leverage is often utilized to increase risk and return.

1.2.12. *Short Biased* funds are either entirely short or have the bulk of their assets sold short. Since the equity and fixed income markets generally trend up over time, few hedge fund managers successfully operate in this category over the long-term. Those that are successful typically focus on small to mid cap firms with company-specific problems.

1.2.13. *Statistical Arbitrage* funds typically employ high frequency computerized trading techniques in order to profit from apparent arbitrage opportunities. True arbitrage opportunities, such as buying IBM in New York and simultaneously shorting it in London for a profit, have no risk and are rare and fleeting if they do exist. The term *statistical* refers to the fact that there may be an arbitrage opportunity according to the fund manager's model; but if the model is not accurate, there remains risk in the trade.

1.2.14. *Multistrategy* funds simultaneously engage in more than one of the previously discussed hedge fund strategies. They attempt to diversify risk by holding a range of strategies, rather than placing all of their capital in a single approach. For example, a merger arbitrage fund would have difficulty attracting capital in the event of a slow period for deals. Conversely, a multistrategy fund could allocate capital towards those hedge fund categories that appear to have the best chance of prospering in the current market environment.

1.2.15. *Fund of Funds* purchase positions in a number of individual hedge funds. They attempt to reduce the damage to the portfolio in the event that a specific fund "blows up," such as with Long Term Capital Management. One disadvantage is that their investors incur a second layer of fees, typically one percent of assets under management and ten percent of profits.

1.3 Paths to Alpha

1.3.1 Is Alpha Possible?

The list of great investors — Buffett, Cohen, Graham, Lampert, Lynch, Paulson, Robertson, Simons, Soros, and so forth — can be theoretically explained by being the economic equivalent of lucky coin flippers, but the more logical explanation is that they simply have or had an ability to consistently generate alpha (α). Let's briefly discuss some relevant studies on investment performance and the most common sources of alpha, or superior risk adjusted returns. A simple equation of alpha is shown below, where the expected return would be obtained with the assistance of a valuation model, such as the Capital Asset Pricing Model or the Arbitrage Pricing Theory.

$$\alpha = \textbf{Actual Return} - \textbf{Expected Return}$$

In *aggregate*, alpha is not possible. Sharpe (1991) demonstrated that the average investor cannot outperform the market average and when transaction costs are taken into account the average investor will actually underperform the average. Nevertheless, several researchers, such as Harri and Brorsen (2004), have found that there is persistence in hedge fund performance. That is, past winning managers have a higher probability of outperforming again and past losers underperform. Losing hedge fund managers that underperform two or three years in a row are likely to be fired or see their fund go out of business. If the fund continues to operate, the departing manager is often replaced with "new blood," which is, at least initially, less experienced and less talented than the *winning* managers. So alpha *is* likely possible for a subset of skilled managers.

1.3.2 Superior Investment Mosaic May Lead to Alpha

I initially came across the Mosaic Theory during my studies in the Chartered Financial Analysts (CFA) program. The theory states that an analyst can create value by combining bits and pieces of public, and in some cases proprietary, information into a unique picture that the market as a whole cannot easily see. By creating a superior mosaic, alpha may be generated. We will create a sample investment mosaic in Chapter 2, whose topic is Hedge Fund Research. In my opinion, based on the hundreds of hedge funds that I have evaluated, the vast majority use the mosaic approach in their quest for alpha.

1.3.3 Superior Information May Lead to Alpha

There is a well known axiom on Wall Street that states, "Orders = Information." Despite the recent billion dollar losses in subprime and credit related securities, trading is the most profitable area for many Wall Street firms. According to Tully (2007), the five biggest U.S. investment banks in 2006 — Bear Stearns, Goldman Sachs, Lehman Brothers, Merrill Lynch, and Morgan Stanley generated $61 billion from proprietary trading, approximately half their total revenue.

The Tully article, which notes the SEC is investigating Wall Street trading practices, discusses how a trade based on information flow might work.

> "Here's a hypothetical example, gleaned from former Wall Street traders as well as outsiders who work closely with them, of how some people think the Street exploits information. Say a fund company, call it Big Dog, wants to buy a million shares of Intel. A Big Dog trader calls a broker at a Wall Street firm — call it Megabux. The broker enters the order into the Megabux trading system. A dozen Megabux 'sales traders' get the info on their computer screens. Their job is to find sellers for the shares. But first they call their top hedge fund clients, giving them the chance to buy Intel before Big Dog pushes up the price. To cover their tracks, the hedge funds don't buy the Intel shares through Megabux, but

they reward their benefactor with a lot of other big trades and by paying higher commissions than the mutual funds do."

The article discusses an additional example where the information of the block trade is passed onto the proprietary trading group. It would be illegal for them to trade in advance of the 1 million share order being completed, but it is very likely that there will be follow up orders at Megabux or elsewhere and the proprietary trader may be able to take a position in advance of a subsequent order. For example, the trader can look at the initial trade size and compare it to a normal full position size of the portfolio manager to get an imprecise estimate of the number of follow up orders in Intel. Wall Street firms state that they have compliance procedures in place to ensure that no front running activity is taking place, but the area is somewhat murky. In the Intel example discussed above, the proprietary trading desk of the Wall Street firm could not be prohibited from trading in Intel forever, leaving a window to execute the trade at some point after receiving the block trade information.

The superior information flow path to alpha is most likely utilized by the largest hedge funds, due to the large commissions that they generate. They often receive the "first phone call" from sell side analysts and traders. In no way do I condone insider trading or any violation of SEC rules. It is merely my wish to point out that, unlike in traditional economic theory, information flow is not instantaneously available to all prospective investors. In many cases there is a time sequence to the dissemination of important information and those at the front of the information chain may have the opportunity to earn alpha.

1.3.4 Superior Execution of Strategies May Lead to Alpha

The rise of electronic communication networks (ECN) and alternative trading systems, such as Liquidnet, have driven down the costs of trading substantially. However, the fragmented nature of the financial markets has created certain pockets or dark pools of liquidity that might not be apparent to the traditional investor. Consider a trade of shares in IBM. Should it be executed on the New York Stock Exchange, Instinet, Tokyo Stock Exchange, Frankfurt Stock Exchange, Liquidnet, or some other venue?

Leinweber (1995) analyzed the "paper" versus actual performance of a mutual fund that attempted to replicate a portfolio of Value Line's highest rated stocks. The "paper portfolio" had an annual return of 26.2% over the 1979–1991 period, but the actual fund, based on the same stock picks, earned only 16.1% per year. Perold (1988) has called the gap between "paper" and real returns the "implementation shortfall." Part of the implementation shortfall in the Value Line study may have been due to the time lag between the publication of the rankings and the date a trade was submitted. Other components of the shortfall are likely related to commissions, bid-ask spreads, and market impact.

The takeaway from the fragmented nature of financial markets and the existence of the implementation shortfall is that superior execution of a strategy may result in alpha. Best execution strategies are especially important for statistical arbitrage and other high turnover strategies. We devote an entire chapter to best execution of hedge fund strategies in Chapter 8.

Of course, some combination of the aforementioned and other techniques may lead to the highest alpha. In sum, alpha is difficult to achieve, but surely possible. The primary purpose of this book is to give hedge fund managers and analysts a framework for generating and understanding it through an analysis of its components — investment research, trade execution, and portfolio management.

Hedge Fund Alpha Tear Sheet — Chapter 1

- There is no uniformly accepted definition of a hedge fund.
  o If we define a hedge fund as a private investment vehicle that charges an incentive fee and (nearly always) asset management fee, then, contrary to popular opinion, A. W. Jones did not start the first hedge fund.
- According to Warren Buffett, Benjamin Graham ran the first hedge fund, since the Graham-Newman Partnership utilized long and short positions and charged an incentive fee.
  o Others may have operated hedge fund like investment partnerships before Graham, but the details of these operations are currently sketchy.
- New hedge fund categories are created each year. Common ones include:
  o Activist, Capital Structure Arbitrage, Convertible Arbitrage, Distressed / Credit, Event Driven, Fixed Income Arbitrage, Global Macro, Long / Short, Managed Futures, Market Neutral, Merger Arbitrage, Short Biased, Statistical Arbitrage, Multistrategy, and Fund of Funds.
- Alpha, or the achievement of superior risk adjusted returns over the long term, is difficult to achieve and sustain, but possible.
  o Alpha equals the actual return of a security or fund, minus its expected return.
  o In aggregate, alpha is not possible, but it is possible for a subset of investors.
  o Several studies have found persistence in performance; that is, winners keep winning and losers keep losing (until they go out of business).
- Common sources of alpha include the following techniques:
  o Creation of a superior investment mosaic.
  o Access to superior information.
  o Superior execution of investment strategies
  o Some combination of the above and other techniques.

References

Harri, Ardian and B. Wade Brorsen, "Performance Persistence and the Source of Returns for Hedge Funds", *Applied Financial Economics*, Vol. 14, January, 2004, pp. 131–141.

Lefèvre, Edwin, *Reminiscences of a Stock Operator*, George Doran & Co., 1923.

Leinweber, David, "Using Information from Trading in Trading and Portfolio Management", *Journal of Investing*, Summer 1995, pp. 40–50.

Loomis, Carol, "The Jones Nobody Keeps Up With." *Fortune* April, 1966, pp. 237–247.

Lowenstein, Roger, *When Genius Failed: The Rise and Fall of Long-Term Capital Management*, Random House, 2001.

Perold, Andre, "The Implementation Shortfall: Paper vs. Reality", *Journal of Portfolio Management*, Vol. 14, Spring, 1988, pp. 4–9.

Sharpe, William, "The Arithmetic of Active Management", *Financial Analysts Journal*, January/February 1991, pp. 7–9.

Taub, Stephen, "Kings of Cash", *Alpha*, April, 2008, pp. 34–49.

Tully, Shawn, "Wall Street's next scandal," *Fortune*, February 19, 2007. http://money.cnn.com/magazines/fortune/fortune_archive/2007/03/05/84 01273/index.htm

2

HEDGE FUND RESEARCH VS. TRADITIONAL RESEARCH

John M. Longo, PhD, CFA

Rutgers Business School & The MDE Group, Inc.

1. Introduction

Research is the lifeblood of any investment process. Without high quality research, *sustainable* alpha is not possible. Although several characteristics, such as rigor, depth, and timeliness, are common to all high quality research processes, hedge fund research is often distinct from traditional "long only" research. We elaborate on these points of distinction below. Subsequently, we give some examples of high quality research and suggest a series of research tools that may aid in adding alpha. We end the chapter by creating a research mosaic or dashboard that may be used as a template by hedge fund managers and analysts.

1.1 Hedge Fund Research Generally Has a Shorter-Term Orientation

Many have heard Keynes' famous quote, "In the long run we are all dead." Most hedge funds don't have the luxury of a client base that will wait years for strong performance. Hedge funds report their returns on a monthly basis and "hot money" will often move away from underperformers as soon as lockup provisions permit. For those hedge funds lucky enough to have more than a one-year lockup, the myopic focus of most hedge funds raises the possibility of a time arbitrage strategy of following momentum in the short run and mean reversion over the long run.

1.2 Hedge Fund Research Has a Greater Focus on Short Selling

As discussed in Chapter 1, many, but not all, hedge funds utilize a material hedge. The hedge is most often accomplished through the short selling of stock or through derivatives such as put options, futures and swaps. The Taxpayer Relief Act of 1997 repealed the "short-short" rule, which prohibited the mutual funds from generating more than 30% of their gross income from gains on stock held less than three months or from short sales. Despite the repeal of the Act, the vast majority of assets in mutual funds remain in traditional long only vehicles. Some notable exceptions include J.P. Morgan Highbridge Statistical Market Neutral, Hussman Strategic Growth, Diamond Hill Long / Short, and TFS Market Neutral.

1.3 Hedge Fund Research Is More Dynamic In Nature

Many mutual funds are characterized by, or some would say chained to, a Style Box, that was popularized by Morningstar. The Style Box looks at an investment from two dimensions: its Size and Style. Size refers to securities of Large, Mid, and Small market capitalization. Style refers to Value, Growth, or Blend, providing an indication of the price of the security relative to its growth prospects. The Style Box for the Fidelity Magellan mutual fund is shown in **Figure 1**. The box indicates that the bulk of the fund's assets fall in the Large Growth category.

Hedge funds too, are often characterized by a specific strategy, such as Long / Short, but their mandates are typically much broader than that of most mutual funds. Accordingly a Long / Short equity manager can more easily roam among Large, Small, Value and Growth names, thus creating the need for a more dynamic research process relative to most mutual funds.

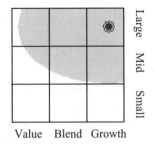

Value   Blend   Growth

Figure 1: Style Box for the Fidelity Magellan Fund

◉ Fund centroid represents weighted average of domestic stock holdings.
⬤ Zone represents 75% of fund's domestic stock holdings.
Source: Morningstar.com

1.4 Hedge Fund Research Often Involves Combinations of Securities

The use of multiple financial instruments and derivatives is much more common in hedge fund strategies, compared to traditional long only vehicles. For example, Convertible Arbitrage hedge funds often have a simultaneous long position in the convertible bond and short position in the common stock of an issuer. More complex strategies, such as Capital Structure Arbitrage, often utilize simultaneous positions in the credit default swaps, bonds, and common equity of an issuer. The carry trade — borrowing money wherever in the world it is cheapest and investing it in areas with the highest expected returns — often involves currency and futures transactions. There are many other examples to emphasize the point that research which describes the *interrelationships* among various markets and instruments is likely to be of greater importance to hedge funds than to traditional long only managers.

2. Examples of Research Useful to a Hedge Fund Manager

We now briefly discuss examples of research that may have been useful to hedge fund managers. Our examples mainly focus on Apple in order to use a company that is familiar to most readers. Two important short-term (i.e. less than one year) issues related to Apple's stock were: 1) a good estimate of their gross margins on the iPhone when it was first introduced and 2) the expansion of the availability of the iPhone to other countries.

Few analysts had rigorous estimates of the gross margins for the iPhone. Not only would this figure have important implications for Apple's stock, but also for its entire supply chain and competitors. An independent research firm, iSuppli, conducted a simple but powerful example of research in obtaining their estimates for Apple's gross margins on the iPhone. Eric Pratt, an analyst at iSuppli, bought an iPhone at its launch and tore it open to examine its components. He estimated that iPhone's initial launch price of $599 for the 8-gigabyte version was approximately double its component cost of $265.83. The 55% gross margin was higher than most analyst estimates. Apple shares rose 5% on the day the iSuppli report was published (July 3, 2007), its largest rise in more than six months, and more than 9% over the span of two days.

Table 1 is extracted from a Bloomberg article discussing the iSuppli report on the iPhone.[1]

Table 1: Selected Components of the iPhone and Estimated Costs

Company	Components	Total Costs
Infineon	Digital baseband Radio Transceiver Power Management	$15.25
National Semiconductor	Display/graphics connecting chip	$1.50
Balda AG	Touch screen module	$27.00
Epson/Sharp/Toshiba Matsushita	Touch screen display	$24.50
Samsung Electronics	Applications processor NAND flash memory DRAM chip	$76.25
Wolfson Microelectronics Plc	Audio codec	N/A
CSR Plc	Bluetooth chip	$1.90
Marvell Technology Group Ltd.	Wi-Fi chip	$6.00
Total Bill of Materials		**$265.83**

Source: Bloomberg article, iSuppli

Although the expansion of the iPhone beyond the United States and the introduction of a new 3G version was inevitable and a foregone conclusion to long-term investors, its timing was of material importance to short-term traders. Kathryn Huberty, a Morgan Stanley analyst, noted in a March 2008 report that over the prior three quarters, Apple Chief Executive Steve Jobs spent $550,000 on air travel, nearly three times more than the average spent over the prior year and a half.[2] She attributed this to Mr. Jobs' integral role in the negotiation of expanding the iPhone overseas. She wrote, "We'd point to a 34 percent year-on-year increase in R&D and 170 percent year-on-year increase in Steve Jobs' airplane expense in the December quarter as signs Apple is preparing for meaningful product launches."

From March 1, 2008 through June 30, 2008, Apple's stock was up 33.9% vs. a rise of 0.9% for Nasdaq. Intense, practical, and timely research may be of interest to long-term investors, but is essential to hedge fund managers forced to defend their investment returns on a monthly basis.

2.1 The Freedom of Information Act (FOIA)

In some cases, it is legal to obtain material *non-public* information about companies. I found this statement to be startling until I became aware of a piece of research published on January 2, 2002 by an independent research firm, SEC Insight. [The firm is not related to the better-known Securities and Exchange Commission (SEC).] SEC Insight requested in November of 2001 the SEC's correspondence with Tyco, under the Freedom of Information Act (FOIA). The SEC refused the FOIA request on the grounds that it may have interfered with law enforcement activities, thereby inferring information that may be useful to short sellers. The SEC did provide FOIA information on Tyco in April of 2001, providing further fuel to the hypothesis that something different had occurred by the time of the November request. Tyco fell 2.8% on the day the SEC Insight report was published. Of course, years later Tyco's stock fell sharply in a series of accounting scandals that eventually threw its former CEO, Dennis Kozlowski, in prison.

According to the SEC's website (http://www.sec.gov/foia.shtml),

> The Freedom of Information Act (FOIA), which can be found in Title 5 of the United States Code, section 552, was enacted in 1966 and provides that any person has the right to request access to federal agency records or information. All agencies of the United States government are required to disclose records upon receiving a written request for them, except for those records that are protected from disclosure by the nine exemptions and three exclusions of the FOIA. This right of access is enforceable in court.
>
> A FOIA request is required to obtain non-public records, such as records compiled in investigations, consumer complaints, and staff comment letters. We will release non-public records, unless the record is protected by one of nine FOIA exemptions. If we can reasonably segregate or delete exempt information from a requested record, we will release to you the rest of the record.

The appropriate contact information for a FOIA request is:

Securities and Exchange Commission
Office of FOIA and Privacy Act Operations
100 F Street, NE
Washington, DC 20549-5100

Phone: 202-551-8300
Fax: 202-772-9336
E-mail: foiapa@sec.gov

An FOIA request may be valuable information to all investors — long, short, short-term, and long-term — in a company's securities.

2.2 Channel Checks

Channel checks refer to the analysis of the product sales of a company with information obtained from talking to distributors, retailers, competitors, and other knowledgeable people in a company's industry. Good channel check strategies may enable an analyst to glean changes in market share, earnings, and industry trends. The process is useful to both short and long term investors, but the emphasis typically relates to the likelihood that a firm will meet its quarterly earnings numbers, a fertile ground for hedge fund strategies. The somewhat related term "channel stuffing" refers to attractive deals that a company will utilize to book sales in order to meet projected quarterly earnings numbers.

Sell-side analysts regularly conduct channel checks as an important part of obtaining their earnings estimates. The larger sell-side firms will often retain independent analysts or consulting firms to supplement their own primary research. Hedge fund managers can leverage off this sell side research to some extent. Fund managers or analysts with limited resources can conduct their own channel checks, by calling representatives of a particular firm, their competitors or the distributors / wholesalers which often act as middlemen between a company and the ultimate seller of a product.

One analyst who works for a mid-sized sell-side firm shared the following technique with me. He would call a distributor using the mundane technique of looking through the yellow pages and ask the distributor questions about sales trends for specific products and a particular industry. In some cases the distributor would be forthcoming with the information. In other cases, the distributor would initially withhold information; the analyst then promised to share the information he received from other distributors, as an incentive to divulge information. His success rate in obtaining relevant information was high and he felt it added material value to the quality of his earnings forecasts. Below, we will discuss the importance of creating a network of experts in the search for sustainable alpha. This network is essentially a superset of the important channel check issue.

2.3 NEGIBOT™ — The Search Engine That Complains About Everything

We are nearly all familiar with the major search engines such as Google, Yahoo!, MSN, and Ask.com. But have you heard of NEGIBOT™, the search engine that complains about everything? In other words, it searches the Internet for negative terms or comments related to the word or phrase entered into its search engine. Its search algorithm is optimized to uncover most types of negative words and connotations, such as "terrible, sucks, poor, bad, hate, etc." and is therefore more precise then entering your own negative phrases in one of the popular search engines. The NEGIBOT™ logo is shown in **Figure 2**. Negative information would be of value to short sellers and also may help long biased funds avoid pitfalls.

Figure 2: NEGIBOT™ Logo

Let's look at a specific example. Amazon's Kindle could be "the next big thing" with some analysts projecting $1 billion in sales by 2010. This figure would represent a relatively small percentage of Amazon's sales, but the ancillary revenue streams of the Kindle platform may prove to be quite valuable for Amazon and demonstrate a halo effect, as it has been the case for Apple with the iPod. **Table 2** lists the search results from NEGIBOT™ for the string "Kindle."

Table 2: Search Results From NEGIBOT™ on "Kindle"

Tynan on Technology (beta) " **Blog Archive** " Amazon's wonderful **terrible** ... The Kindle is amazing and **awful**, grand and **terrible**. ... Two **stupid** things that really pleased me. The RIAA vs. the mothers of prevention ...http://www.dantynan.com/2008/06/15/amazons-wonderful-**terrible**-amazing-**awful**-kindle/ [Yahoo!]
Investing Insights Buy Amazon - Kindle is the iPod of books - Business Week That creates **terrible** chicken-and-egg dilemmas between the devices and the ... take out this basic and **stupid** restriction, the Kindle, so loving gifted to me, ...http://www.businessweek.com/investing/insights/blog/archives/2007/11/buy_amazon_-_ki.html [Yahoo!]
Blogrunner: Amazon Kindle vs. Sony Reader, New eBooks and iPhone: First ... ... important observation about Amazon's new electronic book reader: **It's terrible**. ... eBook readers are **stupid**. Related " Nikhil Pahwa | contentSutra.com ...http://www.blogrunner.com/snapshot/D/3/0/amazon_kindle_vs_sony_reader_new_ebooks_and_iphone_firstlook_comparison/ [Yahoo!]

In case you were wondering, there is also POSIBOT™, the optimistic search engine. In short, vertical search engines, such as deepVertical™, which "search topics an inch wide and a mile deep™" may be of greater value to hedge fund managers and analysts than traditional search engines.

2.4 Google Alerts

The major financial portals, such as Yahoo! Finance, Microsoft Investor, Google Finance, and SmartMoney.com do an excellent job of aggregating national news sources, such as Reuters, Associated Press (AP), PR Newswire and many others. However, in many cases the most comprehensive and valuable information about a firm is uncovered by local news sources, as well as in blogs and user groups. Fortunately, Google Alerts allows you to track companies or phrases "as-it-happens" with emails sent directly to your inbox. Not only does Google Alerts track national and international news articles, but also local articles, blogs, video, and user groups.

The service costs nothing and works best with a Gmail account since the emails on a specific search term (e.g. Goldman Sachs) are aggregated under a single heading despite the fact that one hundred alerts may have occurred on your search string in the past twenty-four hours. **Table 3** shows a sample list of Google Alerts.

Table 3: Google Alerts on Selected Finance Terms

Your Google Alerts

Google Alert - UBS - Google Blogs Alert for: UBS Re: Discussion on Dillon Read Capital Management (UBS) Author: Hedge …
Google Alert - Morgan Stanley - Google News Alert for: Morgan Stanley, Bank of America Cuts Goldman Sachs (GS) and Morgan Stanley …
Google Alert - Lehman Brothers - Google News Alert for: Lehman Brothers, Market Snapshots: US Stocks Turn Mostly Higher As …
Google Alert - Citigroup - Google Blogs Alert for: Citigroup, Citigroup - too big to fail By rss@LiveVideo.com (StocksAtBottom …

2.5 Network of Experts to Help Generate Alpha

One or more highly competent investment professionals manage most hedge funds and a team of analysts often backs the larger ones as well. Regardless of size, hedge funds can and should also tap into the resources of others that can add value to their investment processes — what we shall term as a "network of experts." Let's look at several examples of how many hedge funds tap experts beyond their own walls in their quest for alpha.

One former Head of Research at a bulge bracket sell-side research firm told me one method he used for uncovering experts in a specific industry. During the course of his meetings with people working in a particular field, he would ask, "Who is the smartest person you know in this industry?" He would get a name and then proceed to call the person, stating to the effect, "I heard you are the smartest person in the industry…" Most individuals would be flattered to hear that comment and give you at least a few minutes of their time. To obtain a substantial amount of an expert's time it will likely cost you significant consulting fees (and perhaps be well worth it). At least the initial conversation may tell you enough about whether you would like to proceed further.

There are several specific sources for finding experts in even the narrowest of fields. Let's briefly mention three virtual research firms used widely by hedge fund managers. Gerson Lehrman Group (GLG) (http://www.glgroup.com/) provides a platform to access more than 200,000 subject matter experts on a worldwide basis. According to an article posted on GLG's website, the experts charge their clients anywhere from $50 to $2,000 per hour while GLG earns money by providing clients with access to its database of experts.[3] GLG's fees are $70,000 and up for six months of access to their platform. Other well-known firms that provide access to a virtual network of experts (for a fee) include Standard and Poor's Vista Research (http://www.vistaresearch.com/) and Reuters Insight (http://www.reutersinsight.com/)

It is not a secret that hedge fund managers often share information with other managers about their positions. In fact, many managers are eager to share (primarily long) positions, once they have been established with the expectation that further buying will push up the price of their holdings. For example, David Einhorn of Greenlight Capital in his recent book, *Fooling Some of the People All of the Time: A Long Short Story,* notes the following tense exchange he had with the SEC when they probed his short position in Allied Capital:

> "Have you ever met regularly or irregularly with a group of fund managers that would include Whitney Tilson [of Tilson Capital Partners] and Bill Ackman [of Gotham Partners]?" he asked. 'Well, Bill Ackman was in the Richard Shuster group for a period of time,' I said, referring to an informal quarterly 'idea dinner' of money managers, which I sometimes attend. Richard Shuster ran a small hedge fund called Arbor Partners and organized the dinners. Idea dinners are commonplace. Some, including Richard Shuster's, are self-formed, while institutional salesmen or the investment banks sponsor others. Generally, at an idea dinner each

participant presents one or two investment ideas and gets grilled by the group. 'He hasn't come for a while, maybe several years,' ...

While it is true that I share investment ideas with other fund managers, this works best as a two-way street. No one likes a freeloader. So as a general matter, I share more ideas with others who share back. I don't keep score about who shares what with me, and the practice is quite informal."

Sharing ideas with hedge fund managers is somewhat of a "Catch 22" situation. Star managers might not give a new manager the time of the day. Perhaps one solution is that emerging managers are likely to be able to network with other emerging managers, while larger, more established managers have a high likelihood of networking with most funds.

2.6 Obtaining Alpha Generating Ideas From Websites and Books

Occasionally, it is possible to obtain alpha generating ideas through websites at zero to nominal cost. We distinguish these websites, which present a clear argument for buying or selling a security, relative to the resources that provide specific pieces of an investment mosaic. ValueInvestorsClub.com provides high quality, value oriented ideas to its 250 members, but admission is selective and obtained through an application process. The website, founded by Joel Greenblatt of Gotham Capital, awards *$5,000 a week* to the member with the best investment idea.

SeekingAlpha.com is open to the general public and provides a list of long and short ideas on a daily basis, as well as highlighting investment related articles from other publications. Mark Cuban is majority owner of ShareSlueth.com, a website that primarily uncovers short picks. It has an impressive track record, but the volume of investment ideas is far less than those in ValueInvestorsClub.com and SeekingAlpha.com. A comprehensive, but not exhaustive, list of websites for hedge fund managers and analysts is located in **Appendix A**. Additionally, an annotated reading list is located in **Appendix B**. Hedge fund managers often obtain investment ideas after reading about the thoughts and strategies of successful managers in the industry. The reading list also contains core books in investments, financial statement analysts, short selling, investor psychology, and technical analysis.

3. Putting It All Together In a Hedge Fund Dashboard

This chapter noted how hedge fund research is distinct in many respects from long only research and discussed various resources and techniques that may help a manager deliver sustainable alpha. Disparate information sources and concepts are often best presented in an investment mosaic or dashboard. The CFA Institute promotes the Mosaic Theory, which suggests analysts weave together bits and pieces of public (and sometimes proprietary) information into a unique picture that generates alpha. A sample hedge fund dashboard is shown in **Figure 3**. The dashboard lists macro variables, industry contacts, valuation parameters, watch lists, and so forth. In practice, hedge fund managers may wish to create several dashboards pertaining to different time horizons and securities and have them updated on a real-time basis.

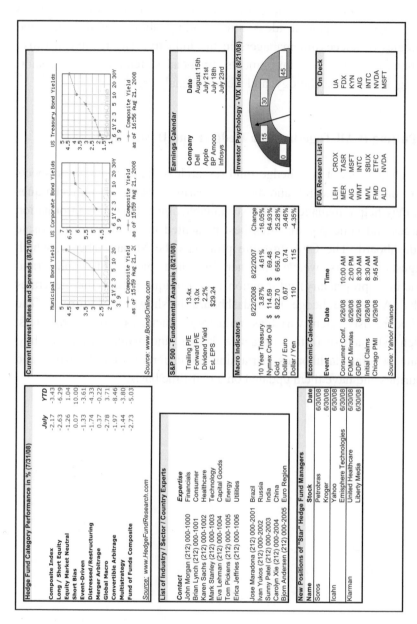

Figure 3: Sample Hedge Fund Dashboard

Hedge Fund Alpha Tear Sheet — Chapter 2

- *Sustainable* alpha is not possible without high quality research.
- Hedge fund research is often distinct from traditional long only research. Some of these differences are listed below:
  - o Hedge fund research generally has a shorter-term orientation.
  - o Hedge fund research has a greater focus on short selling.
  - o Hedge fund research is more dynamic in nature.
  - o Hedge fund research often involves combinations of securities.
- There are many ways a hedge fund manager can utilize research in order to generate alpha. The following techniques were discussed in this chapter:
  - o The Freedom of Information Act (FOIA).
  - o Channel checks.
  - o Negibot™ — the search engine that complains about everything.
  - o Google Alerts.
  - o Network of internal and external experts.
  - o Financial websites.
  - o Creating hedge fund mosaics or dashboards.

End Notes

[1] The Bloomberg article by Cho and Heiskanen (2007) discusses iSuppli's approach to estimating the profit margins on the iPhone.

[2] The Huberty report analyzing Steve Jobs' airline expenditures is discussed in Richards (2008).

[3] An estimate of GLG's fees is discussed in Baird (2008).

References

Baird, Roger, "Investment Matchmaking: A New Industry That Is Beating The Crunch," *City A.M.*, July 21, 2008.

Cho, Kevin and Ville Heiskanen, "Apple's IPhone Sells for Double Costs, ISuppli Says," *Bloomberg*, July 3, 2007. www.bloomberg.com/apps/news?pid=20601087&sid=aGfLsPKqLcTc& refer=home

Einhorn, David, *Fooling Some of the People All of the Time: A Long Short Story*, Wiley, 2008.

Richards, Jonathan, "Apple gears up for June launch of 3G iPhone," *Times Online*, February 29, 2008.

3

ACHIEVING HEDGE FUND ALPHA IN BRAZIL

Jorge Barreiro and John M. Longo, PhD, CFA

Duff and Phelps; Rutgers Business School & The MDE Group

1. Introduction

The purpose of this chapter is to provide a basic overview of the Brazilian (or Brasilian) financial markets and its dynamics, with the ultimate goal of identifying hedge fund strategies that are most likely to generate alpha in this region. Accordingly, it is necessary to discuss some of the common financial instruments that exist in Brazilian markets, regulation, and investor behavior. The global bear market of 2008 has wreaked havoc on nearly all financial markets. However, the enormous foreign exchange reserves of the Brazil, Russia, India, and China (BRIC) countries as of late 2008 puts them in much better position to rebound from the large losses, relative to prior crises in their respective countries. The nascent and rapidly evolving nature of the Brazilian financial markets, as well as with the other (BRIC) countries, may make it a fertile source of alpha in the decades ahead.

Table 1 lists current (2007) GDP and 2050 projected GDP for the BRIC countries and those of other large economies.[1] The projected results, if realized, are simply breathtaking. Brazil's economy, currently ranked (by GDP) 10th in the world, is projected to move to 4th. Russia, currently ranked 11th by GDP is projected to move to 6th. India, currently ranked 12th, is projected to move to 3rd. Incredibly, China's economy in 2050 is projected to be nearly twice the size of the United States', while it currently has less than one quarter of the United States' $13.8 trillion GDP. China, with its $1.8 trillion in reserves is likely to emerge from the global stock market crash of 2008 in a stronger than ever position. We discuss hedge fund strategies for China in Chapter 6.

Table 1: 2007 GDP and Projected 2050 GDP

Rank	Country	2007 Actual GDP ($ Millions)	Rank	Country	2050 Estimate GDP ($ Millions)
1	United States	$13,811,200	1	China	$70,710,000
2	Japan	4,376,705	2	United States	38,514,000
3	Germany	3,297,233	3	India	37,668,000
4	China	3,280,053	4	Brazil	11,366,000
5	United Kingdom	2,727,806	5	Mexico	9,340,000
6	France	2,562,288	6	Russia	8,580,000
7	Italy	2,107,481	7	Indonesia	7,010,000
8	Spain	1,429,226	8	Japan	6,677,000
9	Canada	1,326,376	9	United Kingdom	5,133,000
10	Brazil	1,314,170	10	Germany	5,024,000
11	Russia	1,291,011	11	Nigeria	4,640,000
12	India	1,170,968	12	France	4,592,000
13	South Korea	969,795	13	South Korea	4,083,000
14	Mexico	893,364	14	Turkey	3,943,000
15	Australia	821,716	15	Vietnam	3,607,000

Source: Wilson and Stupnytska (2007)

2. Brazilian Economy

Brazil's economy, with 2007 GDP of approximately $1.5 trillion, is the second largest in the Americas, and among the ten largest in the world. Since 2000, GDP has grown at an astounding 11.7% annual rate. Growth was fueled primarily by a rise in commodities, a decrease in inflation, and expansion of international trade. Although China and India get most of the publicity related to the BRIC countries, it is interesting to note that Brazil's GDP exceeds India's by more than 10%, despite having less than 20% of India's population.

Brazil is well known for its rich natural resources, but surprisingly its largest exports are in the transportation industry. Embraer is Brazil's leading aerospace company, amassing approximately $6 billion in sales in 2007. **Table 2** shows Brazil's leading export industries and markets.

Brazil, rich in sugarcane crops due in part to its warm climate, is the world's leading producer of ethanol. Its petroleum-based exports are certain to increase over the long term after Petrobras' recent discovery of the massive Tupi and Jupiter oil fields in the Santos Basin. Brazilian President Luiz Inacio Lula de Silva, said the country would consider membership in the Organization of Petroleum Exporting Countries (OPEC) once the new oil field discoveries are capable of substantial production. [2]

Table 2: Leading Brazilian Export Industries and Markets

Biggest Exports, 2007	% of Total	Leading Export Markets, 2007	% of Total
Transport Equipment & Parts	12.5	United States	15.8
Metallurgical Products	11.6	Argentina	9.0
Soybeans, Meal & Oils	8.2	China	6.7
Chemical Products	1.9	Germany	4.5

Source: Economist.com

3. Overview of Brazilian Financial Markets

3.1 Brazilian Stock Market

Brazil's only current stock exchange is the Bolsa de Valores de Sao Paulo (BOVESPA), which has roots dating back to 1890. According to De Medeiros (2005), Bovespa and other Brazilian exchanges were at one time official entities linked to finance departments of state governments. The Securities Act of 1965 ushered in the modern era of the stock exchange that exists at present. In 2000, BOVESPA emerged as the monopolistic stock exchange of Brazil after it merged with its primary competitor, Bolsa de Valores do Rio de Janeiro (BVRJ). In May, 2008, BOVESPA merged with Brazil's largest derivatives exchange, Bolsa de Mercadorias & Futuros (BM&F), creating the world's third largest exchange. The combined firm is now known as BM&FBOVESPA.

Equity trading hours are between 10:00 am and 5:00 pm. There is a pre-market trading session from 9:45 am to 10:00 am and an after-hours session from 5:30 pm to 7:30 pm. The aggregate market value of Brazilian stocks was close to $700 billion in mid-October, 2008 and approximately 450 stocks trade on the BM&FBOVESPA.[3] At the same time period, ExxonMobil (a single U.S. based firm) was selling for $375 billion. Petrobras is Brazil's largest company, with a market capitalization of $140 billion as of mid-October, 2008. BM&FBOVESPA has multiple indices which track Brazilian stock market performance, but the most notable is the Bovespa Index that constitutes 70% of all of BOVESPA's companies' market capitalization.

Short-selling is permitted, but uncommon due to the lack of liquidity, outside the largest names. There are approximately 25 Brazilian American Depository Receipts (ADRs) trading on U.S. exchanges. Many of these stocks are shortable in reasonable quantities, but they (like most ADRs) are skewed towards the largest and strongest firms of the country. Hence, they are typically better macro shorts rather than fundamental based.

3.2 Brazilian Bond Market

The Brazilian bond market is not for the fainthearted due to the high historical levels of inflation in the country. Floating coupon rates are more common in Brazilian bonds than in other countries since it reduces the inflation risk of owning a bond during a period of rising interest rates. As we shall discuss later, the high nominal yields and volatility may be a positive for talented fixed income and global macro hedge fund managers.

BM&FBOVESPA is also the primary exchange utilized for trading both government and corporate bonds. Brazil's corporate bond market is relatively small, with approximately $75 billion in debt outstanding as of mid-2007.[4] The average fixed income issue was approximately $112 million.[5] Conversely, the Brazilian government bond market is much larger, with approximately $814 billion in federal debt as of March, 2008.[6]

Leal and Carvalhal-da-Silva (2006) conducted a comprehensive study on the evolution and current state of the Brazilian Bond Market. They find domestic bonds are used as an alternative to bank loans and those firms that issue international bonds tend to view it as one piece of a diversified debt portfolio, which would generally also include domestic bonds and bank loans. They also find several relationships between company characteristics and debt use:

1) Exporters use less international bonds and more asset backed securities.
2) Firms with foreign shareholders use international bonds more often.
3) ADR issuers use international bonds and asset-backed securities less frequently
4) Firms with better corporate governance practices are generally less leveraged

3.3 Brazilian Derivative Market

Not surprisingly, BM&FBOVESPA is also Brazil's primary derivatives exchange. In October 2007, BM&FBOVESPA and The CME Group (CME) approved an agreement of reciprocal ownership. CME owns approximately 10% of BM&FBOVESPA's equity in return for giving the Brazilian exchange a roughly 2% stake in its shares. The transaction was approved by the owners of both firms during the first quarter of 2008.

The following derivatives are traded: equity and index options, and forward / futures contracts on commodities and materials. Swaps, like in most foreign markets, are conducted over the counter (OTC). At the end of 2007, average daily derivatives volume was $1.7 billion with more than $1.2 trillion in open interest.[7] Local currency interest rate derivatives constituted 53% of derivatives trading volume and commodities surprisingly accounted for only 1%.[8] The low activity in derivatives commodities is expected to rapidly change as CME shares its trading technology with BM&FBOVESPA.

4. Unique Dynamics of the Brazilian Financial Markets

4.1 History of High Inflation

The "Achilles' heel" of the Brazilian economy had been its high historical levels of inflation. Brazil's central bank, Banco Central do Brasil has made important strides over the past decade reining in inflation. The actions of the central bank in concert with the rapid rise in its GDP have resulted in Brazil receiving its first ever investment grade rating by a major credit agency. In April, 2008 Standard and Poors (S&P) gave Brazilian sovereign debt its lowest investment grade rating of BBB-. **Figure 1** illustrates the historical levels of Brazil's Consumer Price Index (CPI) and Producer Price Index (PPI) over the past ten years. Brazilian CPI has averaged less than five percent annually over the past five years, a far cry from the persistent double digit levels experienced in the first half of the 1990s. The PPI has been more erratic, but is partially the result of the inherent volatility of production process inputs, such as commodities and materials.

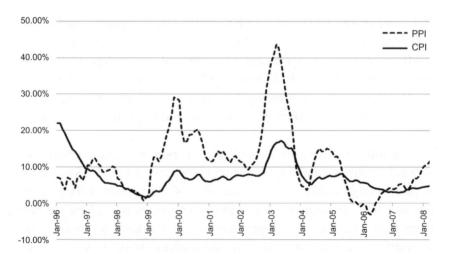

Figure 1: Historical Increases in the Brazilian Consumer Price Index (CPI) and Producer Price Index (PPI)

Source: International Monetary Fund — Data and Statistics

The Plano Real or "Real Plan" was instituted by Brazilian President Itamar Franco and Minister of Finance, Fernando Henrique Cardoso, in 1994 with the primary goal of controlling inflation. The centerpiece of the Plano Real was to peg Brazil's currency to the United States Dollar. The currency peg was removed in January 1999 in order to spur exports and inflation has been generally contained since that time. Brazil's long history of battling inflation has impacted the psyche of domestic and foreign investors alike. We elaborate on the implications of this issue later in this chapter.

4.2 Brazil's Central Role In South America

The Brazilian economy towers over the rest of its South American neighbors, as measured by GDP. **Table 3** lists 2007 GDP for the largest South American economies.

Table 3: Estimated GDP for Leading South American Countries [9]

World Rank	Country	2007 GDP Millions $
10	Brazil	$2,131,608
25	Argentina	741,713
32	Colombia	426,063
36	Venezuela	335,000
46	Chile	245,617
54	Peru	217,971
60	Ecuador	98,280
66	Bolivia	39,780
96	Uruguay	37,280
98	Paraguay	35,310
168	Guyana	4,129
173	Suriname	3,690

Source: CIA World Factbook

Brazil's GDP is nearly triple that of Argentina's, its closest competitor. In fact, Brazil's GDP is roughly as large as the next ten biggest South American economies *combined*. Brazil's size provides it with an important export advantage relative to other countries in the region. Furthermore, its South American roots give it an advantage over North American, European, and Asian countries when selling goods and services to countries in the Latin American region. A key takeaway for hedge fund managers is, similar to China, Brazil has the capacity to grow domestically and regionally, despite the global slowdown that has engulfed much of the developed world in 2008.

The European Union (EU) and North American Free Trade Agreement (NAFTA) are well known international trading blocs. Several South American countries formed in 1991 a trade bloc called Mercosur; whose English translation is the "Common Market of the South." Mercosur's short-term goal is to eliminate barriers to trade among member countries. Its' long-term goal is complete South American economic integration. Mercosur's members account for 75% of South American GDP and it is the fourth largest trading bloc in the world behind the EU, NAFTA, and the Association of South East Asian Nations (ASEAN).[10]

Brazil has sought to increase its power in South America and throughout the rest of the world through a number of initiatives, in addition to its primary role in Mercosur. Soares de Lima (2008) points to the following recent moves that demonstrate Brazil's increasingly global ambitions:

- Its active campaign to obtain a permanent seat on the UN Security Council.
- The formalization of relations among the BRIC countries.
- Its formation of the ISBA (India, Brazil, and South Africa) coalition.
- Its role in the creation of the Union of South American Nations (Unasul).
- Its command of the UN peacekeeping mission in Haiti.
- Its role in the creation of the G-20, which focuses on agriculture-related issues in the WTO.
- Its proposal to create a South American Defense Council as a mechanism to prevent conflict in the region.

4.3 Brazilian Investor Profile and Behavior

Brazilians' wealth has been growing at a rapid pace. According to the 2008 edition of the annual Capgemini Merrill Lynch *World Wealth Report*, the number of Brazilians with $1 million or more in liquid net worth increased 19% over the prior year to 143,000. Clearly, the global bear market of 2008 will reduce these numbers, but many viable, cash flow positive businesses in Brazil have been created over the past decade. These businesses will continue to generate wealth for their owners. As noted previously, less than 500 stocks trade on the Brazilian stock exchange, BM&FBOVESPA, so the magnitude of the decline in privately held businesses is likely to be less precipitous.

A 2005 study by Instituto Brasileiro de Opinião Pública e Estatística (IBOPE) and Associação Nacional dos Bancos de Investimento (ANBID) discussed the profile of the typical Brazilian investor. The typical Brazilian investor is an upper middle class to wealthy citizen (usually male) in his late 50s, earning between $24,000 and $48,000 per year. This income range is approximately 3 to 5 times that of the average Brazilian citizen. These investors allocate the bulk of their investments to mutual fund type vehicles with the overall goals of preserving capital, earning a reasonable return, and having strong liquidity.

Brazilian investors place a high premium on liquidity due to their long dated experiences with the ravages of inflation. Furthermore, transparency for Brazilian firms is lacking relative to other firms around the world. For example, Brazil has not yet implemented international financial reporting standards (IFRS), in contrast to virtually all of Europe, India, Russia, Singapore, Hong Kong, and many other countries. The CVM has declared that listed Brazilian firms should comply with IFRS by 2010 so the transparency issue is likely to improve over time.

Despite the transparency concerns, many investors are willing to take the plunge into the Brazilian markets due to their long term secular trends. International investors account for the largest share (37%) of trading volume of Brazilian equities, according to BOVESPA's Facts & Figures (2008). These investors fall into two broad categories, long-term and short-term. The long-term investors in general desire exposure to the Brazilian financial markets and base their decisions to a large extent on fundamentals and secular trends. Conversely, hedge funds (Portuguese translation: fundos multimercado) domiciled in Brazil are required by the Comissão de Valores Mobiliários (CVM), the regulatory agency of Brazilian financial markets, to provide their investors with *daily liquidity*. This constraint results in a strong preference for hedge funds to engage in active trading strategies.

Fundos multimercado and other Brazilian money managers also have a short term focus due to the manner in which they quote their returns. In order to induce investors, mindful of the days of high inflation, portfolio returns are quoted on the basis of CDI (Certificado de Deposito Interbancario) a daily interbank rate, instead of the traditional total return or net asset value approach.

De Medeiros (2005) finds that Brazilian investors overreact to positive shocks or good news and underreact to negative shocks or bad news. He cites "one possible explanation is that the Brazilian market is small as measured by the number of securities listed, quantity of investors, and market capitalization. Usually, such relatively small stock exchanges are dominated by speculative investors who respond to long-run rather than short-run market fluctuations."

5. Hedge Fund Strategies in Brazil

The unique dynamics of the Brazilian financial markets make some hedge fund strategies more likely to outperform than others. Rather than listing a specific trade, that would likely be obsolete by the time of publication, our goal is to discuss hedge fund strategies that have the increased likelihood of earning alpha for the decade ahead. Our approach is to link Brazilian cultural issues and market microstructure to common hedge fund strategies. In our view, the following strategies are most likely to generate significant alpha for hedge funds trading in Brazil in the decade ahead.

5.1 Global Macro

The high levels of volatility of the Brazilian equity and fixed income markets are well suited to the strategies of Global Macro hedge funds. One estimate finds that 70%–75% of the hedge funds operating in Brazil in 2006 were Global Macro hedge funds.[11] BM&FBOVESPA operates a sophisticated electronic system with ample liquidity for macro related trades, such as equity indexes, fixed income indexes, and currency related trades. Furthermore, the daily liquidity requirement of Brazilian hedge funds places primary emphasis on entering and exiting positions quickly. In short, Global Macro hedge funds have and will continue to find fertile ground for generating alpha in Brazil.

5.2 Fixed Income / Credit

High nominal and real interest rates on Brazilian debt are enticing to both Fixed Income hedge funds and traditional investors. Exchange rate changes also add to or detract from returns. **Figure 2** shows yields on Brazilian Government Bonds as of mid-November, 2008. The nearly unprecedented turmoil in the global credit markets has pushed annual yields on 8-year Brazilian debt to almost 19%. Brazilian sovereign debt is generally limited to maturity dates of eight years or less due to investor weariness with the country's historical bouts of high inflation. Corporate bonds are relatively thinly traded in Brazil since their yields are generally 300 to 1000 basis points higher than sovereign debt. Accordingly, traditional corporate bond issuance is extremely expensive and not a common form of financing. Brazilian firms generally prefer bank debt and equity for their external financing needs. Fixed income hedge funds can employ typical arbitrage strategies on sovereign Brazilian debt and derivatives. To a lesser extent, they can go long Brazilian corporates and hedge with fixed income indexes or derivatives.

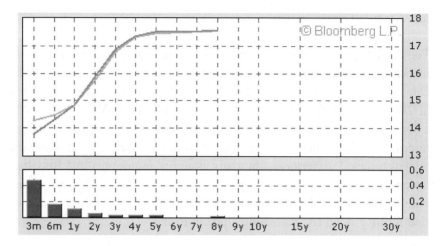

Figure 2: Yields On Brazilian Government Bonds, November 14, 2008

Note: The upper curve represents the current yield curve and the lower curve represents
the yield curve at the close of the prior day, October 23, 2008.
Source: Bloomberg

5.3 Event Driven

Hedge funds that focus on event driven strategies should find attractive
alpha opportunities in the Brazilian financial markets. The previously
cited work finding overreaction in the presence of good news and
underreaction to bad news provides a strong framework for alpha
generating strategies. Brazil's expected adoption of IFRS by 2010 will
likely increase the opportunity for earnings based event studies. In
addition, the continued growth of and interest in the Brazilian financial
markets will surely result in more sell side research on Brazilian firms in
the decade ahead, creating alpha generating opportunities for event
strategies based on security upgrades, downgrades, and earnings estimate
revisions.

5.4 Statistical Arbitrage

The technological infrastructure of BM&FBOVESPA is quite advanced and it is expected to continue to progress upward due to the reciprocal ownership relationship with CME. Most trading is done electronically, but an open outcry floor is still available for trading derivatives. BM&FBOVESPA's website states that 99.5% of orders sent to its Mega Bolsa system take less than 0.62 seconds to be processed and that its Global Trading System is capable of executing 250 transactions per second. Hence, high frequency statistical arbitrage hedge funds should find that their strategies are executed efficiently.

One advantage of the near monopolistic nature of BM&FBOVESPA is that trading across asset classes and financial instruments is somewhat seamless, relative to similar strategies conducted on foreign exchanges. Strong technology in concert with high volatility creates fertile alpha ground for Statistical Arbitrage hedge funds. The daily liquidity requirement of Brazilian hedge funds, make Statistical Arbitrage a more economically viable strategy than Distressed, Short Selling and other less liquid strategies. The primary impediments to achieving alpha at this time are the limited number of individual securities and relatively low trading volume for securities outside the largest 50 to 100 names, especially on the short selling side of the hedge fund book.

5.5 Multistrategy

Multistrategy funds can turn the relative illiquidity of the Brazilian financial markets into an advantage, by telling their investors that they can allocate capital towards the most promising areas of the market. A Multistrategy fund that emphasizes the strategies discussed above — Global Macro, Fixed Income / Credit, Event Driven, and Statistical Arbitrage — is likely to generate the best results. Brazil's primary role in South America may enable Multistrategy funds to expand into related markets, since each additional market is likely too small to accommodate traditional hedge fund strategies. In other words, a South American Multistrategy Fund, with a Brazilian focus may maximize alpha opportunities and allow for reasonable capacity.

Hedge Fund Alpha Tear Sheet — Chapter 3

- The economies of Brazil Russia India and China (BRIC) are expected to be near the top of world GDP charts by 2050. Accordingly opportunities in Brazil and the rest of the BRIC countries may make it a fertile source of alpha in the decades ahead.
- Brazil's economy, with 2007 GDP of approximately $1.5 trillion, is the second largest in the Americas, and among the ten largest in the world.
  - o Brazil's GDP is projected to rank the fourth largest in the world by 2050.
- The vast majority of Brazilian financial market trading activity is conducted on BM&FBOVESPA, the third largest exchange in the world by market capitalization.
- Investors in Brazilian financial markets have dealt with many bouts of high inflation and remain wary of its risks.
  - o This wariness is one reason for the daily liquidity requirement forced upon hedge funds domiciled in Brazil.
- Brazil's prominent role in South America provides it with a strong platform for growth, despite the global credit crisis of 2008.
- Transparency in Brazilian financial markets is lacking, but is expected to improve markedly by 2010 with the adoption of the International Financial Reporting Standards (IFRS).
- Empirical studies have found Brazilian investors overreact to positive news and underreact to negative news.
  - o These persistent behaviors may form the basis for alpha generating strategies.
- In our view, the following hedge fund strategies in Brazil are best poised to deliver alpha in the decade ahead.
  - o Global Macro
  - o Fixed Income / Credit
  - o Event Driven
  - o Statistical Arbitrage
  - o Multistrategy

End Notes

[1] The 2050 GDP forecasts come from Wilson and Stupnytska (2007) of Goldman Sachs.

[2] Hargreaves (2008) discusses Brazil's interest in joining OPEC.

[3] The BM&FBOVESPA website provides various statistics on trading in the Brazilian financial markets.

[4, 5] Leal, Ricardo and Andre Carvalhal-da-Silva, "The Development of the Brazilian Bond Market," Working Paper, Federal University of Rio de Janeiro (UFRJ), September 13, 2006.

[6] Hugh (2008) cites the Brazilian national debt figures.

[7, 8] These statistics are from Basar (2008).

[9] The differences in Brazil's 2007 GDP figures in Tables 2 and 3 may be explained by the different sources (Goldman Sachs vs. CIA World Factbook) and currency adjustments. Additionally, the Goldman Sachs figure is actual, while the CIA Factbook number is estimated.

[10] These statistics are from Klonsky and Hanson (2007).

[11] WealthNet is the source of the estimate.

References

Amante, André, Araujo, Márcio, and Serge Jeanneau, "The Search for Liquidity in the Brazilian Domestic Government Bond Market" *BIS Quarterly Review*, June 2007, pp. 69–82.

Basar, Shanny, "Brazilian Exchange plans to take on the world", *Dow Jones Financial News Online*, June 23, 2008.
http://www.efinancialnews.com/homepage/content/2451018916

BOVESPA's Facts and Figures, June, 2008.
http://www.bovespa.com.br/pdf/FactsFigures.pdf

BOVESPA Homepage.
http://www.bovespa.com.br/indexi.asp

Capgemini Merrill Lynch *World Wealth Report*, 2008.

CIA World Factbook, GDP Purchasing Power Parity.
https://www.cia.gov/library/publications/the-world-factbook/
rankorder/2001rank.html

De Medeiros, Otavio R., Reaction of the Brazilian Stock Market to
Positive and Negative Shocks, December 5, 2005.
http://virtualbib.fgv.br/dspace/bitstream/123456789/1587/1/invest-
112.pdf

Economist.com, Country Briefings: Brazil.
http://www.economist.com/countries/Brazil/profile.cfm?folder=Profile-
FactSheet

Embassy of Brazil in London website.
http://www.brazil.org.uk/economy/gdp.html

Goldman Sachs, *Market Profile, Brazil*, June 22, 2007.

Hargreaves, Steve, "Brazil Dances with OPEC," February 22, 2008.
http://money.cnn.com/2008/02/22/news/international/brazil_opec/index.
htm

Hugh, Edward, "Brazil Debt Raised To Investment Grade By Standard
and Poor's," Thursday, May 01, 2008.
http://brazileconomy.blogspot.com/2008/05/brazil-debt-raised-to-
investment-grade.html

IBOPE Opinião. (2005, June 3). RADIOGRAFIA DO INVESTIDOR
DE FUNDOS NO BRASIL. Retrieved May 18, 2008, from IBOPE.
http://www.ibope.com.br/opiniao_publica/downloads/opp046_anbid_jun
05.ppt

International Monetary Fund — Data and Statistics.
http://www.imfstatistics.org/imf/

Klonsky, Joanna and Stephanie Hanson, "Mercosur: South America's Fractious Trade Bloc," Council on Foreign Relations, December 7, 2007. http://www.cfr.org/publication/12762/

Leal, Ricardo and Andre Carvalhal-da-Silva, "The Development of the Brazilian Bond Market," Working Paper, Federal University of Rio de Janeiro (UFRJ), September 13, 2006.

Soares de Lima, Maria Regina, "Brazil Rising".
http://www.ip-global.org/archiv/2008/autumn2008/brazil-rising.html

The WealthNET, "Brazilians lured by booming hedge fund industry".
http://www.anbid.com.br/institucional/documentos_download/fundos/estudos%20e%20estat%C3%ADsticas%20mundiais/brazilians%20lured%20by%20booming%20hedge%20fund%20industry%20-%202006.doc

Wilson, Dominic and Anna Stupnytska, *The N-11: More than an Acronym*, Global Economics Paper:153, Goldman Sachs, March 28, 2007.

4

ACHIEVING HEDGE FUND ALPHA IN RUSSIA

Irina Samoylova and John M. Longo, PhD, CFA

Goldman Sachs; Rutgers Business School & The MDE Group

1. Introduction

The purpose of this chapter is to provide a basic overview of the Russian financial markets and its dynamics, with the ultimate goal of identifying hedge fund strategies that are most likely to generate alpha in this region. Accordingly, it is necessary to discuss some of the common financial instruments that exist in Russian markets, regulation, and investor behavior. Our primary focus is on the financial markets in Russia, but when appropriate, we will also discuss the related economies and markets of Eastern Europe. The nascent and rapidly evolving nature of the Russian financial markets, as well as the other BRIC countries, may make it a fertile source of alpha in the decades ahead.

2. Russia's Economic Growth

Russia's economy has experienced a rapid rise over the past 10 years, largely on the basis of the strong leadership (some would argue too strong) of President and now Prime Minister Vladimir Putin and the secular bull market in commodities. Russia, of course, is rich in natural resources and has used these valuable assets at times to reassert its political power. Russian Gross Domestic Product (GDP) has increased at approximately 7% per year since Putin's rise to power. Although not quite as high as China's 10% annual GDP growth over the same period, Russia's growth is quite impressive given the lack of a smoothly functioning financial system and less foreign direct investment (FDI) capital flows.

One particularly noteworthy accomplishment is that the Russian government has very little debt and a foreign exchange reserve surplus in excess of $560 billion, as of September 2008. Many in the hedge fund community can readily recall the dramatic 1998 period, when Russia defaulted on $40 billion of its national debt. This default was one of the early dominos that resulted in the spectacular downfall and Wall Street supported bailout of "star" hedge fund, Long Term Capital Management (LTCM). The recent unraveling of the credit bubble has resulted in a dramatic 60% drop to the Russian stock market through the third quarter of 2008. However, the country is in a much stronger financial position to deal with the current crisis, relative to prior ones. In addition, the excessive volatility is a positive for hedge fund managers, as long as the markets continue to operate and onerous restrictions are not placed on foreign capital.

3. Evolution of Russian Economy

According to Dabrowski et al. (2005), the stagnation and ultimate collapse of communist regimes throughout the former Soviet Union and Eastern Europe did not result simply from a fatal coincidence of circumstances or political error, but rather from their deeply rooted economic inefficiencies. The painful, but ultimately successful, transition from a planned economy to a market based economy increased the need for the development of Russia's financial markets.

The early post-privatization period reestablished the need for functioning exchanges and for the development of other core infra-structure activities. The widespread ability to effectively convert the Russian Ruble (or Rouble) into other mainstream currencies in 2006 was an important step in Russia's continued growth and a proud moment for many Russian citizens. In some respects, the Ruble's convertibility represented a "coming out" party for Russia, now firmly ensconced as an important G8 member, the club of the most powerful economic nations on Earth.

The "Achilles heel" of Russia's economy is its nascent banking system. A smoothly functioning financial system is central to effective economic growth, since financial intermediaries perform the function of transferring surplus savings to those that need capital to grow. A recent United States State Department report (2008) provides the following statistics.[1] The Russian Banking system had aggregate capital of only $59 billion, as of January, 2007. Approximately one third of Russians have such distrust for the banking system that they would rather keep their savings "under the mattress." Of the nearly 1,200 banks in Russia, approximately only 50 are foreign owned. Sberbank is by far the largest bank in Russia, but it faces emerging competition from Vneshtorgbank, Gazprombank, Alfa Bank, MDM Bank and Austrian bank, Raiffessen.

4. Overview of Russian Financial Markets

4.1 Russian Stock Markets

There are more than 14 stock exchanges in Russia, but the majority of trading takes place in the Moscow Interbank Currency Exchange (MICEX), Open Joint Stock Currency Russian Trading System Stock Exchange (RTS OJSC), St. Peterburg Interbank Currency Exchange (SIPBCEX), and the Moscow Stock Exchange (MSE). The aggregate stock market value of Russia is relatively small, at less than $1 trillion near the end of 2008. By way of comparison, ExxonMobil, a single U.S.-based stock, is worth slightly more than $400 billion at the same point in time. We briefly discuss the two largest exchanges below.

4.1.1 Moscow Interbank Currency Exchange (MICEX)

Despite its name, the MICEX is an active stock exchange in Russia. Its chief advantages are its relatively robust technological infrastructure, which allows for effective remote trading, and ability to trade large blocks of securities. MICEX electronically trades a wide variety of financial instruments, including stocks, government and corporate bonds, derivatives, and of course currencies. In trades more than 50 equities, including the largest, state-controlled natural gas monopoly, Gazprom. A pre-trading period of 10:15 am–10:30 am helps determine the opening price. Regular trading hours are conducted between 10:30 am and 5:45 pm. Trading activity during the last 30 minutes of the day determines the closing price.

The MICEX Index is a value-weighted index that provides a benchmark for Russian stock market returns. Since Gazprom dominates the MICEX Index, the need for other more representative indexes has arisen. The MICEX 10 is a price weighted index and consists of the 10 most liquid stocks of Russia, regardless of the exchange that they trade upon. It is the Russian index most similar to America's Dow Jones Industrial Average.

4.1.2 Open Joint Stock Company Russian Trading System Stock Exchange (RTS OJSC)

The Open Joint Stock Company Russian Trading System Stock Exchange (RTS OJSC) is the most active Russian market for trading equities. It was previously known as the RTS Exchange. According to a recent Goldman Sachs Report (2007), approximately 60% of shares are traded over the counter through RTS OJSC. Its architecture closely resembles Nasdaq's "PORTAL" system. The exchange is currently a non-profit entity owned by its 250 members, but it is in the process of transforming into a public, for-profit entity.

RTS OJSC trades nearly 1700 securities, across all asset classes.[2] The RTS Index an important equity benchmark barometer. It consists of 50 securities on a value-weighted basis, but the weight of the largest firms is capped at a maximum value of 15%.

4.2 Russian Bond Markets

The Russian bond market is attractive to hedge fund managers due to its double-digit nominal yields, and corresponding high inflation rates. As a result, Russian bonds are generally more volatile than their Western counterparts, raising the prospect of significant alpha for savvy fixed income hedge funds. The absence of a well functioning banking system has led many major Russian firms to seek fixed income financing through the capital markets, rather than from a traditional commercial bank. MiG, Russian Railways, and Gazprom are among the higher profile Russian firms to have issued bonds in recent years.

Issuers include the national government, municipalities, and corporations. The MICEX Corporate Bond Index (MICEX CBI) is one of the leading measures of tracking the performance of Russian bonds. Russian bonds are generally marketed as Eurobonds, or denominated in Rubles. A report by Credit Europe Bank Ltd (2008) finds that 57% of Russian Bonds are denominated in Rubles and the remaining 43% in Euros. Nearly 43% of Ruble-denominated bonds consisted of sovereign and municipal debt, 20% finance oriented companies, and the remainder spread across various industries. Conversely they find that issues relating to oil and gas accounted for the largest share (33%) of Russian Eurobonds.

The turmoil in the credit markets has taken its toll on bond markets around the world, including those in Russia. Trading in the Russian financial markets has been suspended several times in September 2008 in an effort to ward off a financial panic. The Finance Ministry has pledged $60 billion to help an already fragile Russian banking system. Despite the short-term turbulence, Russia's bond market should continue its sharp upward trajectory with respect to the number and size of issues. The developing Russian mortgage market is expected to be a key contributor to its growth as the country continues to rollout its Affordable Housing National Project.

4.3 Russian Derivative Markets

Given Russia's commodity driven economy, its derivatives markets are arguably more important than the country's equity and fixed income markets. Futures and Options on RTS (FORTS) is the major derivatives exchange in Russia and it has experienced rapid growth. Fairless (2008) finds that the value of contracts on FORTS increased nearly 200% over the first six months of 2008 to 6.6 trillion Rubles, relative to the same period a year earlier. According to Goryunov (2007), a 2006 law passed by the Duma, Russia's lower parliamentary chamber, provided the derivatives market with important legal protections and was a major factor in its exponential growth.

More than 64 futures and options contracts trade on FORTS including currency, interest rates, indexes, oil, gold, silver, and sugar. Domestic firms are now actively utilizing derivatives contracts as a way to reduce risks inherent in running their businesses. The convertibility of the Ruble has also substantially increased demand for currency hedging by foreign enterprises doing business in Russia.

5. Unique Dynamics of the Russian Financial Markets

5.1 Heightened Political Risk

Political risk and emerging markets go hand in hand. Yet, politics seems to play a greater role in Russian financial markets, relative to most other countries. Of course, one of the most dramatic examples of political risk was the aforementioned default on Russia's sovereign debt that occurred in 1998. Such an event seems unlikely in more recent times, due to Russia's strong foreign exchange position, but other troublesome events have emerged.

5.1.1 Yukos

Yukos, founded in 1993, emerged from the privatization process that occurred in the transition from a planned to market-based economy. It grew to become one of the largest energy companies in the world, producing nearly 20% of Russia's oil. In 2004, the Russian Government charged Yukos with evading nearly $7 billion in taxes. This judgment eventually resulted in Yukos declaring bankruptcy and landed its CEO, Mikhail Khodorkovsky, in prison for tax evasion. Our point is not to comment on the merits of the case against Yukos, but rather the speed at which one of the largest companies in the Russian market can virtually disappear due to its still evolving legal and property rights systems.

5.1.2 Mechel

A feared replay of the Yukos case emerged with Mechel, a vertically integrated Russian mining company, in the summer of 2008. Prime Minister Putin, speaking at an industry conference, said concerning Mechel, "Meanwhile, it is known that in the first quarter this year the company exported raw materials abroad at half the domestic, and world, price. And what about the margin tax for the government?"[3] Mechel's stock, which closed at $36.61 on the day prior to Putin's comments, tumbled $13.77 after them, closing at $22.84. Kramer (2008) notes, "When Vladimir Putin talks, investors in Russia listen. And some head for the door." Mechel was trading at approximately $13.00 a share in September 2008, amid a sharp drop in the value of materials stocks worldwide.

5.1.3 Hermitage Capital Management

Hermitage Capital Management, an activist hedge fund, is one of the world's largest investors in Russian securities. Hermitage's CEO, William Browder, has long been critical of the management of Gazprom, Russia's largest company, which has a virtual monopoly on its country's natural gas market. Browder's Russian visa was revoked in 2005 for unspecified national security reasons. Initial reports claimed that in April, 2008, Browder was charged with tax evasion by the Russian Government. However, Adelaja et al. (2008) quotes Moscow Police spokeswoman, Anzhela Katuyeva, as saying, "The Moscow police issued no arrest warrant for Browder and no tax evasion case is pending against him as far as we know." The case has not yet been resolved as of the third quarter of 2008, but bears close watching for hedge funds trading in Russia — especially those of the activist variety.

5.2 Current Lack of Effective Insider Trading Laws

Capital markets function best when they are open and trustworthy. Nothing creates mistrust as much as a lack of insider trading rules, or their effective enforcement. The "On Securities Markets" law limits trading on "office information" but is far more vague than traditional laws on insider trading, and is rarely enforced. Vladimir Milovidov, the head of Russia's Federal Service for Financial Markets, stated a law to prevent insider trading is "the number one task,"[4] A draft of a law prohibiting insider trading and market manipulation was said to be circulating within the Duma in 2008. However, as of October, 2008, there were no effective laws prohibiting insider trading in Russia.

5.3 Russian and Eastern European Investor Behavior

The Russian financial markets are not yet as well developed as their western counterparts with respect to the collection and dissemination of accurate financial information. As a result, market prices are often driven by rumors and investor sentiment. Russian investors are very risk-averse, due in part to the country's relatively high corruption levels. Transparency International ranked Russia 147 of 180 countries on the group's annual survey of the most transparent countries.[5] Russian prosecutors estimated, in late 2006, that $240 billion worth of bribes change hands every year in Russia.[6] The high levels of corruption and distrust have led most Russian citizens to keep the bulk of their liquid assets in bank deposits or "under the mattress", rather than in investment oriented vehicles.

McCarthy and Puffer (2003) find that Eastern Europeans have a strong reticence to share knowledge, a significant preference to work with familiar individuals, and to generally exclude those they consider outsiders. As a result, individuals from these regions tend to safeguard valuable information to a greater extent than others. Elenkov (1998) argues that Russia's traditional bureaucratic structure, high levels of risk aversion, and lack of interpersonal trust, predisposes its individuals and institutions to provide minimal disclosure of company-related information.

Michailova and Husted (2003) find that the potential value of information sharing is often defeated by what they term "knowledge sharing hostility." In other words, they find that Eastern Europeans generally do not view information sharing as a "win-win" scenario and therefore have a general preference to withhold valuable information. They also find that the "Not-Invented-Here" Syndrome, which often results in the rejection of even valid ideas from others, is especially strong in Eastern European individuals. Accordingly, it is exceptionally important for hedge funds trading in Russia to have a strong network of "locals."

6. Hedge Fund Strategies in Russia

Not all hedge fund strategies are equally likely to generate alpha in Russia. For example, activist hedge funds are rarely welcomed anywhere, but may receive an especially unfriendly response in Russia. The Russian stock market is highly concentrated, with limited liquidity (outside the largest firms), and has limited history. Government officials have halted trading during especially volatile times in the stock market, making proper hedging and risk management somewhat problematic. Trading was halted three times during the turbulent month of September, 2008. Therefore, traditional equity strategies may not be as successful as in other emerging markets. In our view, the following strategies are most likely to generate significant alpha for hedge funds trading in Russia in the decade ahead.

6.1 Managed Futures / Commodity Trading Advisors (CTAs)

Russia's vast natural resource reserves ensure it will be a major player in the commodities market for years to come. Recall the original purpose of derivatives markets — namely, to help producers and consumers of various commodities reduce risk. Accordingly, there is strong fundamental demand for many commodity-oriented financial instruments in Russia.

Although trading volume is currently small compared to the activity of the Chicago Mercantile Exchange, Russia's FORTS system is among the 20 most active futures markets in the world.[7] FORTS volume has grown exponentially over the past three years, with few signs of slowing down. Accordingly, several of its 64+ contracts contain enough liquidity for Managed Futures / CTA oriented hedge funds.

By definition, commodities should be similarly priced around the world, raising the prospect of arbitrage opportunities between Russian and foreign commodity exchanges. Lastly, global banks, such as UBS, Societe Generale, and Deutsche Bank are among the clearing firms on FORTS, simplifying the operational process for U.S. or European based hedge funds.

6.2 Global Macro

The high levels of volatility of the Russian and Eastern European financial markets and their dependence on commodities create fertile alpha ground for Global Macro hedge funds. As noted previously, the convertibility of the Ruble was an important step in Russia's economic growth. Additionally, the triangular currency relationships, among the Ruble, Eastern European currencies, and the Euro create some interesting speculative opportunities. For example, Global Macro hedge funds can estimate the likelihood of various Eastern European countries being admitted to the European Union, and ultimately having their currencies be converted to the Euro. Russia's economic ties to European countries, especially through the Energy sector, create some unique macroeconomic relationships that can be effectively modeled by Global Macro hedge funds.

6.3 Fixed Income / Credit

The absence of an effective banking system in Russia has increased the importance of the country's fixed income capital markets. Unlike in Asia, where the bank loan market is the preferred vehicle of companies for raising fixed income capital, Russian firms are much more open to issuing securities to meet their financing needs. The nascent Russian banking system has come under severe stress in late 2008, in the aftermath of the global credit bubble.

The main drawback of the credit markets, thus far, is the limited liquidity in most issues. The federal law "On Joint Stock Companies," requires that the volume of a bond issue not exceed a company's authorized capital, resulting in a "Catch 22" situation. That is, it is easer for firms to issue debt after they grow, but they need the capital before they can effectively grow.

High levels of inflation in Russia, estimated to be at 15% annualized in October, 2008, have dramatically increased volatility of fixed income instruments and the corresponding alpha possibilities that go with it.[8] Amazingly, Moscow is now the third most expensive real estate market in the world, trailing only London and Monaco, having risen six-fold since 2003.[9] Russia's real estate bubble appears to be unraveling, creating fertile alpha ground for fixed income hedge funds. Furthermore, the significant gap between market prices, and government subsidized rents, creates exciting alpha opportunities for those hedge funds able to do fundamental research on the space.

6.4 Event Driven

At present, it would be difficult to create an effective Event-Driven hedge fund based on a single assets class, due to the limited liquidity of most market sectors. However, our earlier cited studies documented the collective behavior tendencies of Eastern European investors, potentially resulting in an attractive alpha opportunity. Given these behavioral tendencies, a momentum oriented strategy may add alpha once a particular event (e.g. crash in the Russian real estate market) is revealed. Additionally, the relative homogeneity of the Russian capital markets, due to its large focus on natural resources, creates a purer play trade relative to event strategies in more diverse economies, such as that in the United States.

6.5 Statistical Arbitrage

Russia has 14 stock exchanges and the largest firms, such as Gazprom, Rosenfelt, Rosneft, and Lukoil trade on more than one of them. Although the universe of Russian American Depository Receipts (ADRs) is currently limited to less than 10, several others trade on the "Pink Sheets" with material volume. For example, Gazprom, which does not have an ADR, trades approximately 1 million shares per day. Accordingly, there are likely to be divergences in prices among exchanges for the same security until the inevitable consolidation occurs.

Hedge funds with detailed knowledge of Russian market microstructure, and with access to institutional brokers at the various exchanges, may be able to uncover some pure arbitrage opportunities. Additionally, the lack of synchronicity among the exchanges may result in lead-lag relationships that can be exploited. The more technologically advanced exchanges, or those with the higher levels of trading volume, may act as leading indicators for the "lagging" exchanges.

6.6 Multistrategy

Multistrategy funds can turn the relative illiquidity of the Russian financial markets into an advantage, by telling their investors that they can allocate capital towards the most promising areas of the market. A Multistrategy fund that emphasizes the strategies discussed above — Managed Futures / CTA, Global Macro, Fixed Income, Event Driven, and Statistical Arbitrage — is likely to generate the best results. Those funds promoting a Russian *and* Eastern Europe theme will have a wider opportunity set, nearly always finding some attractive alpha generating opportunities and sufficient liquidity to execute their strategies.

Hedge Fund Alpha Tear Sheet — Chapter 4

- Russia's economy has experienced a rapid rise over the past 10 years, largely on the basis of the strong leadership of President and now Prime Minister Vladimir Putin and the secular bull market in commodities.
- The "Achilles heel" of Russia's economy is its nascent banking system.
  - o A recent U.S. State Department report cites that 1/3 of Russians keep their money "under the mattress" given their distrust of the current banking system.
- The aggregate stock market value of Russia is relatively small, at less than $1 trillion near the end of 2008.
- The volatile Russian bond market is attractive to Global Macro hedge fund managers due to its double digit nominal yields, and corresponding high inflation rates.
- Given Russia's commodity driven economy, its derivatives markets are arguably more important than the country's equity and fixed income markets.
- Unique dynamics of the Russian financial markets include:
  - o Heightened political risk.
  - o Current lack of effective insider trading laws.
  - o Investor behavioral biases that may differ from their Western counterparts.
- In our view, the following hedge fund strategies in Russia are best poised to deliver alpha in the decade ahead.
  - o Managed Futures / CTAs
  - o Global Macro
  - o Fixed Income / Credit
  - o Event Driven
  - o Statistical Arbitrage
  - o Multistrategy

End Notes

[1] Statistics on the Russian banking system may be obtained at the following, http://www.state.gov/e/eeb/ifd/2008/101005.htm

[2] Safonov (2007) provides some statistics on the RTS market.

[3] Kramer (2008) discussed Putin's comments on Mechel and their impact on the company's stock price.

[4] Vladimir Milovidov's quote on insider trading may be found at the following, http://74.125.113.104/search?q=cache:kkVmp4ID-58J:www.interfax.com/3/428217/news.aspx+russia+insider+trading+laws&hl=en&ct=clnk&cd=1&gl=us

[5, 6] These statistics may be found in the Dow Jones Newswire article entitled, "Russia Corruption Levels Worst In Eight Years — Watchdog."

[7] FORTS' volume and growth is discussed in Safonov (2007).

[8, 9] The inflation figures and price of Moscow real estate come from Hugh (2008).

References

Adelaja, Tai, Delany, Max, and Catrina Stewart, "Hermitage Hits Back Over Tax Allegations," *Moscow Times*, April 4, 2008. http://www.cdi.org/russia/johnson/2008-69-36.cfm

Credit Europe Bank, *Russian Bond Market*, March 25, 2008.

Dabrowski Marek, Mau Vladimir, Yanovskiy Konstantin, Sinicina Irina, Antczak Rafal, Zhavoronkov Sergei, and Shapovalov Alexei. *Russia: Political and Institutional Determinants of Economic Reforms*. Working Paper — Center for Social and Economic Research. Moscow–Warsaw, May 2005.

Editor, "Russia Corruption Levels Worst In Eight Years — Watchdog," *Dow Jones Newswires*, September 23, 2008.
http://news.morningstar.com/newsnet/ViewNews.aspx?article=/DJ/2008
09231154DOWJONESDJONLINE000462_univ.xml

Elenkov, Detelin, "Can American Management Concepts Work in Russia: A Cross-Cultural Comparative Study," *California Management Review*, Vol. 40, No. 4, 1998, pp. 133–162.

Fairless, Tom, "Investors Pile into Russian Derivatives," *Dow Jones Online Financial News*, July 4, 2008,
http://www.rts.ru/s964

Goryunov, Roman. "From the land of the bear, a bull emerges." *Special Report on Russia and Hedge Funds*, 2007, p. 9.

Goldman Sachs, *Market Profile: Russia*, June 20, 2007.

Kramer, Andrew, "Putin's comments drive a company's stock down," *International Herald Tribune*, July 25, 2008.
http://www.iht.com/articles/2008/07/25/business/steel.php

Hugh, Edward, "Russia's Crisis Spreads Right Across The Domestic Credit Market," October 3, 2008.
http://fistfulofeuros.net/afoe/economics-and-demography/russias-crisis-spreads-right-across-the-domestic-credit-market/

McCarthy, Daniel and Sheila Puffer, "The Emergence of Corporate Governance in Russia." *Journal of World Business*, Vol. 38, No. 4, pp. 284–298.

Michailova, Snejina and Kenneth Husted. "Knowledge-Sharing Hostility in Russian Firms," *California Management Review*, Berkeley, Vol. 45, No. 3, 2003, pp. 59–81.

Safanov, Oleg. "RTS plans raft of new derivatives." *Special Report on Russia and Hedge Funds*, 2007, pp. 6–7.

United States Department of State, "Russia".
http://www.state.gov/e/eeb/ifd/2008/101005.htm

5

ACHIEVING HEDGE FUND ALPHA IN INDIA

Ali Jaffery and John M. Longo, PhD, CFA

Aeneas Capital; Rutgers Business School & The MDE Group, Inc.

1. Introduction

The purpose of this chapter is to provide a basic overview of the Indian financial markets and its dynamics, with the ultimate goal of identifying hedge fund strategies that are most likely to generate alpha in this region. Accordingly, it is necessary to discuss some of the common financial instruments that exist in Indian markets, regulation, and investor behavior. The nascent and rapidly evolving nature of the Indian financial markets, as well as the other BRIC countries, may make it a fertile source of alpha in the decades ahead.

1.1 Overview of Indian Financial Markets

The Indian financial markets have been an abundant source of alpha generation for hedge funds over the last ten to fifteen years. The reasons are clearly the Indian economic boom, bull market for equities, and market liberalization.

The Securities and Exchange Board of India (SEBI) recognizes 22 stock exchanges in the country. The most prominent of these are the Bombay Stock Exchange (BSE) and the National Stock Exchange (NSE). The BSE is the largest and oldest exchange in the country

(10th largest in the world as of mid-2008) and has over 5000 listed companies, while the NSE has approximately 1300 listed companies. The two have a combined market capitalization of approximately $2 trillion. The BSE and NSE today have about 840 and 1014 members, respectively[1].

The major indices on these exchanges are the BSE Sensitive Index (SENSEX 30) and the S&P CNX NIFTY. Members of the SENSEX 30 are chosen on the basis of liquidity, depth and industry representation. The NIFTY has some overlap with the SENSEX 30, and consists of 50 large capitalization companies, representing 24 sectors within the NSE[2]. Other popular indexes include the BSE Mid-Cap Index and the BSE Small-Cap Index.

1.2 Financial Instruments Traded

In 2000 the BSE created its first exchange traded index futures contract on the capital markets benchmark index, the BSE Sensex[3]. Today, the securities available for trading and investment include equities, bonds, index funds and exchange traded and OTC derivatives. Within the derivative universe, participatory notes, commonly called P-notes, are derivative instruments that are issued against an underlying security, permitting holders to get a share (or all) of the income from the security. P-notes are the most commonly used vehicle by hedge funds to invest in the Indian markets due to their enhanced liquidity relative to ordinary shares. They are issued by large domestic and foreign brokerage houses that are permitted to own and trade Indian equities. Brokerage houses purchase equities on behalf of hedge funds and then issue P-notes against these equities to the same funds. Historically, P-notes have been particularly attractive to hedge funds because they did not require the holder to be a registered Foreign Institutional Investor (FII). However, in accordance with recent SEBI regulations, even P-note holders must now be registered FIIs. The importance of P-Notes is highlighted by the fact that they constituted about 46 per cent of cumulative net investments in equities by FIIs as of August 2004[4]. In October 2007, SEBI Chairman M. Damodaran was quoted in an interview with *Business Standard* as saying that 25–30% of foreign investment coming into India was through P-notes.[5] This number is unofficially thought to be as high as 50%.

Management sometimes chooses to aggressively market their shares to international investors and thus often elect to dual list their companies in the U.S. as American Depository Receipts (ADR) or in Europe as Global Depository Receipts (GDR). Hedge funds have often used ADRs and GDRs to invest in India as they can be bought or sold short directly in their respective markets and usually cost significantly less in fees and commissions than P-notes. Drawbacks with most ADRs and GDRs are that they typically are available only for large companies and often trade at a premium to their corresponding ordinary securities. Less than twenty Indian ADRs traded on American exchanges, as of late 2008.

Another common investment vehicle in India is the Foreign Currency Convertible Bond (FCCB). FCCBs have been an avenue for Indian firms to raise capital at attractive interest rates and usually boost share liquidity at attractive valuations. Indian FCCBs have two peculiar features that make them interesting and unique; it is compulsory to convert the bonds into equity and the conversion terms are not specified at the time of issue but are left to be determined subsequently by the Controller of Capital Issues (CCI), the government entity regulating capital market instruments in India.[6]

1.3 Difficulty in Effective Hedging

Hedge funds have often struggled to effectively hedge their long exposure in India. Previously, equities could only be shorted if brokers had inventory of stock and were willing to create a synthetic short through P-notes. Traditional short selling is just beginning to emerge under SEBI's modernization plan, but liquidity remains thin. Hedge funds can short GDRs and ADRs as long as liquidity is meaningful enough to provide adequate exposure. Given these limitations, hedge funds have often chosen to hedge themselves by being on the short side of index futures, and options. These instruments have exhibited considerable liquidity but tend to be more of a hedge against overall market risk and are not usually an effective hedge against sector or company-specific risks.

2. Evolution of the Indian Markets

Until the mid to late 1980s, the Reserve Bank of India (RBI) and SEBI had a protectionist stance and demonstrated a reluctance towards foreign investment. India's development strategy at the time was focused on self-reliance and import substitution.[7] However, Indian financial markets have gone through a significant evolutionary process over the last 20 years. The government has taken several policy initiatives to modernize operations and expand options for investors with the purpose of attracting global foreign and portfolio investment. In 1998, SEBI worked hard to popularize dematerialization (the move from physical securities certificates to electronic trading), draw up regulations for derivatives, develop credit rating agencies and amend the Takeover Regulations of 1997 Act. In more recent years, the regulatory body has implemented policy measures such as Qualified Institutional Participation (QIP) guidelines, Real Estate Investment Trusts (REITs), cross-collateralization across cash and derivative markets, all of which have been conducive to both local and foreign investment.

2.1 Restrictions on Ownership

SEBI has also moved to formalize the role that foreign institutional investors (FIIs), Non-resident Indians (NRIs) and Persons of Indian Origin (PIOs) can play in the system. The ceiling for overall investment as a percentage of paid up capital of an Indian company for FIIs and NRIs/PIOs has been set at 24% and 10%, respectively.[8] However, these limits are subject to change in accordance with government and board approval.

2.2 Required Registration of Foreign Institutional Investors

In a move that was considered protectionist by many, SEBI now requires funds to be registered FIIs before they are eligible to trade in the local market. These restrictions are also enforceable on P-notes which historically have been the preferred avenue for FIIs to indirectly invest in, and sometimes short sell, securities on the BSE and NSE. The government argues that this regulation will stem speculation and control volatility in the Indian markets. The registration process is not particularly difficult, as evidenced by the more than 800 FIIs registered in India.[9] As noted earlier, the government is currently in the process of implementing a new short selling policy. According to SEBI, the new regulations will permit all classes of investors (including FIIs) to short sell subject to a broad framework specified by the Secondary Market Advisory Committee.[10]

2.3 Growth in Indian Economy

Policy initiatives have not been constrained only to the capital markets. The RBI and the Ministry of Finance have also drawn upon monetary and fiscal policy strategies that have contributed to economic growth. **Table 1** shows selected macroeconomic metrics that detail the dramatic progress the Indian economy has made over the past several years.

Table 1: Selected Macroeconomic Metrics for the Indian Economy

	2000	2005	2006
GNI per capita, PPP (current international $)	1,500	2,210	2,460
GDP growth (annual %)	4.0	9.2	9.2
Market capitalization of listed companies (% of GDP)	32.2	68.6	89.8
Fixed line and mobile phone subscribers (per 100 people)	4	13	19
Internet users (per 100 people)	0.5	5.5	..
Merchandise trade (% of GDP)	20	30	32
Foreign direct investment, net inflows (BoP, current US$) (millions)	3,584	6,677	17,453
Workers' remittances and compensation of employees, received (US$) (millions)	12,890	21,293	25,426

2.4 Rapid Increase in Foreign Investment

New policy initiatives and old policy amendments have indicated India's stance towards gradual and cautious liberalization. As a result, the Indian stock markets have arguably seen one of the greatest bull runs in the world over the past decade. Its fundamentals were also strong, as evidenced by the 9% growth in India's GDP in fiscal year 2007.[11] The SENSEX 30 was up 168% from 2000 through mid 2008 and the NIFTY was up 172% for the same period. Both the indices are down approximately 29% over the first half of 2008, due to a global stock market correction / bear market. Cumulative FII investment also increased from $11.3 billion in 2000 to $39.3 billion in 2006. This increase, coupled with the fact that net FII inflows into India have been less volatile compared to other emerging markets, provides one measure of the attractiveness of the Indian financial markets.[12]

Below the top line aggregate investment numbers, interest in Indian equity and fixed income securities has been robust. Net equity investment in India has grown from $8.0 billion in 2006 to $17.2 billion in 2007. Net debt investments have grown from $0.9 billion to $2.3 billion for the same period. The year over year growth has been impressive, and is well above the corresponding net equity and debt investment numbers from 2002 of $0.7 billion and $23 million, respectively.[13]

3. The Importance of Manager / Owners in Indian Publicly Traded Companies

The primary beneficiary of India's financial policy evolution has been its burgeoning middle class. This group has benefited from a stronger educational system, increased employment and a broader menu of consumer goods. Traditionally, Indian business owners have preferred debt over equity as the primary means of financing and growing their businesses. The underlying reason for this behavior has been the desire to keep absolute control of a company. This psyche has carried through to public companies where it is not uncommon for a manager-owner, or so-called "promoter", of a public limited company to own more than 50% of the company's stock. Promoters often fund capital expenditures, working capital, and acquisitions through credit lines, term loans, and "plain vanilla" debt instruments.

The analysis of Indian firm ownership structure is of crucial importance since family-owned companies constitute approximately 70% of India's market capitalization, making India among the more highly concentrated markets by ownership in the world. Most of the large family-owned businesses have been built over a few generations and it is not uncommon for these families to want to keep control and wealth within the family. Ingrained in the Indian culture, the pride associated with building up a business is only surpassed by the pride associated with owning and controlling a business of a relatively significant size.

Equity dilution and public offers have historically been seen as an unnecessary distribution of wealth and control. This mindset is linked to India's landownership structure, which existed before land reforms. Landowners divided their holdings among their children, who ultimately did the same, diluting family holdings over the course of generations. This led to subsequent generations with fewer land holdings and lesser wealth than their forefathers. It should be noted that this phenomenon is not isolated to India. The country's neighbors have a very similar ownership culture.

As the need for greater and more sophisticated capital grew, promoter psyche evolved with it. To put it very simplistically, many promoters who were previously satisfied with a big piece of a small pie now prefer a smaller piece of a much larger pie. The change in attitude can be attributed to a desire to see growth extend beyond Indian borders and the requirement of foreign capital and knowledge to do so. Promoters realize that absolute returns are much higher and stock prices more rapidly approach their fundamental values when sophisticated investors purchase securities, and correspondingly increase their profile and liquidity. The transformation in the psyche of Indian promoters is exhibited in the record number of IPOs, Foreign Currency Convertible Bonds (FCCBs) and foreign investor ownership filings in recent years.

4. Indian Investor Behavior

India has traditionally exhibited a very high savings rate among its citizens, with much of the savings channeled into the stock market. As a result, the country has developed a significant retail investor base. As is the case with most emerging market retail investors, trading on many occasions tends to be rumor based, investments are often made on asymmetric information, and there are a significant number of margin traders.

Generally speaking, the retail investor base in India also tends to be a little cynical and very risk averse which leads it to be cautious when there is good news and overreactive when there is bad news. It is not uncommon to see significant retail inflows on the back of market rumors and news of local or foreign institutional interest. Retail investors have become savvier in recent years as Indian markets have moved towards maturity. Part of this transformation is due to the widespread availability of financial-oriented information through over 10,000 brokers and the proliferation of the Internet. Investors are increasingly sensitive to macro indicators and company specific metrics, such as earnings and credit ratings. The increase in institutional ownership has also accelerated the learning curve of retail investors, with their desire to follow the "smart money," resulting in the increased need for financial education.

Numerous studies on investor behavior in the Indian financial markets have been conducted. Our goal here is to provide a brief discussion of studies that may broadly describe how investors react to certain market events. In short, alpha generation may be possible by taking advantage of movements of the masses.

Marisetty, Marsden, and Veeraraghavan (2007) examine price reactions to the announcement of rights issues by listed Indian firms.[14] Their study spans the 1997–2005 time period and reveals that, although investors react positively to such an announcement, the reaction is statistically insignificant in aggregate. Beneath the surface, the study reveals two important observations:

1) The price reaction to an announcement of the rights issue was more negative for firms affiliated with a family group.

2) Higher levels of individual holdings are associated with a more positive price reaction to the rights issue announcement.

Hence, if the results still hold, a simple strategy of shorting (through P-notes, ADRs, GDRs, or ordinary shares) family controlled shares after a rights offering would generate alpha. This strategy can be enhanced by simultaneously buying securities of non-family controlled firms after a rights offering. The number of rights issues in India may not be significant enough to run an entire fund on this strategy, but it might be an element of an event-driven or statistical arbitrage strategy.

Gordon and Gupta (2003) suggest a multifactor model to describe capital flows to India. They find that the most important external factors are interest rates, as measured by LIBOR, and emerging market stock returns, whereas the primary domestic factors are lagged stock returns and changes in credit ratings.[15]

A study by the Ministry of Finance (2005) on FII investment patterns documents a common concern that FIIs may generate "herding" due to the asymmetry and integrity of information.[16] The paper argues that this behavior can lead to positive / negative feedback trading loop which can exacerbate volatility in markets. The feedback mechanism is further amplified by retail investors that often try to emulate the behavior of "smart money" institutional investors.

5. Hedge Fund Strategies in India

It is difficult to define the *modus operandi* of hedge funds in India due to the wide spectrum of strategies being deployed in its markets. Unlike in the United States and other developed markets, high quality Indian financial data does not span several decades, making it difficult for quantitative funds to form and backtest their algorithms with a high degree of statistical validity. Conventional convertible arbitrage techniques are also difficult to carry out as effectively in the United States due to the difficulties of shorting in size and the mandatory conversion feature discussed previously.

Given the strong long-term fundamentals of the Indian economy, a short biased strategy may be especially risky. In our view, the following strategies are best positioned to deliver sustainable alpha in India over the next decade.

5.1 Long / Short Equity

Long / short has probably been one of the most successful hedge fund strategies in India to date, due to the secular upward trend combined with high levels of volatility. The real estate, retail, informational technology, agriculture and materials industries have been prime beneficiaries of India's growth. Funds that have been able to create long positions and simultaneously short company specific ideas have enjoyed the greatest risk adjusted returns. Until recently, short selling was limited either due to liquidity constraints or regulatory restrictions, partially explaining the long bias of many funds.

In the current Indian market environment, beset by high levels of volatility, a long / short strategy may become even more effective. As noted above, the reduction in world economic growth has resulted in a 29% correction in the two major Indian indices over the first half of 2008. Long / short funds are poised to benefit from this situation as they can become *tactically* short biased (short-selling equities that they feel will be most affected by bear market conditions) while holding onto a smaller percentage of what they feel might be long-term value and / or growth investments.

5.2 Activist Funds

Activist hedge funds use their ownership in companies to influence management's actions in ways that are believed to enhance shareholder value. Activist funds usually take at least a 5% position in a company's shares in order to be viewed seriously by management. Once these funds buy into a company, they use their holdings to create shareholder value through their interventions.[17] Sometimes, these interventions can take on an aggressive form where hedge funds try to oust senior management, attempt to change business strategy by holding a seat on the board, restructure, sell the entire company, or spin-off a specific division.

Non-aggressive activist hedge funds are likely to be most successful in India. As discussed in previously, Indian firms are often family controlled, but they may require foreign capital and insight to achieve their growth plans. In this respect, the activist investor is more akin to a private equity investor, providing capital and know how in return for upside participation in growth. Family controlled firms are often willing to dilute their ownership to the 51% range to long-term activist hedge funds with appropriate connections and favorable track records.

5.3 *Statistical Arbitrage*

There exists a window of opportunity, perhaps short in duration, to profit from the fragmentation of India's numerous financial exchanges. There are 22 stock exchanges in India and SEBI has encouraged cross listing as one solution to the fragmentation problem.[18] Each exchange varies in its listings, volume and technological infrastructure, creating nonsynchronous trading effects. So, if the same security is listed on two exchanges, and they differ in price, a statistical arbitrage opportunity arises.

Another arbitrage opportunity may exist since it is impossible for 22 exchanges to move in perfect synchronicity. The more technologically sophisticated exchanges, such as BSE, are generally more efficient than some of the smaller exchanges, creating a lead-lag effect. Accordingly, an alpha generating statistical arbitrage strategy would be to buy (sell) securities on the less technology efficient exchanges when the BSE is rising (falling) sharply. The same financial indicators, such as changes in interest rates, government policy, and currency values, should affect all exchanges in roughly the same manner. However, if each separate market does not efficiently incorporate the change in macro variables into stock prices an arbitrage opportunity will arise.

5.4 Global Macro

The Indian financial markets have almost always been beset by high levels of volatility. We have discussed India's stock market gyrations over the past decade and the country has had a long history of rapid changes in inflation, interest rates, and currency prices. Furthermore, the monsoon season can greatly affect agricultural prices. When combined with the high rate of growth in the economy, the Indian financial markets are ideal alpha hunting grounds for Global Macro hedge funds.

5.5 Special Situations / Distressed Equities

The 2008 correction in the Indian stock markets and the global credit crunch has caused difficulty for a significant number of mid and small cap firms. Many of these firms have strong long-term fundamentals, but lack the capital to fund the working capital and capital expenditures that are crucial to their growth. The capital markets are essentially "cut off" for a whole host of firms, creating a raft of distressed debt and equity securities. Hedge funds flush with capital can earn alpha from two areas: 1) provide capital, via a Private Investment in Public Equity (PIPE) transaction, to high potential distressed firms and participate strongly in the upside as these firms are nursed back to health; 2) purchase securities on the exchanges of high quality small and mid firms that were unfairly punished — in essence, "separating the wheat from the chaff."

5.6 Multistrategy

Multistrategy funds with a focus on all the strategies noted above — Long / Short, Activist, Global Macro, Statistical Arbitrage, Special Situations / Distressed — might provide the best risk adjusted returns since they could dynamically alter their portfolio weights to the strategies that are performing the best. In addition, their diversified nature has the effect of dampening overall portfolio volatility. Multistrategy funds could make a strong case to potential investors that, due to the rapidly evolving Indian financial landscape, it pays to not be locked into a single hedge fund strategy and to adroitly capitalize on the efficiencies in the market as they occur.

6. Sustainability and Evolution of Alpha

The maturation of Indian capital markets may erode some current alpha opportunities, such as cross listing statistical arbitrage. However, the same path to maturity may also create alpha generation opportunities that have not existed previously. For example, Capital Structure Arbitrage, and Convertible Arbitrage are unlikely to be highly successful in the present, because of a limited number of instruments in conjunction with the regulatory restrictions on those instruments. However, if regulation of the Indian financial markets continues on the same upward trajectory, these and other strategies might be able to generate considerable alpha in the future.

Hedge Fund Alpha Tear Sheet — Chapter 5

- The Indian financial markets have been an abundant source of alpha generation for hedge funds over the last ten to fifteen years.
- Securities available for trading and investment in India include equities, bonds, index funds, and derivatives.
  - o Within the derivative universe, participatory notes (P-notes) are the most commonly used vehicle by hedge funds to invest in the Indian financial markets due to their enhanced liquidity relative to ordinary shares and historical restrictions on short selling.
- Indian firms have historically been family owned and majority controlled.
  - o The manager / owner of a family business is often known as a "promoter."
- In the past, promoters had little interest in diluting their company stake. At present many promoters are willing to accept a smaller piece of a larger pie, and are thereby welcoming *value added* institutional ownership.
- Generally speaking, the retail investor base in India tends to be a cynical and risk averse, which leads it to be cautious when there is good news and overreactive when there is bad news.
- In our view, the following hedge fund strategies in India are best poised to deliver alpha in the decade ahead.
  - o Long / Short
  - o Activist
  - o Global Macro
  - o Statistical Arbitrage
  - o Special Situations / Distressed
  - o Multistrategy

End Notes

[1] These statistics come from Goldman Sachs (2007).

[2] Our sector categorization comes from Bloomberg.

[3] History on the BSE Sensex may be found at the website of the Bombay Stock Exchange, http://www.bseindia.com/

[4] Report of the Expert Group on Encouraging FII Flows and Checking the Vulnerability of Capital Markets to Speculative Flows.

[5] The quote of the SEBI Chairman comes from Rediff (2007).

[6] Barua and Jayanth (1991) discuss the valuation of Indian Convertible Bonds

[7] Report of the Expert Group on Encouraging FII Flows and Checking the Vulnerability of Capital Markets to Speculative Flows.

[8] The statistics come from the Reserve Bank of India.

[9] Report of the Expert Group on Encouraging FII Flows and Checking the Vulnerability of Capital Markets to Speculative Flows.

[10] Ernst & Young (2008) discusses short selling in India.

[11] Bloomberg is the source of our Indian GDP figure.

[12] Report of the Expert Group on Encouraging FII Flows and Checking the Vulnerability of Capital Markets to Speculative Flows.

[13] Goldman Sachs (2007) discusses growth in the Indian capital markets.

[14] Marisetty, Marsden, and Veeraraghavan (2007) analyze Indian rights offerings and their corresponding impact on stock prices.

[15] See Gordon and Gupta (2003) for a model that forecasts Indian capital flows.

[16] Report of the Expert Group on Encouraging FII Flows and Checking the Vulnerability of Capital Markets to Speculative Flows.

[17] Brav, Jiang, Partnoy, and Thomas (2008) discuss the returns of activist funds.

[18] Jain and Sharma (2007) discuss SEBI's advocacy of cross listing.

References

Barua S K and Varma Jayanth. "Indian Convertible Bonds with Unspecified Terms: A Valuation Model," *IIMA Working Papers 991*, Indian Institute of Management Ahmedabad, Research and Publication Department, 1991.

Bombay Stock Exchange.
http://www.bseindia.com/

Bloomberg Terminal.
http://www.bloomberg.com/

Brav, Alon, Jiang, Wei, Partnoy, Frank and Thomas, Randall S., "The Returns to Hedge Fund Activism," *ECGI — Law Working Paper* No. 098/2008, March 2008.

Ernst & Young, Global Financial Services, "Short Selling of Securities and the Scheme for Securities Lending and Borrowing" *Global Financial Services Industry Alert*, p. 1, January, 2008.

Goldman Sachs, *Market Profile: India*, June 20, 2007.

Gordon, James P. and Gupta, Poonam, "Portfolio Flows into India: Do Domestic Fundamentals Matter?" *IMF Working Paper* No. 03/20, January, 2003.

Government of India Ministry of Finance Department of Economic Affairs New Delhi, "Report of the Expert Group on Encouraging FII Flows and Checking the Vulnerability of Capital Markets to Speculative Flows," November, 2005.

Jain, Tarun and Sharma, Raghav, "Cross Listing of Stock Exchanges: Strengthening Self-Regulation?," *Company Law Journal (India)*, Vol. 3, p. 64, 2007.

Marisetty, V., Marsden, A., Veeraraghavan, "Price Reaction to Rights Issues in the Indian Capital Market" *Pacific-Basin Finance Journal*, 2008, Vol. 16, Issue 3, pp. 316–340.

Rediff Business Desk, "What are P-Notes?" October 17, 2007. http://in.rediff.com/cms/print.jsp?docpath=//money/2007/oct/17spec.htm

Reserve Bank of India. http://www.rbi.org.in/home.aspx

6

ACHIEVING HEDGE FUND ALPHA IN CHINA

John M. Longo, PhD, CFA, Wei-Kang Shih, and Ben Sopranzetti, PhD

Rutgers Business School & The MDE Group; Rutgers Business School;
Rutgers Business School

1. Introduction

The purpose of this chapter is to provide a basic overview of the Chinese financial markets and its dynamics, with the ultimate goal of identifying hedge fund strategies that are most likely to generate alpha in this region. Accordingly, it is necessary to discuss some of the common financial instruments that exist in Chinese markets, regulation, and investor behavior. Our primary focus is on the mainland financial markets in Shanghai and Shenzhen, but when appropriate, we will also discuss the more developed markets of Hong Kong and Taiwan. The nascent and rapidly evolving nature of the Chinese financial markets, as well as the other BRIC countries, may make it a fertile source of alpha in the decades ahead.

2. China's Economic Growth

China's economic growth has been nothing short of remarkable. It currently has the second largest economy in the world, behind that of the United States, with a GDP of more than $6.9 trillion. Its GDP has compounded at an annual rate of nearly 10% per year since its modern economic reforms were enacted in 1978. China has amassed an enormous trade surplus with nearly the rest of the world and continues to benefit from strong inflows of foreign direct investment. As a result, by mid-2008, it held nearly $1.8 trillion in foreign exchange reserves. This figure is by far the largest of any other country, including Japan, whose reserve value China surpassed in 2003.

Siegel (2005) "conservatively" estimates that the economy of China will be nearly twice as large as that of the United States by 2050. In fact, by the same time period, Siegel predicts China's economy will be as large as that of the United States, Europe, and Japan combined. He arrives at this prediction by assuming the typical Chinese worker's income must only rise to one-half the level of the average American's income. Currently, the average Chinese now earns only about one-eighth the income of the average worker in the United States. To reach one-half of the American income level, China's productivity has to grow 3 percent per year faster than that of America's. He believes that China's adoption of western technologies and infrastructure ensures China's productivity will not drop much below 5 percent for decades to come.

3. Evolution of Mainland Chinese Financial Markets

The Shanghai Stock Exchange has a rich history. It was founded in 1882 and began trading foreign stocks as early as 1891. The Shanghai Securities and Commodities Exchange was established in 1920. Due to the agricultural focus of the Chinese economy at that time, it quickly became the biggest exchange market in China. Shanghai emerged as the financial center of the Far East by 1930. The communist revolution of 1949 and corresponding founding of the People's Republic of China (PRC) resulted in the closure of all mainland Chinese stock markets.

As China's economic reforms of the late 1970s and early 1980s began to take root, the need for well functioning capital markets emerged. It was therefore inevitable that stock and other exchanges would return to mainland China. By the mid-1980s several state owned and private companies (many of which were supplied with foreign capital) evolved into large organizations, but their shares were not publicly traded. The

Shanghai Stock Exchange was reestablished in 1990 and joined by the Shenzhen Stock Exchange (whose members had strong trading ties to Taiwan) in the same year. The number of firms listed on mainland China stock exchanges grew from a mere 10 in 1990 to the nearly 2000 firms that trade today.

4. The Importance of State Owned Publicly Traded Companies in China

There are two types of shares being issued in China's mainland stock markets: 1) non-tradable state-owned and corporate-owned (legal persons) shares and 2) tradable publicly owned shares. The publicly owned shares can take on several forms, including A-shares, B-shares, H-shares (shares listed on the Hong Kong Stock Exchange), and N-shares (shares listed on the New York Stock Exchange). Only the publicly owned shares are listed and tradable. State-owned shares and the corporate-owned shares can be converted into publicly owned shares with approval from the China Securities Regulatory Commission (CSRC).

Non-tradable shares currently comprise two thirds of the total market capitalization. The Chinese government is speeding up the reform to allow more companies to sell state-owned or corporate owned non-tradable shares to the public. By the end of January 2006, more than 450 companies either started or completed the sales of their conversion.[1]

5. Overview of Chinese Stock Markets

5.1 Mainland China Stock Markets

The two stock exchanges in mainland China are the Shanghai Stock Exchange (SHSE) and the Shenzhen Stock Exchange (SZSE). The China stock markets are segmented into A-share (for domestic investors) and B-share (for foreign investors) classes. However, after a series of reforms, domestic investors can now invest in the B-share market and the

A-share market is also open to Qualified Foreign Institutional Investors (QFIIs). Accordingly, the arbitrage spread that periodically exists between the two markets is expected to diminish over time. At the end of July 2008, SHSE has 853 companies listed in the A-share market with a market capitalization of Renminbi (RMB) 15.3 trillion and 54 companies in the B-share market with market capitalization of RMB 73 billion. The SZSE lists 715 companies in the A-share with market capitalization of RMB 3.6 trillion and 55 companies in the B-share market with market capitalization of RMB 73 billion

Both SHSE and SZSE use a computerized trading system, the electronic consolidated open limit order book (COLOB). Trading hours are from 9:30 am to 11:30 am in the morning and from 1:00 pm to 3:00 pm in the afternoon. The process of determining the opening price differs from that used to obtain prices at other points in the day. The opening price is based on a centralized competitive pricing process that takes place from 9:15 am to 9:25 am. Subsequent to the opening price, prices are then determined according to a continuous bidding process. The closing prices of the stocks are the weighted average of the trading prices of the final minute.

The minimum tick size is RMB 0.01. There is a minimum requirement of 100 shares for purchases, but no size requirement for sales. Both exchanges employ price limits; halting trading if the change in price exceeds a 10% drop or rise. Short sales are currently prohibited on SHSE and SZSE but investors can sell short in Hong Kong and in the United States through ADRs and ETFs. Finally, margin trading was introduced in August 2006 and its use has gradually increased over time.

5.2 Hong Kong Stock Market

Hong Kong's stock market is the seventh largest in the world on the basis of market capitalization. At the end of 2007, there were 1039 companies listed on the Main Board of the Hong Kong Exchange and Clearing (HKEx). Another 194 companies were listed on the Growth Enterprise Market (GEM). Total market capitalization of all securities listed hit an all time high of HK$20 trillion near the end of 2007. Most of the foreign money invested in China flows through Hong Kong's equity market, in part due to its more advanced legal system relative to the mainland markets. H-shares (shares of mainland-incorporated companies listed on HKEx) and red-chips (similar to H-shares, but the companies are not registered in China) from China state entities raised HK$232.6 billion in IPOs on the Main Board of HKEx in 2007. This figure represented 85% of total IPO funds raised on the Main Board during the year.[2]

5.3 Taiwan Stock Market

The Taiwan Stock Exchange (TSE) and The Gre Tai Securities Markets (GTSM, the over-the-counter stock market) are the two primary stock exchanges in Taiwan. As of the end of May of 2007, there were 680 companies listed on TSE with a total market capitalization of NT$20.2 trillion and 533 companies listed on the GTSM with a total market capitalization of NT$2.17 trillion. In 2003, the QFII system was abolished. Therefore, foreign institutional investors can now directly invest in the Taiwan stock markets without upper limits. According to the statistics from the Ministry of Finance, there were approximately 720 QFIIs before the abolishment of the QFIIs system.

6. Overview of Chinese Bond Markets

6.1 Mainland China Bond Market

China has the potential to be the largest corporate bond market in Asia, but it is currently quite small relative to those in the United States and Europe. The major types of bonds currently trading in China include Treasury bonds, financial bonds, and corporate bonds. The bond market is theoretically closed to foreign investors. Currently, only a limited number of foreign invested enterprises, with at least two Chinese state-owned partners, have access to the bond market. However, the Chinese government is working on opening up the market and reserving more issuing quotas for domestic companies. As of July 2008, there were 68 financial and corporate bonds listed on SHSE with market capitalization totaling RMB 178.9 billion. SZSE has 40 financial and corporate bonds listed with a market capitalization totaling RMB 32.01 billion.

6.2 Hong Kong Bond Market

The bond market in Hong Kong is relatively small compared to its equity markets. According to Hong Kong Monetary Authority, the outstanding amount of the private sector debt at the end of September 2007 was approximately HK$620.7 billion. Public sector debt, or Exchange Fund Bills and Notes, stood at HK$136 billion at the same time period.[3] Because of the bond market's small size and other limitations, many firms prefer to issue debt in the more liquid Eurobond and Yankee-bond markets. However, a glimmer of hope for the Hong Kong bond market lies in the growing debt financing needs of mainland-incorporated companies that are too small for international offerings.

6.3 Taiwan Bond Market

The bond market in Taiwan has grown in popularity in recent years, but bank loans are still the primary financing choice for most companies. The major market for bond trading is GTSM, an over-the-counter market. At the end of 2007, the outstanding amount of Treasury bonds and corporate bonds were NT$3.52 trillion and NT$1.09 trillion, respectively.[4] One current trend is the increase in convertible debt.

7. Overview of Chinese Derivative Markets

7.1 Mainland China Derivatives Markets

The financial derivatives markets are not yet developed well in mainland China. Currency forwards and commodities futures are the primary derivative vehicles. Swaps are mostly confined to non-renminbi currencies and options are not traded at all. There are now four futures exchanges in China: Dalian Commodity Exchange (DCE), Zhengzhou Commodity Exchange (ZCE), Shanghai Futures Exchange (SHFE), and the newly established China Financial Futures Exchange in Shanghai. All of the existing contracts are related to metal or agricultural commodities. The China Financial Derivatives Exchange launched stock index futures in 2007. Treasury bond and currency futures are currently under development.

7.2 Hong Kong Derivatives Markets

Hong Kong has one of the most active derivatives market in Asia. HKEx offers various stock index products, stock futures, interest-rate products, and other equity linked instruments. In 2007, the trading volume of futures contract in HKEx was 31 million, with 68% of that total coming from Hang Seng Index futures. Stock options trading volume equaled 44 million contracts. Additionally, funds raised by derivative warrants hit an all time high of HK$738 billion.

The swap market in Hong Kong centers primarily on interest-rate and currency swaps. The Renminbi Swap Offer Rate Fixing serves as a market-based floating rate benchmark for the RMB. Its importance lies in that it can help corporations and financial institutions to hedge interest rate risk on their RMB exposures.

7.3 Taiwan Derivatives Markets

The Taiwan Future Exchange (TAIFEX) is the major exchange for trading futures and options in Taiwan. TAIFEX offers a total of 18 products consisting of index futures, index options, and so forth. The total trading volume was approximately 115 million contracts by the end of 2007. The swaps market in Taiwan is dominated by foreign banks such as ABN AMRO, Citibank, UBS, and Bank of America.

8. Unique Dynamics of the Chinese Financial Markets

8.1 Chinese Corporations Trading the Stock of Other Firms

There is an interesting dynamic responsible for a significant percentage of the earnings of Chinese companies. Namely, many Chinese companies purchase stock in other Chinese firms and benefit from market rises and suffer from market falls. Of course, many companies around the world trade in the securities of others, but not to the same extent as in China. Furthermore, the Chinese model differs from the Japanese keritsu model of interlocked sister companies where formal business ties exist. The Chinese companies trade in other companies predominantly for investment or speculative purposes.

For example, Jerry Lou, head of China research at Morgan Stanley, calculated in late 2007 that "noncore" earnings from stock, real estate, and other ventures accounted for an amazing 54.1% of profits in China's health-care sector and 64.6% in its consumer goods sector. Said Lou, "People overestimate Chinese investors' sophistication. Somebody needs to point out that the emperor has no clothes."[5] This activity creates an interesting momentum strategy for hedge funds. When the Chinese stock market rises, earnings are likely to be better than expected and the opposite will be true when earnings fall.

8.2 Chinese Investor Behavior

Wang, Sun, and Chee (2005) find that individual investors dominate the Chinese stock market, owning more than 90% of the tradable shares. Moreover, due to the unreliable public information on listed companies, the market is mainly driven by rumors and investor sentiment. This dynamic creates an interesting platform to study how individual investors' behaviors affect the movement of stock prices and the feasibility of certain hedge fund strategies.

Chinese investors behave differently from the Western investors in many ways because of their unique cultural backgrounds. Gong (2003) finds Chinese society is more collective-oriented and better defined by a set of Confucian principles, such as conservatism and moderation. These doctrines or "cult of restraint" guide Chinese people in every aspect of their lives, including the investment decision making process. As a result, Chinese investors exhibit a more asymmetric reaction to news, either positive or negative, from those observed in the more developed markets in the Western world.

Chen, Kim, Nofsinger, and Rui (2007) find that in the face of good news, Chinese investors exhibit a great "disposition effect." That is, they tend to sell those stocks that have been increasing in price but hold on to those have been decreasing in value. Chinese individual investors react slowly to the good news because they are reluctant to believe the news is actually true. This phenomenon can be attributed to the Confucian doctrines that discourage risk-taking (conservatism) and support prudence (self-control) when making an important decision. The early sales of these winning stocks depress their prices, making it longer for them to reach their true fundamental values. Hence, Chinese investors underreact to good news and the slow information travel results in a post-announcement drift in stock prices.

Conversely, Chinese investors exhibit overreaction to bad news, which tends to induce panic selling after the announcement. Liu, Wang, and Zhang (2002) studied stock price movements around recent earnings warnings in China's stock market.[6] They found that stock prices drop substantially in the 3 day-period immediately after the announcement of the earnings warning but exhibit a price reversal over medium term (i.e. 30, 60, and 90-day) periods. Investors' sentiment plays an important role in explaining this phenomenon. According to Moore (1998) and Yao (1998), Chinese investors rely heavily on distributional information and word-of-mouth communication. In particular, investors' past experiences in the market, and those of their peers, are given significant weight when making financial decisions. Chinese investors want to minimize social risk (i.e. losing "*face*"[7] because of the loss in the stock market) by acting in the same manner as their peers. This collective selling depresses stock prices and drives the prices further away from their fundamental values.

The underreaction to good news and overreaction to bad news have important implications for hedge fund strategies in the Chinese stock markets. Grinblatt and Han (2005) find the underreaction to good news provides opportunities for short-term momentum trading strategies, given that prices slowly adjust to their higher fundamental values. The overreaction to bad news on the other hand gives contrarian investors a potential alpha opportunity when oversold securities reverse course and eventually revert to their higher fundamental values.

9. Hedge Fund Strategies in China

Not all hedge fund strategies are equally likely to generate alpha in China. For example, China's bond market is not well developed, even in regions such as Hong Kong, so traditional fixed income hedge fund strategies might have a difficult time deploying large sums of capital. In addition, the relatively short trading day in Shanghai and Shenzhen give statistical arbitrage funds less time to generate returns. In our view, the following strategies are best positioned to deliver sustainable alpha in China over the next decade.

9.1 Global Macro

Astute Global Macro funds can benefit from the high volatility that is characteristic of Chinese financial markets. For example, the Shanghai Stock Exchange Composite increased 130% in value in 2006, 97% in 2007 and has fallen 56% more through the third quarter of 2008. Such wide swings are tailor made for Global Macro managers. Furthermore, the decision by the leaders of the People's Republic of China (PRC) to allow the value of the RMB to be tied to a basket of foreign currencies will create some interesting foreign exchange opportunities over the long-term. Most economists find the RMB is substantially undervalued on a Purchasing Power Parity (PPP) basis.

　　The PRC has stated that the basket of reference currencies, to which the RMB is tied, primarily consists of the U.S. Dollar, Euro, Japanese

Yen and South Korean won. The RMB's value is driven to a lesser extent by the other currencies in the basket, including the British Pound, Thai Baht, Russian Ruble, and Australian Dollar. The daily change in the price of the RMB is currently limited to 0.5%. However, China's persistent trade surplus with the western world has resulted in political pressure to allow the RMB to float more freely.

Currently, forward contracts are the most convenient way for Global Macro funds to trade the RMB. Hedge funds, who prefer to trade exchange traded funds (ETFs) can also purchase the Wisdom Tree Dreyfus Chinese Yuan ETF, whose symbol is CYB. The Wisdom Tree Dreyfus product utilizes forward contracts and currency swaps and is designed to create a position economically similar to a money market security denominated in Chinese Yuan, plus the appreciation of the RMB relative to the U.S. Dollar.

9.2 Long / Short Equity

The lack of widespread and high quality financial information has created a gap in the "perfect information" hypothesis discussed in most Economics 101 classes. Therefore, substantial inefficiencies likely persist in the Chinese equity markets. The lack of short selling and underdeveloped derivatives markets in Shanghai and Shenzen make precise risk management a problem. However, hedge funds can go long stocks they like in these markets and short with an index or ETF. Commonly used ETFs that have exposure to the Chinese equity markets include the iShares FTSE / Xinhua China 25 Index (FXI), PowerShares Golden Dragon Halter USX China (PGJ), and SPDR S&P China (GXC) Additionally, there are more than 70 shortable Chinese ADRs trading on American stock exchanges as of late 2008. Short selling may also be done in Hong Kong and Taiwan.

9.3 Equity Arbitrage

Multiple share classes and the cross listing of many Chinese firms on different exchanges around the world has created numerous arbitrage opportunities, on the surface. Structural impediments, that are slowly eroding, often prevented these arbitrage opportunities from disappearing.

Perhaps the most dramatic example was the price of PetroChina after its IPO on the Shanghai Stock Exchange in November, 2007. Previously, it traded in Hong Kong and on the New York Stock Exchange. PetroChina sold only 2.2% of its shares in its Shanghai IPO, resulting in enormous oversubscription from Chinese retail investors. PetroChina was valued at more than $1 trillion on its first day of trading in Shanghai, more than double that of the next most valuable company in the world, ExxonMobil. However, in Hong Kong and New York, PetroChina was valued at approximately $400 billion. The divergence was caused by the inability of many mainland Chinese citizens to trade in Hong Kong and New York and the absence of short selling techniques in China. As noted previously, the fixed segmentation among A-share, B-share, and H-Share classes are slowly dissipating, resulting in a window of arbitrage opportunities for astute hedge fund managers.

9.4 Event Driven

The cultural elements of Chinese society discussed previously, suggest hedge funds focused on event study strategies might be highly profitable. For example, Chinese investors typically underreact to good news and overreact to bad news. Hence, hedge funds could generate alpha by purchasing securities that had good news, and (if possible) by shorting companies that provided bad news. After the stock reporting bad news had bottomed, the hedge fund manager could go long to capitalize on its oversold nature.

The underdeveloped Chinese bond market makes it difficult for hedge funds to have a clear focus on distressed securities. However, the notion of not losing "face" may result in an interesting hedge fund strategy. It would be a major embarrassment for state-owned Chinese firms to declare bankruptcy, especially those listed on Western exchanges. Therefore, hedge fund managers could invest in high profile state owned Chinese firms with less than perfect finances, under the assumption that they will receive the necessary cash infusions or governmental support to remain viable. For example, China Eastern Airlines is largely state owned, but is laboring under Debt to Equity ratio of nearly 12:1, as of late 2008.It may be an attractive distressed purchase under the "too high profile to fail" theory.

9.5 Multistrategy

Multistrategy funds with a focus on all the strategies noted above — Global Macro, Long / Short Equity, Equity Arbitrage, and Event Driven — might provide the best risk adjusted returns since they could dynamically alter their portfolio weights to the strategies that are performing the best. In addition, their diversified nature has the effect of dampening overall portfolio volatility. Multistrategy funds could make a strong case to potential investors that, due to the rapidly evolving Chinese financial landscape, it pays to not be locked into a single hedge fund strategy and to adroitly capitalize on the efficiencies in the market as they occur.

Hedge Fund Alpha Tear Sheet — Chapter 6

- China has exhibited remarkable economic growth over the past 30 years, growing its GDP by nearly 10% per annum since 1978.
  - o Jeremy Siegel of Wharton estimates by 2050, China's economy will be double the size of that of the United States' and more than the size of the economies of North America, Europe, and Japan combined.
- There are two types of shares being issued in China's mainland stock markets: 1) non-tradable state-owned and corporate-owned (legal persons) shares and 2) tradable publicly owned shares.
  - o The publicly owned shares can take on several forms, including A-shares, B-shares, H-shares (shares listed in Hong Kong Stock Exchange), and N-shares (shares listed in New York Stock Exchange).
  - o Non-tradable shares currently comprise two thirds of the total market capitalization
- China's financial markets include a mix of equity, debt, and derivative securities.
  - o The financial markets in Hong Kong and Taiwan are generally more in line with those of western exchanges and allow for short selling and a variety of derivative instruments.
  - o Short selling individual securities is still restricted on the Shanghai and Shenzhen exchanges.
- Chinese firms actively purchase the shares of other Chinese firms, for speculative or investment reasons. Therefore, there is often a material divergence between "core" earnings and reported earnings.
- Deep-rooted cultural values often result in Chinese retail investors overreacting to bad news and underreacting to good news.
- In our view, the following hedge fund strategies in China are best poised to deliver alpha in the decade ahead.
  - o Global Macro
  - o Long / Short Equity
  - o Equity Arbitrage
  - o Event Driven
  - o Multistrategy

End Notes

[1] 2008 Main Report of China, *Economists Intelligence Unit.*

[2] 2008 Main Report of Hong Kong, *Economists Intelligence Unit.*

[3] Both private sector and public sector debt amounts are obtained from 2008 Main Report of Hong Kong from the *Economists Intelligence Unit.*

[4] *Highlight of Bond Issuance in 2007,* Financial Supervisory Commission, Taiwan, 2007.

[5] A *Business Week* article entitled, "China Inc. Is Out on a Limb" discusses Morgan Stanley's research on the earnings quality of Chinese companies.

[6] China Securities Law Rule 65 specifies that listed companies which plan to report a substantial loss, or loss that will cause losses in three consecutive years, issue a statement prior to their financial report announcement.

[7] The definition of the concept "face" is vague because it is a direct translation from Chinese. According to Ho (1975), "face" is similar to *prestige* in an American sense. Also, "face" represents the confidence of society in the integrity of ego's moral character. The loss of "face" makes it virtually impossible for a person to function properly within the community.

References

Chen, Gongmeng, Kenneth A. Kim, and John R. Nofsinger, Oliver M. Rui, 2007, "Trading Performance, Disposition Effect, Overconfidence, Representativeness Bias, and Experience of Emerging Market Investors", *Journal of Behavioral Decision Making,* forthcoming.

Editor, "China Inc. Is Out on a Limb", *Business Week,* November 26, 2007.
http://www.businessweek.com/magazine/content/07_48/b4060064.htm

Frazzini, Andrea, 2006, "The Disposition Effect and Underreaction to News", *Journal of Finance*, 61, pp. 2017–2046.

Gong, W., 2003, "Chinese Consumer Behavior", *Journal of American Academy of Business,* 3, 1/2, pp. 373–380.

Grinblatt, Mark, and Han, Bing, 2005, "Prospect Theory, Mental Accounting, and Momentum", *Journal of Financial Economics*, 78, pp. 311–339.

Ho, David Yau-fai, 1976, "On the Concept of Face", *The American Journal of Sociology*, Vol. 81, No. 4, pp. 867–884.

Hong, Harrison, Stein, Jeremy C., 1999, "A Unified Theory of Underreaction, Momentum Trading, and Overreaction in Asset Markets", *Journal of Finance* 54, pp. 2143–2184.

Kang, Joseph, Ming-Hua Liu, and Sophie Xiaoyan Ni, 2002, "Contrarian and Momentum Strategies in the China Stock Market: 1993–2000", *Pacific-Basin Finance Journal*, Vol. 10, pp. 243–265.

Li, Ji., Kevin Lam, and Gongmian Qian, 2001, "Does Culture Affect Behavior and Performance of Firms? The Case of Joint Venture in China", *Journal of International Business Studies*, Vol. 32, No. 1, pp. 115–131.

Liu, Li, Zheng Wang, Zheng Zhang, 2002, "Subsequent Excess Return After Loss Warning Announcement in China's Stock Market", SSRN Working Paper.

Moore, Eric G. 1998, "Competitive Judgment in a Business Simulation: A Comparison Between American and Chinese Business Students", *Psychology and Marketing*, Vol. 15, No. 6, pp. 547–562.

Siegel, Jeremy, "Move over USA", *The Future for Investors*, Yahoo! Finance, September 22, 2005.
http://finance.yahoo.com/expert/article/futureinvest/986

Shi, Pei-Gi, Yin-Hua Yeh, Shean-Bii Chiu, and Hsuan-Chi Chen, 2005, "Are Taiwanese Individual Investors Reluctant to Realize their Losses?", *Pacific-Basin Finance Journal*, Vol. 13, pp. 201–223.

Wang, J., B.M. Burton, and D.M. Power, 2004, "Analysis of the Overreaction Effect in the Chinese Stock Market", *Applied Economics Letters*, 11, pp. 437–442.

Wang, Changyun, Qian Sun, and Su Ling Chee, 2005, "The Behavior and Performance of Individual Investors in China", Working Paper, National University of Singapore.

Yao, Oliver H.M., 1988, "Chinese Culture Values: Their Dimensions and Marketing Implications", *European Journal of Marketing*, Vol. 22, No. 5, pp. 44–57.

7

USING DERIVATIVES TO CREATE ALPHA

Sanjeev Khullar

Auriga Partners LLC, & TradeGames.com

1. Introduction

The primary objective in trading and investing is to make money, ideally in as risk-free a manner as possible. In financial-speak, the objective is to create alpha. This holds true whether someone is hedging existing positions, speculating on prices, or arbitraging different markets. Derivatives are an important instrument class in this regard. Used effectively, they can be a money manager's best friend; when they are not, they can be devastating. This chapter explores the multi-faceted use of derivatives to create alpha. We start with an introductory background and then lay out various derivatives strategies aimed at creating alpha. We illustrate with a few examples, and wrap up with methodologies for managing derivatives portfolio risk in order to preserve alpha.

The motivation for studying alpha stems from the very reason people engage in trading, to make money, explicitly or implicitly, ideally without taking much risk. Alpha is a measure of returns adjusted for risk. The attempt is to determine skill in trading / investment management performance, as opposed to performance attributed to luck or stemming from general market exposure. It is typically calculated as the rate of return on a security or portfolio in excess of what would be expected based on an equilibrium model such as the capital asset pricing model. The portfolio alpha (α) can be represented formally as:

α = Actual Return – Expected Return

Expected return can be computed from the Capital Asset Pricing Model (CAPM) or the Arbitrage Pricing Theory (APT). This formulation works well for linear portfolios. However, as pointed out by various researchers, this CAPM alpha overestimates the value added by managers with short option positions, and underestimates value when managers are long options. This is the case even when the managers have no superior skill or information. Leland (1999) suggests a modified measure that removes this bias. The Leland formula explicitly accounts for the lognormal distribution of returns.[1]

Another statistic that relates to investment performance is beta. While alpha is aimed more at the excess returns aspect of the risk-return tradeoff, beta parallels the volatility or risk aspect. Beta is a measure of co-movement, between the expected return of a security or portfolio and its corresponding overall market. The higher the beta value of security, the more sensitive it is to movements in its corresponding market. The formula for the beta of a security i, (β_i) relative to the market (Mkt) is:

β_i = Covariance (Returns$_i$, Returns$_{Mkt}$) / Variance (Returns$_{Mkt}$)

An asset with a beta of zero means that its price is uncorrelated with the market. A positive beta means that the asset generally follows the market. A negative beta shows that the asset moves opposite to the market; the asset generally decreases in value if the market goes up. Beta is coupled tightly with alpha, both conceptually and mathematically, and needs to be untangled in order to determine the part of performance that can be attributed to alpha value creation. Many derivative strategies are also aimed explicitly at generating performance that is uncorrelated with the market.

There are also a host of other very useful statistics — Sharpe ratio, Capture ratios, Sortino ratio, Tracking error, Information ratio, to name a few. One way or other, they are all looking to qualify a strategy or portfolio in terms of either historical or expected performance and risk.

2. Derivatives

Derivatives are financial contracts or instruments whose value is tied to other assets. The contracts can be based on different assets such as bonds, interest rates, equities, commodities, currencies, property market indices or economic statistics, as well as a combination of these assets (as in the case of dual currencies additionally linked to different interest rates). They run the gamut of instruments, from futures, swaps and options, to more complex OTC instruments, with payoffs that range from plain-vanilla to exotic. We shall explore the use of these derivatives in creating alpha.

2.1 Derivatives Strategies

Derivatives serve the alpha-beta needs of different classes of investors-active trader, fund manager, speculator, hedger, arbitrageur, fund of funds. Before we delve into examples, let us examine how.

2.1.1 For the Hedger

Hedging is the classical motivation for using derivatives — a tool to transfer risk from the hedger to the speculator. The hedger takes the derivative position opposite to his position in the underlying asset. For example, an airline company which is concerned about rising jet oil prices' negative impact on its operational efficiency can enter into a futures contract to lock in future prices of fuel. The derivatives trade in this case is a risk-reduction activity.

Beyond single-trade hedges, which are how derivatives hedging is most often described, the bigger hedging need that derivatives address is in terms of portfolio-wide hedging. Exchange-traded derivatives are usually the fastest and most liquid way to cut down systematic exposure when positions are too many to reverse, or when it makes sense to hold on to core positions in, say, multiple equities, but hedge because of short-term concerns.

2.1.2 For the Active Trader

The active trader is interested in identifying profitable trading opportunities as defined by "what to buy, what to sell, when to buy, when to sell." They are constantly scavenging for profitable trades, looking to trade in and out on a frequent basis. Derivatives are often a key to their trading- futures and options often lead the cash markets and offer a low-capitalization way for traders to implement their ideas and to actively trade different markets. In fact, commodities trading advisors (CTAs) focus their trading around exchange futures.

2.1.3 For the Mutual-Fund Manager

Mutual funds are generally constrained by size considerations and can at best trade only a small percentage of their holdings on an active basis. They rely primarily on their "stock picking and asset allocation" skills in order to deliver value to their clients. Active rebalancing is generally not viewed as a core alpha element of their strategy. Derivatives such as exchange-traded funds and sector indices expand the playing field for investors who follow a mutual fund strategy. S&P or other futures can also be used to transport alpha that some mutual funds create to other markets.

2.1.4 For the Hedge-Fund Manager and Arbitrageur

Market-timing is a de facto requirement everywhere. In the case of the active trader or the macro hedge fund, timing is an explicit part of strategy. But even when someone is following a sophisticated hedge–fund arbitrage strategy, timing is key, even if implicitly so. Derivatives provide the ability for the manager to quickly put on sizeable directional / hedge trades and coordinate timing with other trades.

Derivatives are also the building blocks that underlie most cross-product arbitrage trades. The price information embedded in various derivatives is an integral part of the pricing and risk models used by arbitrageurs. In summary, *derivatives complete the markets and help expand the alpha opportunity set.*

3. Examples Illustrating Strategies to Create Alpha

Alpha creation involves beating the market based on ability in terms of forecasting, valuing and hedging. It involves skill. Alpha opportunities can be pure or they can be statistical in nature. Below we present examples from different derivatives markets, which illustrate how alpha can be created. Our goal here is to sketch out the alpha generating logic of each possible trade and not to provide detailed quantitative calculations.

3.1 Alpha From Futures Arbitrage

A contract might be bought in, say the CBT, at one price and sold in the Philadelphia Stock Exchange at a higher price. This is an example of a purely hedged transaction, where price differences in the same contract are exploited. Obviously, these trades are hard to find, especially in mature liquid markets, and in today's world where the slightest differences are quickly arbitraged away through sophisticated technologically driven order-execution platforms. But when they are found, they represent alpha in one of the purest profit forms.

3.2 Alpha From Realized / Implied Volatility Arbitrage

The more common futures and options arbitrages are statistical. An example from the futures options arena would be when the market is pricing the options at a volatility level lower than what the trader expects going forward. To take advantage of this mis-estimation, the gamma risk is not hedged, but the delta (directional) risk is continuously hedged, allowing the spread between pricing and realized volatilities to be captured. Alpha is being created here because of the trader's expertise in forecasting volatilities, in understanding the nuances of the market and skill in managing the underlying exposure.

3.3 Alpha From Volatility Skew Trades

In many markets, different options on even the same underlying instrument trade at substantially different Black-Scholes implied volatilities. In the equity area, for example, lower strikes (out-of-the-money puts) often have implied volatilities much higher than options that are at-the-money. To the extent that underlying price distributions should be lognormal (as assumed in the Black-Scholes model), volatility skews represent a source of pure profits. The trade can be constructed by buying the cheaper implied strikes, selling the more expensive ones (thereby creating a vega / volatility neutral position), and going delta neutral by trading in the underlying. OEX backspreads or put ratio spreads are case in point. These trades again rely on skill in predicting volatilities and the likely price distributions. But rather than relying on convergence in volatility levels to historical values (as was the case above), volatility skew trades are based on exploiting differentials in the shapes of the price distributions — the distribution implied from option prices and the distribution expected to prevail.

3.4 Alpha From Cash Futures Basis Trade

The cash futures basis trade exists in almost all markets. The general principle is to buy (or sell) the cash instrument and sell (or buy) the futures on it, with the objective of exploiting price differences between the two, after accounting for any hidden costs or imbedded options. In the US government bond market, for example, the futures seller implicitly owns various options stemming from the seller's ability in terms of cheapest-to-deliver — quality option, end-of-month option, afternoon or wildcard option, timing option and new issue option. The option to decide which of these to exercise and make the cheapest possible delivery depends on yield levels, yield spreads between alternative cash bonds, realized bond volatility and cost of carry. The fair price of the futures contract vis-à-vis the cash bond is determined after stripping off these options, and can be arbitraged away by buying futures and selling options and cash bonds, or the reverse.

3.5 Alpha From Trading the Optionality in Bonds

Callable bonds, range accrual notes, period caps and indexed amortizers are bonds that embed negative optionality and that pay higher coupons than the non-option counterparts. Callable bonds, for example, are structured in a Bermuda style, where the issuer / seller can exercise the call at different times after an initial period. These bonds often also have derivative equivalents — the Bermuda swap is a synthetic variation on the callable bond — and are motivated by the need for someone to hedge their cash bond exposure, or because of transaction costs, or the need to keep trades off-balance sheet and reduce margin requirements. In any case, it is possible to construct relative value trades that exploit volatility differences between different markets and that rely on superior modeling skills to create alpha. In the callable bond example, one can buy different European swaptions that synthetically mimic the short Bermuda option exposure. To the extent that these swaptions can be bought cheaply enough, and the Bermuda / European mismatch managed effectively, there is a possibility of locking in alpha profits.

3.6 Alpha From Trading the Optionality in Convertible Bonds

The core convertible bond strategy entails purchasing convertible bonds and shorting the underlying stocks, leaving a net long volatility position. The hedge neutralizes equity risk but is exposed to interest rate and volatility risk. Income is captured from the convertible coupon and the interest on the short position in the underlying stock. This income is reduced by the cost of borrowing the underlying stock and also the dividends payable to the lender of the underlying stock. The non-income return comes from the long volatility exposure. Rebalancing will add to or subtract from the short stock position, and will be driven by transaction costs and risk appetite. The core arbitrage comes down to the implied volatility of the convertible bond vis-à-vis' actual volatility over the life of the position.

The strategy, as outlined, does not necessarily entail the use of derivatives, since one can simply buy the converts and short stocks. But derivatives technology still is a must — the techniques that enable the imbedded options to be priced and risk managed properly. In addition, in markets where shorting stocks is difficult, derivatives can play an explicit role. One can buy puts or sell calls, synthetically creating short equity exposure. This synthetic transaction may result in arbitrage opportunities that depend on differences in the implied volatilities between the options and convertible bonds, two different (though theoretically correlated) markets. The possibility of generating alpha returns can be significant, given that this is not a widely understood asset class.

3.7 Alpha From Macro Interest Rate Trades

A lot of hedge fund strategies are arbitrage-driven, seeking to exploit perceived mispricing across different products and markets. The other strategies are explicitly directional such as macro bets on interest rates in different countries, directional plays on yield curve spreads, etc. The instruments used for these trades range from both cash bonds to futures, including U.S. T-Bond futures, U.S. T-Note futures, German Bunds, Japanese JGBs, and British Gilts. Constant maturity swaps (CMSs) and derivatives that pay based on differences in CMS rates between two points on the yield curve are also instruments that can be used to implement specific views and to trade in size. The trades are conceptually simple, requiring someone to either go long or short these instruments, and represent pure alpha by following an active management strategy.

3.8 Alpha From Relative-Value Trades: Mortgage-Backed Securities vs. Treasuries

An example of a mortgage-backed relative-value trade is going long (short) an MBS pass-through security or a tranche of a CMO, selling (buying) a duration-adjusted equivalent of treasuries (notes or futures), and buying (selling) OTC treasury options. The idea is to capture the option-adjusted spread between the mortgage-backed security and treasuries. Value is created based on someone's ability to develop a good hypothesis of how pre-payments, interest rates and cash flows interact in these markets, and the ability to translate that hypothesis into sophisticated pricing and risk management models. More often than not, relative value trades come with imbedded options and basis risk. They require taking an integrated view of different markets within a consistent cross-product pricing framework that covers both cash and derivatives markets. In this case, one needs to look at Eurodollar prices and swap rates (to create the forward curve), cap and swaption prices (to incorporate volatility and optionality into rates), and IO / PO prices (to calibrate prepay models).

3.9 Alpha From Credit Derivatives

Credit derivatives have been pounded over the 2007–2008 period and are not likely to get back to previous form. The risk in credit derivatives stems from the fact that models are grossly incapable of predicting default rates. The complexity in some of the structures also makes it hard computationally to drill down to pool-level data and derive cash flows that flow through the tranching waterfall. Credit default data that covers a long history of extreme market environments, which one can use to build reasonable models, is also hard to get, especially in the subprime space that has been so problematical. Finally, there is a paucity of hedging instruments that one can use. Most dealers have been caught on the same side, and need to hedge using the same instruments.

That being said, credit derivatives should remain a useful tool in terms of completing financial markets as well as in mitigating counterparty risk of default. As long as trading involves two counterparties, credit risk is not going away. In theory at least, it should also be possible to find greater pricing dislocations in the market in the current environment, dislocations that can be acted upon profitably. CDO tranches that are pricing in extreme levels of defaults are potential buys. To the extent that some of the collateral might be better than the collateral underlying standard ABX / TABX indices, and to the extent that one can understand and properly model those differences, one can buy into structures that are trading lower than the indices, all else equal, using the indices as a hedge.

3.10 Alpha From Energy Derivatives

One of the more unusual derivatives in the energy world is the swing option — an option that allows the energy quantities delivered or used to vary. These options have historically been embedded in the legal contracts written by energy producers and require a good understanding of the stochastic price dynamics that drive energy markets, including the ability to model distinctive price spikes, volatilities and seasonal movements. They present opportunities for alpha creation simply because they have not always been priced using that level of sophistication. There is also value that can be created by integrating these financial options more closely with the physical options inherent in operating physical plants, and by looking at both as a portfolio.

3.11 Alpha From Long / Short Strategies

Long-short trades are very common in arbitrage-oriented strategies, relying as they do on price convergence on both legs of the trade. But they have traditionally not been used as extensively in putting together funds or in stock market investing. Mutual funds for the most part are long-only, often by mandate. This limitation reduces the potential opportunity set.

Assume the following long-only portfolio allocations which use ETFs for broad-based market exposure: 40% US Stock (symbol SPY), 20% US Bonds (IEF), 20% Commodities (IAU), 15% Real Estate (IYR), and 5% Money Market (VMFXX). This is an example of a diversified portfolio for a U.S. investor.

Now, instead of 40% allocation in SPYs, an alternative would be to employ leverage and use shares in, say, the ProFund Ultra Bull (ULPIX). With 2 times leverage, a 20% allocation in ULPIX would provide the same exposure as a 40% allocation to S&P500. This strategy frees up 20% capital, which can then be allocated for a long-short alpha play. A portion of this capital could be used to target sectors that are expected to outperform S&P500s, with the remainder invested in inverse sector fund ETFs (such as PHPIX) that are expected to do well in a declining market. To the extent that the long-short sectors perform as expected, the strategy would add alpha over and above what could be generated with the long-only portfolio.

Of course, skill is required in this example, as in other alpha trades. But when portfolio solutions can be long-short, the strategy set is widened, returns become potentially uncorrelated with the market, portfolio volatility is lowered, and one can profit from not only the longs, but also the shorts.

4. Using Derivatives to Transport Alpha

Alpha transport is the process of transferring an investment manager's ability to add alpha in one investment strategy to another market. Consider the following: long a fund which excels at picking US stocks, short S&P futures, long FTSE futures. The strategy of going long the fund and shorting S&P futures creates essentially a US market-neutral position. Any value that is added is due to the manager's ability with regard to selecting US stocks that outperform the S&P index. Overlaid with FTSE futures, the net effect is a portfolio, which is subject to the exceptional returns (over S&P index) offered by the US manager on top of the returns of the core FTSE position. Alpha transport allows participants to go beyond their traditional orientation and add value from other sources.

5. Risk Management of Derivatives Portfolios

Finding alpha-generating strategies is one side of the coin. Preserving alpha is the other, and that is where risk management shines. Derivatives are subject to the following investment risks:

Leverage risk. The use of derivatives can result in large losses due to the use of leverage. Derivatives allow investors to earn large returns from small movements in the underlying asset's price. However, investors could lose large amounts if the price of the underlying moves against them significantly. There have been several instances of massive losses in derivative markets, including Long Term Capital Management (LTCM) and Orange County.

Take the case of an arbitrage fund. A good arbitrage pricing model can at best suggest what is rich or cheap today. But by itself, it cannot predict whether things will not get richer or cheaper tomorrow. Arbitrages often take time to converge, whereas leverage and mark-to-market pressures necessitate good timing, even in the short-term. Many funds that have destructed over the years used excess leverage and they got their timing wrong as well.

Factor risk. The risk in equity derivatives is not only systematic market exposure, but also exposure to various other factors: industry, sector, country, momentum, P/E, to name a few. In fixed income, duration bond-equivalents, convexity, option-adjusted spreads, exposure to different points along the yield curve, are the usual yardsticks. The optionality inherent in many derivatives portfolios also necessitates a close look at the various Greeks- delta, vega, gamma, theta, rho etc.

Correlation risk. Correlation is a key input when it comes to multi-asset class portfolios. A lot rides on realized correlations turning out the same as the ones that are input. In times of extreme market stress, asset correlations break down, often catastrophically. Models that assume a constant correlation dynamic are fraught with pricing and risk management errors; a risk that can perhaps be mitigated by the use of sophisticated correlation Multi-Garch forecasting algorithms.

Model risk (leading to both incorrect valuation and risk numbers). Market prices for exchange-traded derivatives are mostly transparent. They can be viewed on trading screens the world over, and are often published in real time by the exchanges. Price discovery is a simple matter. Model risk does not come into play for these trades. For other derivatives, however, the arbitrage-free price for a derivatives contract is complex, and there are many different factors to consider. Valuation becomes model-driven, and is subjected to someone's ability to accurately model price, volatility and correlation dynamics. It is not uncommon then to find that on most trades, both counterparties show profits. Problematical as that is, it happens because each is marking their positions to their respective models. In fact, it is this model discrepancy that drives the two sides to trade.

There are of course other risks in derivatives — *operational risk, counter-party risk, and liquidity risk.* These however are not unique to derivatives. A more complete discussion of risk is discussed in Chapter 12.

The ability to effectively manage these risks is important. The specific methodologies for doing so vary from market to market. In general, given that so much of derivatives trading is model-driven, models have to be vetted against market prices wherever available. Stress testing the inputs, scenario analysis, and netting exposures into different exposures, all have to be part of the risk management models. Interactive risk management interfaces that enable users to track benchmark indices, and quickly change trade size and determine hedges, are also key.

6. Conclusion

Derivatives are an integral part of most trading strategies. They offer the ability to quickly put on sizeable directional bets and hedges across different markets. For the arbitrage-oriented hedge fund, they also serve as the building blocks for cross-product strategies. They complete the cash markets and provide price information that is essential to the valuation and risk management of complex strategies and portfolios. In sophisticated hands, they can be used to systematically create alpha, transfer alpha and preserve alpha.

Hedge Fund Alpha Tear Sheet — Chapter 7

– Derivatives are financial contracts or instruments whose value is tied to other assets.
– Derivatives are the building blocks that underlie most cross-product arbitrage trades.
– Derivatives complete the markets and help expand the alpha opportunity set.
– We briefly discussed the following alpha generating strategies via derivatives:
   o Alpha from futures arbitrage
   o Alpha from realized / implied volatility arbitrage
   o Alpha from volatility skew trades
   o Alpha from cash futures basis trade
   o Alpha from trading the optionality in bonds
   o Alpha from trading the optionality in convertible bonds
   o Alpha from macro interest rate trades
   o Alpha from relative-value trades: Mortgage-backed securities versus Treasuries
   o Alpha from credit derivatives
   o Alpha from energy derivatives
   o Alpha from Long / Short strategies
– Derivatives are used in alpha transport strategies, the process of transferring an investment manager's ability to add alpha in one investment strategy to another market.
– In sophisticated hands, derivatives may be used to systematically create alpha, transfer alpha, and preserve alpha.

End Notes

[1] If one does not use leverage, the maximum loss for an investment is 100%, while the maximum gain is unlimited (or several thousand percent in practical terms.) Given this dynamic, the lognormal distribution provides a better estimate of security returns than the normal distribution. The net result is that a procedure that measures alpha, adjusted for lognormal returns, is generally more accurate than the traditional linear method.

References

Leland, Hayne, "Beyond Mean-Variance: Risk and Performance Measurement in a Nonsymmetrical World", *Financial Analysts Journal*, January–February 1999, pp. 27–36.

8

BEST EXECUTION OF HEDGE FUND STRATEGIES

Saad Rathore

Algorithmic Capital Markets

1. Introduction

October 19th 1987, was a calamitous day in financial markets history. Stock markets crashed around the world. The Dow Jones Industrial Average (DOW) dropped a whopping 22.6% in a *single* session. This event was later called The Great Crash of 1987 or simply Crash of 1987. It resulted in the largest daily percentage decline in the modern United States financial market history. Its aftermath was complete chaos — not only were huge sums of money lost, but also the confidence in the financial markets was utterly shattered. Friedrich Nietzsche, the famous German philosopher, is attributed to have said that out of chaos comes order. The financial markets chaos that resulted from the Crash of 1987 forced regulators to bring about changes that resulted in the advent of modern securities trading systems and procedures.

Many theories have been presented as to what caused the Crash of 1987. One theory, relevant to our study of best execution of hedge fund strategies, is that the slew of orders coming into the marketplace for execution were not handled effectively and this failure created a self fulfilling panic among investors. On October 19th 1987, investors sent orders, via telephone and electronically, to trading desks for execution. In the mayhem, many orders went unexecuted. Many thought that they had closed their trades and were startled to find out later that their trades remained open. There were many complaints that market makers simply refused to pick up their phones (the dominant approach to sending in trading orders in 1987) during the Crash of 1987. Regulators were flooded with complaints from angry investors and knew it was necessary to institute major changes in order to significantly reduce the likelihood of a similar event happening in the future. The changes in market microstructure, which details how trades are entered and executed, instituted after the Crash of 1987 gave rise to modern day electronic-based markets. Today transaction costs are significantly less and execution speed is exponentially faster relative to the systems that were in force during 1987. We elaborate on these changes in the next section.

The efficient implementation of hedge fund trades, the process known as best execution, was once an afterthought for many hedge fund managers. Good hedge fund managers realize that best execution of trades can result in alpha. Indeed, for Statistical Arbitrage, Event Trading, and other active hedge fund strategies, there can be no alpha without strong trading processes. Furthermore, best execution matters greatly to longer term oriented hedge funds as well, since effective trading processes safeguard anonymity and minimize the market impact of a hedge fund's trades. Accordingly knowledge of best execution is of prime importance to all hedge fund managers and not simply to those manning trading desks.

2. Market Microstructure Evolution

2.1 Small Order Execution System (SOES)

NASDAQ instituted the Small Order Execution System (SOES) in 1988 and its main purpose was to provide prompt, automated executions of small investors' orders. Investors who sent trade orders via SOES forced market makers to honor their obligation of filling orders at their quoted bid and ask prices. All market makers were obligated to continuously provide two-sided (bid and ask) quotes and therefore could not do the electronic equivalent of not answering their phones. Market officials believed the proper execution of investor trades would result in increased confidence in the financial system and ultimately greater trading volume. SOES was a giant leap towards the open and efficient execution paradigms that would later emerge. The system was used for orders of 1000 shares or less for active stocks and 200 shares or less for more illiquid issues. Today, SOES has been supplanted by other electronic systems, but one of its key features still remains in force. Namely, SOES pioneered the order obligation system now viewed as the backbone of modern electronic markets. Prior systems, such NASDAQ's SelectNet, enabled market makers to enter bid and ask quotes, but did not obligate them to trade at those prices. Today, orders posted on Electronic Communication Networks (ECNs) are posted on a "full obligation" basis, meaning that if the orders are posted then anyone can 'hit' those quotes to get a fill of their trading order(s).

2.2 Christie-Schultz Study of "Implicit Collusion" By Market Makers

Many financial professionals view academic research as "ivory tower" and not of practical relevance. A study by Christie and Schultz (1994) contained results that jolted the "business as usual" mindset of the trading powers on Wall Street. The Christie-Schultz paper presented evidence that the market makers were "implicitly colluding" to avoid odd eighth quotes. Taking a step back for a moment, U.S. stock markets for many decades operated under the "Spanish system" of quoting prices in fractions, such as 1/16, 1/8, and 1/4. If market makers avoided odd eight quotes — 1/8, 3/8, 5/8, and so forth — it would create high bid-ask spread, and greater profits for market makers. Traders who enter market orders pay the bid ask spread as part of the cost of getting a trade executed promptly. In theory, the number of odd eighth quotes should be roughly equal to the number of even eighth quotes, but the Christie-Schultz study found this to be far from the truth.

After the Christie-Schultz findings were verified by regulators, NASDAQ quickly instituted new order handling rules. One of the main features of the new rules was the integration of ECN prices into NASDAQ quote books. In essence, individual investors, hedge funds, and others were now empowered with the opportunity to quote prices alongside of traditional market makers. Individuals or institutions with this capability are characterized as trading with Direct Access. In most cases, Direct Access is conducted via ECNs, which also have the important benefit of trading anonymity. Trades through ECNs appear to the observer to be coming from a brokerage firm and not an individual or particular hedge fund.

Some of the more active ECNs today include Archipelago, Island, BATS and Knight Trading's Edge ECN. The market share gain of ECNs proved to be so rapid that traditional exchanges, such as The New York Stock Exchange and NASDAQ, purchased Archipelago and Island, respectively. ECNs account for the majority of volume on U.S. exchanges today due to their speed, anonymity features, and low transaction costs.

2.3 Decimalization of U.S. Markets

The U.S. Securities and Exchange Commission (SEC) ordered in 1997, partially due to the findings of the Christie-Schultz study, that all stock markets convert their quotation systems to decimals by April 2001. Moving from a system that quotes prices in fractions to one that quotes in dollars and cents is known as decimalization. The idea behind decimalization was that it would bring several benefits to small investors, most notably a shrinking of the bid-ask spread. Then NYSE Chairman, Richard Grasso, testified to a Congressional Committee in June 2000 that such a move could save investors a billion dollars or more.

The decimalization of the price quotes created a massive increase in exchange volume since orders in many cases were now executed with a penny difference. For example, a trade size of 1,000 shares would result in a bid-ask spread cost of $125 using eighths or $10 using pennies. Decimalization in concert with increased trading via ECNs resulted in a massive increase in stock market volume. The decimalization process also enabled investors to better compare prices with exchanges globally, where trading was already conducted in decimals.

2.4 Regulation National Market System (Reg NMS)

The traditional market maker model fell out of favor with the advent of decimalization, the narrowing of spreads, and the growth of ECNs. The profitability at market maker / specialists firms declined precipitously. Previously, the trading function of many hedge funds was outsourced due to high costs. Specifically, it was costly for hedge funds to maintain their own trading desks (beyond the simple clerk function of sending trades) since discovering trading interest and employing sophisticated trading algorithms required a significant capital commitment and access to trading order flow. Well-capitalized wholesale execution trading firms, which benefited from a massive amount of variegated order flow, previously added significant value when executing trades. The emergence of ECNs resulted in more hedge funds favoring the Direct Access model over the outsourced trading function through traditional market makers and institutional trading desks.

The popularity of ECNs resulted in another obstacle to best execution — the "fragmentation" of trading interest. In short, it was difficult for investors to get a complete picture of liquidity in the market unless they could simultaneously view prices on all relevant exchanges and ECNs. A trader may have missed the best possible price by not being able to "see" the trading interest throughout various venues on the marketplace. The SEC became concerned with the market fragmentation problem and enacted Regulation National Market System, or Reg NMS. Under Reg NMS, market makers and execution agents were now obligated to sweep through the entire fragmented marketplace to provide the best execution. The process of finding and executing at the best prices among several exchanges is called "smart order routing."

3. Best Execution of Hedge Fund Trades

The increased use of electronic trading and mathematical algorithms has resulted in additional layers of complexity to the best execution process. This complexity is an alpha opportunity for astute hedge funds. Modern financial theories, such as those pioneered by Markowitz, Sharpe, Black, and Scholes are largely silent on the process of best execution. The process of best execution takes on increasing importance in "crowded trades" or those where many hedge fund managers are following the same core strategy. For example, a common trade for many Long / Short hedge funds over the 2007 to mid-2008 time period was to be short Financial stocks and long Energy stocks. Akin to a game of musical chairs, the Darwinian process of weeding out weaker hedge funds in crowded trades may ultimately come down to the execution prowess of a particular hedge fund.

4. Transaction Costs

Ronald Coase was awarded the 1991 Nobel Memorial Prize in Economics for his groundbreaking research on the nature of transaction costs. Although the bulk of his research was conducted several decades ago, its framework still applies well to the process of best execution of hedge fund trades. Coase (1937) states that cost of obtaining goods or services through the market is actually more than just the price of the good. There are several related costs such as discovery, bargaining, searching, trade policing, and enforcement that all might add to the total cost of the good or the asset being purchased. Coase's ideas apply to the modern day traders who not only consider price, but also venue, negotiation costs and the market impact of their trades.

Wagner (2003), Chairman of the trading firm Plexus Group, estimated that the transaction costs faced by institutional traders were as much as 1.5% per transaction. It is readily apparent that active trading may entail substantial transaction costs and overwhelm much of the expected alpha of a trade. In order to better understand the components of trading, we will break total costs into explicit and implicit pieces.

4.1 Explicit Costs

Explicit costs are readily observable and quantifiable and include commissions, ECN costs for removing liquidity, ECN rebates for adding liquidity, taxes, bid-ask spreads, payments for data services and so forth. Traders have always paid special attention to explicit costs since it is one of the easiest ways for supervisors to gauge their effectiveness. However, the previously cited study by Wagner, and those conducted by others, found that implicit costs generally make up the largest component of transaction costs.

4.2 Implicit Costs

Implicit transaction costs are determined by estimating the change in market factors such as price, information content, and liquidity, due to the act of trading or an expression of trading interest. In other words, it is the movement in the price of a security due to the actions of a particular trader or investor. For example, a hedge fund seeking to buy 1,000,000 shares of IBM may end up moving the market adversely if the marketplace becomes aware of pending block trades. A good trader will discretely chop the block up into several smaller pieces and execute the trade with minimal impact over time. However, if the market rapidly moves up in the interim, the trader may incur an opportunity cost due to delaying. IBM is a large and liquid stock, so the delay issue comes into greater focus when trading smaller issues. Nevertheless, it would be unwise to dismiss implicit or market impact costs when examining large stocks, since many institutional managers tend to hold the same securities. This herding behavior may result in a large and seemingly liquid stock dropping sharply in value, as exhibited by many world equities in October, 2008.

An astute trader will therefore have to make several decisions in order to achieve best execution for his fund. He may ask the hedge fund manager about the urgency of execution. If timeliness is of high priority, perhaps due to an impending earnings report, then the trader may have to pay up in transaction costs in order to get the full position established before a particular event date. Conversely, if there is no immediate urgency, the trader can break up the order into smaller sizes to reduce market impact by not showing his hand. For example, the trader could engage in a patient style of trading using not only limit orders, but also capturing ECNs rebates for providing liquidity. One helpful way to model the best execution process is to create a matrix of preferences with respect to price, liquidity, time, cost, and other relevant dimensions. **Table 1** lists a simple trading preference matrix.

Table 1: Trading Preference Matrix

	Preferences		
Security	Price	Liquidity	Time
IBM	Low	High	High
TEX	High	Moderate	Low
VIP	Medium	Low	Medium

5. Pre, During and Post Trade Analyses

Statistical techniques provide traders with many tools to analyze costs for analyzing the best execution process. It is helpful to break the best execution process into three components — pre, during, and post trade analyses. Best execution is a never-ending process since the market is a self-learning and adjusting mechanism. In other words, today's best execution process, may not be optimal next month or year.

Wall Street has embraced in recent years the importance of best execution and is putting in significant intellectual, financial and technological resources behind providing an execution solution that best fits a particular trader or hedge fund's needs. Hedge fund traders of the past primarily focused on forecasting market movements, but today's traders must also be familiar with proprietary and third party capability with respect to trading algorithms. Many trading desks have algorithms tailored to a particular hedge fund strategy, such as Statistical Arbitrage, Distressed, and Event Driven.

5.1 Pre-Trade Analyses

Pre-trade analyses may include the historical volatility of the security, technical analysis, money flow, correlation to fund's benchmark, tracking error (if internal records from previous executions are kept), investigation into news flow surrounding the company, put / call activity, and other aspects of market sentiment. Pre-trade analyses should provide traders with insight into the best method of executing a trade before the "send" button is selected. Pre-trade analyses may also help traders find out what algorithm offered by external brokerage firms is best suited for their particular trade. Over time, a scorecard or "report card" should be kept in order to analyze the effectiveness of the trader's decisions and the performance of external trading desks. Accordingly, it is important for hedge funds to keep a data warehouse to analyze the effectiveness of all of its trading related decisions.

The field of Pre-trade analyses is growing rapidly as firms increasingly compete to execute their trades with minimal impact. In many ways, Pre-trade intelligence is somewhat similar to an information knowledge advantage the firm may develop by investing in hiring more qualified and insightful analysts. For example, many traders will argue that certain stocks exhibit price behavior that is idiosyncratic to the security. Pre-trade analyses may help to identify these patterns. Some stocks move slowly, while others are more reactive to news and earnings announcements. A trader may be able to get a fill for 1,000,000 shares in IBM without significantly moving the market but not be able to sell 50,000 shares of an illiquid security without creating a massive market impact. In short, pre-trade analyses may help a trader sketch out his strategy of best execution while being cognizant of the trading mandates of time, size and price.

5.2 During Trade Analyses

During trade analyses focus on the segment of time when an order is being filled. Given that explicit transaction costs have fallen sharply in recent years, its main focus is on reducing implicit costs, such as market impact. One commonly adopted method of minimizing market impact is to split up a large order into smaller orders designed to leave a minimal footprint of trading activity. In our IBM example, instead of posting a complete 1,000,000 shares in the market, the order would be presented in smaller waves of perhaps 50,000 shares over a period of time, or other trading volume amount that is not expected to generate friction.

Another technique to minimizing market impact is to post the order as "not held," which indicates the price of the order may be altered at the discretion of the executing trader. In recent years, the marketplace has become very reactive to "not held" orders due to their typical large size. The contents of limit order books — a list of buy and sell orders at specific prices — were once the exclusive domain of the market makers or the specialists on the exchange floor. However, the limit order book of ECNs and some exchanges are now freely viewable to all and the information contained in these electronic books are valuable for during trade analyses. Traders can glean insight into the depth and breadth of interest in each security as a trade works its way to completion.

Perhaps the most important trading innovation over the past ten years is the growing use of trading algorithms in the execution of institutional trading orders. Trading algorithms are most effective through ECNs due to their open architecture systems, lightening quick executions, and guaranteed anonymity. ECNs enable one to receive price quotes, send orders, cancel orders and receive confirmations through their programmable computer interfaces. This computer architecture facilitates the writing of quantitative and artificial intelligence-based routines to predict, send, cancel and adjust execution orders to the marketplace. According to research by the Aite Group (2006), algorithmic trading is now contributing as much as a third of all volume in US and European Union exchanges and is expected to grow to 53% of the total volume by the year 2010. Broker provided trading algorithms have taken on increased importance in recent years and some of these algorithms are quite complex. However, it may also be helpful to discuss some of the more traditional execution techniques offered by brokers. We discuss these metrics in the next few subsections.

5.2.1 Volume Weighted Average Price (VWAP)

Many sell side-trading desks offer Volume Weighted Average Price (VWAP) services. VWAP orders are sliced and diced into a smaller number of shares that are gradually presented to the marketplace. It measures the ratio of the total dollar value traded to total volume traded within a specific time window. VWAP is calculated as follows:

VWAP = ∑ (Number of Shares Executed * Price) / (Total Shares Executed)

VWAP is the most commonly used algorithm and has become a benchmark for execution quality. Index funds are some of its largest users. Some brokers have offered "Guaranteed VWAP" services, but this practice has declined in recent years since VWAP is not a trivial benchmark to clear. Most brokers are now offering VWAP on "best efforts" basis.

5.2.2 Time Weighted Average Price (TWAP)

Time Weighted Average Price (TWAP) orders are sliced based on the percentage of daily value traded within a given time window selected for execution. The TWAP strategy is purely a time slicing strategy. For example, the amount of trading at the first and last hours of the trading day far exceed those around the lunch period. Accordingly, larger orders are more likely to be executed with the TWAP strategy at either end of the day. Traders may provide the time slicing parameters they want to use, such as the maximum percentage of volume during the specified time window.

5.2.3 Target Volume Strategies (TVOL)

Target Volume Strategies (TVOL) orders are executed in proportion to market volume and are not tied to a specific time window or price. The trader may specify he wants to purchase approximately 10% of the average volume of a company's securities and the executing broker will carry out the trades over the course of the day. The average price may be better than or worse than VWAP or other quantifiable execution benchmark. The trader can be assured of having a trade get done, but execution price remains a concern and should be closely monitored.

5.2.4 Proprietary Advanced Execution Strategies

Several brokers provide other proprietary execution strategies and claim they perform better than some of the aforementioned techniques. The most common way of evaluating proprietary execution strategies it to compare their effectiveness to VWAP. It is difficult to beat VWAP on consistent basis, so a proprietary execution strategy that has done so may provide an edge worth paying for.

5.2.5 Dark Pools and Crossing Networks

Market impact is the major obstacle for most hedge fund trades, and at times it may be optimal to transact away from traditional exchanges and ECNs via "dark pool" trading networks, such as those run by ITG, Liquidnet, Goldman Sachs SigmaX, Pipeline Trading, and others. Dark pools are computer networks that are designed to facilitate the exchange of large quantities of shares away from the public exchanges through private transactions between subscribers. Sometimes these trading venues are called crossing networks, since if two opposite orders (buy and sell) for a particular security occur in the same time window they match or cross each other, resulting in a completed trade. Dark pools are open to a select group of institutional subscribers and their orders are not displayed on any public limit order books, hence the "dark" part of the name.

Dark pools enable traders to move large blocks of shares without revealing their identities while minimizing market impact. In many cases, the nature of your order (buy or sell) is not revealed, reducing the risk of front running. For example the dark pool operated by Pipeline Trading does not allow traders to indicate whether they are a buyer or a seller in the stock, but rather allows them to post an expression of interest. If Pipeline determines that one side is a natural buyer and the other side is the natural seller, the two parties are allowed to complete the transaction. Liquidnet is a peer to peer network where parties can negotiate among themselves a price at which to exchange shares, once the buyer and seller link is established. ITG works by accumulating trading interests over a specific time interval and then exchanges shares if there is a match. The execution however is not guaranteed when the order is accepted by ITG, as the natural contra side may not exist. The probability of not executing the trade is the major drawback of trading in dark pools, relative to trading on the public exchanges which are mandated to continuously provide bid and ask quotes.

The major advantage of using dark pools is to reduce the implicit cost related to market impact. An exchange is only possible if there is a large buyer or a large seller of a stock at a mutually agreeable price. Institutional traders can use dark pools to move large blocks of securities without artificially depressing their prices. Orders are disseminated in a manner such that there is no leakage of information to an outside broker or ECN, or public. Dark Pools are therefore an essential and efficient mechanism for executing hedge fund trades.

Dark pools have gained popularity in recent years since the average trading size on exchanges and ECNs dropped precipitously after the advent of decimalization. A liquidity driven institutional trader may not see liquidity in conventional markets and therefore might be nervous about offloading a position through these venues. In other words, the likelihood of an institutional trader matching a large order on the exchange has recently become more limited. They are better served by finding other institutions with large position to exchange shares, rather than going into the market and "spraying" the market with their orders.

There are several dark pools in operation today. Almost all are different from each other as to how they make the buyers and the sellers come together. Some are set up as independent companies with patented methods, such as Pipeline, while others are offered by large institutional brokers, yet others are offered by the exchanges such as NYSE Euronext (Matchpoint) and NASDAQ. According to the Aite Group, in Q3 of 2007, 25% of US exchange volume flowed through dark pools.[1]

The most active dark pools today are Morgan Stanley Trajectory Cross and MS Pool, Direct Edge, Citi LIQUIFI, Credit Suisse CrossFinder, Knight Capital Group's Knight Match, Fidelity Capital Markets' CrossStream, Goldman Sachs' SIGMA X, Instinet, Merrill Lynch's APX and MLXN, Bank of New York's ConvergEx VortEx,

LavaFlow, BIDS Trading, Pipeline Trading, ITG Posit, Jones Trading and UBS' Price Improvement Network (PIN).

5.2.6 Technology for Best Execution

The discussion of the myriad of trading options leads one to wonder what may be the best approach to executing a particular trade. Wall Street has created useful tools through software programs that go by the name of Order Management System (OMS) and / or Execution Management System (EMS). EMS and OMS are computer applications that let traders see market data, position blotters, market value exposures and interact with relevant trading systems. An OMS is the trader's gateway to the markets and the plethora of execution services that it offers.

OMS was one of the major technological advancements of the late 1990s and has provided traders with a screen based tool to enter, cancel and replace orders through mouse clicks or keyboard inputs and then to deliver those orders to different brokers via an industry standard messaging protocol. The industry standard messaging protocol for electronic communication is known as Financial Information Exchange FIX).

Let us continue with our example of a hedge fund trader that wishes to execute a buy order of 1,000,000 shares of IBM. The order might be submitted through the hedge fund's OMS to different brokers and get distributed in the following tranches:

a) 200,000 shares sent for execution by Goldman Sachs VWAP Algorithm.

b) 200,000 shares sent to a sales trader at Morgan Stanley for execution.

c) 100,000 shares sent to a sales trader at Merrill Lynch & Co for execution.

d) 250,000 shares sent to ITG's Posit crossing network for execution.

e) 100,000 shares sent for execution via CSFB's execution algorithm.
f) 150,000 shares sent for execution using a Direct Market Access connection.

After the trader enters these orders through the hedge fund's OMS platform, the other parties, in real-time, will send him copies of execution reports indicating the price and quantity for those orders which have been filled. The trader may cancel unexecuted orders at any given time. He will continue to get these reports from different execution brokers, but is required to fill out reports for orders that he sent to the market. Order Management Systems also provide compliance and post trade reporting tools, such as adherence to leverage limits, legal regulations, and other pertinent items.

5.3 Post-Trade Analysis

An effective best execution regimen must be constantly evaluated to determine if indeed the process is delivering on its expected advantages. Post-trade analysis, in essence, is the jury's verdict on how well the investment execution was carried out. We can observe from our analysis if performance was driven by our execution approach, hampered by it, or benefited from luck. Several firms have developed software for post-trade transaction cost analysis. These programs primarily focus on two issues, Transaction Cost Analysis and Performance Analysis.

5.3.1 Transaction Cost Analysis (TCA)

Transaction Cost Analysis (TCA) centers on measuring implementation shortfall, which is the difference between the actual price of execution and the price of the security at the time the order was first entered. In some cases, the implementation shortfall is adjusted for movements in the market while the trade was being completed. The realized return includes costs related to commissions, bid-asks spreads, transfer and holding fees, opportunity, and delay. Implementation shortfall is commonly known as "slippage" in Wall Street terms. Hedge funds should keep track of implementation shortfall numbers and try to improve them over time through their best execution processes.

5.3.2 Performance Analysis

Performance analysis measures the execution results of the trader versus industry benchmarks. For example, commissions are an explicit cost the hedge fund has to pay and is unavoidable. However, it is still worthwhile to examine the commission rates of the hedge fund versus a comparable industry average. Firms typically have limited data to determine how their own costs stack up against industry costs, so they will often rely on reports from industry consultants, such as Plexus Corp, who maintain large databases of these records, while safeguarding anonymity.

5.3.3 Reporting on Post Trade Analysis

Portfolio managers are judged relative to their performance versus an industry benchmark, such as the S&P 500. Hedge fund traders who carry out the wishes of their fund manager(s) are often evaluated through TCA and Performance Analysis. Ideally, the trader will be contributing to alpha as well. It is not a trivial task to estimate the value added by a trader, since certain strategies are more difficult to implement than others. For example, a mean reversion strategy is relatively easy to implement since the trader is usually buying when the market is selling and visa versa. Conversely, the trader for a momentum strategy initiates a position only after it begins to move in one direction. These traders may have difficulty in executing trades at a price close to that which appeared when the trade was initiated.

Hedge Fund Alpha Tear Sheet — Chapter 8

- The financial markets chaos that resulted from the Crash of 1987 forced regulators to bring about changes that resulted in the advent of modern securities trading systems and procedures.
- The efficient implementation of hedge fund trades, the process known as best execution, was once an afterthought for many hedge fund managers.
  - o Good hedge fund managers realize that best execution of trades can result in alpha.
- Important events in the evolution of U.S. trading systems included the creation of the Small Order Execution System (SOES), the publication of the Christie-Schultz study on market maker implicit collusion, Decimalization, and Regulation National Market System (Reg NMS).
- Transaction costs not only include explicit costs, such as commissions and bid ask spreads, but also implicit costs, such as market impact.
- Our framework for best execution of trades involves the creation of a Trading Matrix and divides the process into pre-trade, during trading, and post-trading analyses.
- Pre-trade analyses may include the historical volatility of the security, technical analysis, money flow, correlation to fund's benchmark, tracking error, investigation into news flow surrounding the company, put / call activity, and other aspects of market sentiment.
- During trade analyses focus on the segment of time when an order is being filled and include topics such as Volume Weighted Average Price (VWAP), Time Weighted Average Price (TWAP), Target Volume Strategies (TVOL), dark pools, and crossing networks.
- Post trading analyses place primary emphasis on transaction cost analysis and performance analysis.
  - o These techniques focus on the performance of the trader and fund versus appropriate industry benchmarks.
- Best execution is a continuous process due to the constant evolution of trading systems, technology, mathematical models, and hedge fund investment strategies.

End Notes

[1] Numerous statistics on dark pools of trading may be found in the Aite Group report (2007).

References

Aite Group, "Algorithmic Trading 2006: More Bells and Whistles," November, 2007.

Aite Group, "Rise of Dark Pools and Rebirth of ECNs: Death to Exchanges," September, 2007.

Christie, William and Paul Schultz, "Why do NASDAQ Market Makers Avoid Odd-Eighth Quotes?" *Journal of Finance*, Vol. 49, No. 5, December 1994, pp. 1813–1840.

Coase, Ronald H., "The Nature of the Firm," *Economica*, Vol. 4, 1937, pp. 386–405, 1937.

Wagner, Wayne, Presentation to the House Committee on Financial Services, U.S. Government, March, 2003.

9

GROWTH OF THE HEDGE FUND MANAGEMENT COMPANY: EVOLVING FROM A SINGLE STRATEGY FUND TO A MULTISTRATEGY FUND OR MULTIPLE FUNDS

John M. Longo, PhD, CFA

Rutgers Business School & The MDE Group

1. Introduction

The average life of a hedge fund is approximately three years.[1] If the hedge fund management company is not viable, there cannot be any sustainable alpha. The best investment managers in the world can see their businesses dramatically shrink due to external factors beyond their control. For example, mergers and leveraged buyouts (LBOs) have largely dried up during the period from late 2007 through 2008 due to the fallout resulting from the problems in the credit markets. In a difficult market environment, it would be a challenge for managers to put fresh money to work in these areas, and justify their high fees.

Although the best path for some funds may be to stick to their particular niche within a single strategy hedge fund format, many firms have the desire to expand. A single strategy hedge fund is akin to "a farmer putting all of his eggs in one basket," so to speak. Understandably, this is how most hedge funds start. However, the largest hedge fund management companies, such as Highbridge or SAC Capital, often evolve into a multistrategy fund or series of distinct hedge funds. Which is the best approach to evolution: multistrategy or multiple funds? One approach does not dominate the other and the best answer depends on the views and skill set of the principal(s) of the firm.

The purpose of this chapter is to explore different approaches to growing and ensuring the viability of the hedge fund management company. The main discussion focuses on evolving from a single strategy fund to a multistrategy fund or multiple funds. We also explore the topic of keeping all of the fund management company's capital in house, or using part of it to invest in other promising hedge funds, typically in return for an equity stake in the external company.

Table 1 shows the largest hedge fund management companies in the world. All of the fund management companies operate several funds

Table 1: Largest Hedge Fund Management Firms, December 31, 2007

Rank	Firm / Subdivision or Fund	Assets Under Management
1	**JP Morgan Asset Management**	**$44.7 Billion**
	Highbridge Capital Management	*$27.8 Billion*
	JP Morgan Asset Management	*$16.9 Billion*
2	**Bridgewater Assocaties**	**$36.0 Billion**
	Pure Alpha Strategy	*$36.0 Billion*
2	**Farallon Capital Management**	**$36.0 Billion**
4	**Renaissance Technologies Corp**	**$33.3 Billion**
	Institutional Equities Fund	*$22.0 Billion*
	Medallion	*$7.5 Billion*
	Institutional Futures Fund	*$3.8 Billion*
5	**Och-Ziff Capital Management Group**	**$33.2 Billion**
6	**D.E. Shaw Group**	**$32.2 Billion**
7	**Goldman Sachs Asset Management**	**$29.2 Billion**
8	**Paulson & Co.**	**$29.0 Billion**
	Advantage Plus	*$5.6 Billion*
	Credit Opportunities	*$4.3 Billion*
	Advantage	*$3.6 Billion*
	Enhanced	*$3.4 Billion*
	Paulson International	*$2.7 Billion*
9	**Barclay's Global Investors**	**$26.2 Billion**
	Equity Long / Short	*$12.8 Billion*
	Global Macro and Currency	*$9.9 Billion*
	Fixed Income Long / Short	*$3.6 Billion*
10	**GLG Partners**	**$23.9 Billion**

Note: Only the largest funds are shown for those firms with sub-detail.
Source: *Alpha*, May 2008.

or run a multistrategy fund. In contrast, the Vanguard 500 Index Fund, a single mutual fund, has aggregate assets of more than $100 billion. The simple reason for the disparity in size is that there is only so much alpha that can be wrung out of a single hedge fund strategy. The capacity for each strategy varies by a number of factors including liquidity, growth prospects, the ability to trade anonymously, and the presence of derivative securities allowing for synthetic hedging, speculation, or replication. Naik, Ramadorai and Strömqvist (2007) find evidence of capacity constraints for a number of common hedge fund strategies and support the thesis that increased capital flows to specific hedge fund segments ultimately reduces its alpha potential.

2. Methods of Single Strategy Fund Expansion

There are several methods for moving beyond a single strategy hedge fund. Here, we will discuss two. (For now, we will not make any distinction between a multistrategy fund and multiple funds). This distinction will be the focus of our next section. The two methods are:

1. Expand to other strategies related to the initial fund's core competence.
2. Expand to other strategies uncorrelated to the firm's initial strategy.

One advantage to the first approach is that managers are less likely to make mistakes by investing in strategies that they may not fully understand. The case of Amaranth Advisors provides one extreme example of this point. Amaranth began primarily as a convertible arbitrage hedge fund. Amaranth expanded into other hedge fund strategies as the convertible arbitrage trade became crowded around the year 2000 time frame. By the summer of 2006, Amaranth had $9 billion in assets under management and was regarded by many as one of the top multistrategy hedge funds in the industry. However, a look beneath the surface of their portfolio revealed that leveraged energy trades drove the bulk of the fund's assets and profits — a market with vastly different dynamics relative to convertible arbitrage. Brian Hunter, who was not one of the original principals of Amaranth, led the firm's energy trading efforts. In September, 2006 disaster struck, with many of Amaranth's leveraged trades in the natural gas market going against it. The fund lost at least 65% of its assets in a matter of a single week and ultimately had to be liquidated.

Table 2 shows the hypothetic evolution of a single Long / Short Domestic Equity Fund to a total of five strategies likely within the core competence of existing management. The first two extensions of the original strategy may be done without significant incremental work. For example, the Market Neutral Domestic Equity fund would simply force managers to keep the beta of the portfolio close to zero and possibly place some constraints on sector exposure. The 130/30 hedge fund, which uses $1.30 Long and $0.30 Short for each $1.00 of capital, would force managers to hold a roughly constant long / short ratio. In both cases, the list of securities would be similar or identical to the ones in the original strategy.

Table 2: Sample Evolution of Long / Short Domestic Equity Fund To Five Strategies

Original Long / Short Domestic Equity
⇓
Market Neutral Domestic Equity
⇓
130/30 Domestic Equity
⇓
Long / Short Global Equity
⇓
Long / Short International Equity

Expanding into a Long / Short Global Equity fund may require incremental or substantial additional resources. The more quantitative the fund, the lower the extra costs of extending into the global realm. However, if the hedge fund management company is primarily fundamental in nature, it may require an investment in new staff and resources on a worldwide basis. The fifth strategy, a Long / Short International Equity Fund, will almost certainly require an investment in overseas staff, or an extensive travel budget. In all cases, the core investment process of the domestic strategy may be portable to the "evolved" strategies, albeit with incremental to significant extra costs. Once again, the chief strength of this approach is that the evolution is likely to remain within management's circle of competence, reducing the likelihood of an "Amaranth-like" mistake. The weakness of this "core competence" approach to evolution is, if the style of the original strategy goes out of favor, the other strategies are likely to be impacted as well, due to their relatively high levels of historical correlation.

A second approach to expansion beyond the initial hedge fund strategy is based on Markowitz Portfolio Theory. Harry Markowitz shared the 1990 Nobel Memorial Prize in Economic Science for his pioneering work in portfolio theory. Prior to Markowitz's seminal work in the early 1950's, risk was considered to be of far less importance than return in the portfolio construction process. Furthermore, the mindset prior to Markowitz was that risk was best mitigated by naïve diversification across many securities and not the correlation or interaction approach that played a central role in his theory. In a nutshell, Markowitz created an approach for finding the optimal risk-return combination of all investment possibilities and then matched individual preferences to this investment opportunity set in order to tailor a portfolio to a client's objectives. **Figure 1** graphically illustrates Markowitz Portfolio Theory.

The goal of Markowitz Portfolio Theory is to create an efficient portfolio — one that maximizes return for a given level of risk, or minimizes risk for a given level of return. The correlation among securities, or portfolios, is the driving result of obtaining an efficient portfolio. Correlation mathematically is bound between +1 on the upside and −1 on the downside. The lower the correlation, the greater the diversification benefits and lower the risk of the portfolio. Accordingly, a second path to evolution from the initial hedge fund strategy is to add new strategies that are uncorrelated to the initial one and then to continue to add strategies that create an efficient overall hedge fund management company portfolio.

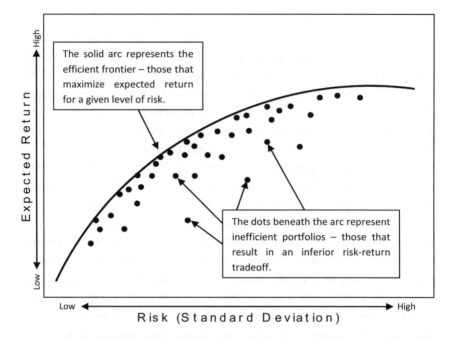

The solid arc represents the efficient frontier – those that maximize expected return for a given level of risk.

The dots beneath the arc represent inefficient portfolios – those that result in an inferior risk-return tradeoff.

Figure 1: Markowitz Portfolio Theory

Table 3 shows the correlation of returns among various hedge fund strategies over the January 1994 – July 2008 time period. Continuing with our earlier example of evolving beyond the initial Long / Short strategy, the first new strategy may be the one with the lowest correlation to Long / Short, or Short Biased in this case. Given that there is a paucity of Short Biased managers, Fixed Income Arbitrage might be the next viable candidate. The next strategy for expansion may be the one that has the lowest correlation to this portfolio, and so forth.

The Markowitz approach to evolving beyond the initial hedge fund strategy has the advantage of having at least one strategy likely to be performing well while the others are faltering, due to internal or external factors. The disadvantage includes the need to find additional talent, since the new strategy will likely be outside the core competence of the original, and the increased likelihood of making a mistake in a strategy that may not be fully understood by the principals of the original fund.

Table 3: Correlation Among Various Hedge Fund Investment Strategies

Strategy	Str 1	Str 2	Str 3	Str 4	Str 5	Str 6	Str 7	Str 8	Str 9	Str 10	Str 11	Str 12
Convert Arb	1.00											
Short Bias	-0.29	1.00										
Emerging Mkts	0.33	-0.55	1.00									
Equity Mkt Neut	0.36	-0.32	0.24	1.00								
Event Driven	0.59	-0.62	0.68	0.38	1.00							
Distressed	0.52	-0.61	0.60	0.36	0.93	1.00						
Multistrategy	0.59	-0.55	0.67	0.35	0.94	0.76	1.00					
Risk Arb	0.37	-0.50	0.43	0.32	0.65	0.54	0.62	1.00				
Fixed Inc Arb	0.62	-0.15	0.28	0.16	0.41	0.34	0.43	0.13	1.00			
Global Macro	0.29	-0.13	0.42	0.24	0.38	0.31	0.41	0.15	0.41	1.00		
L/S Equity	0.33	-0.72	0.61	0.37	0.69	0.61	0.67	0.52	0.25	0.43	1.00	
Managed Futures	-0.07	0.08	-0.04	0.15	-0.07	-0.05	-0.08	-0.09	-0.01	0.28	0.05	1.00

Key: Str 1 = Convert Arb; Str 2 = Short Bias; Str 3 = Emerging Mkts; Str 4 = Equity Mkt Neut; Str 5 = Event Driven; Str 6 = Distressed; Str 7 = Multistrategy; Str 8 = Risk Arb; Str 9 = Fixed Inc Arb; Str 10 = Global Macro; Str 11 = L/S Equity; Str 12 = Managed Futures.
Source: Credit Suisse Tremont Index LLC

Correlation is a single number, often estimated from a historical time series. A more sophisticated approach to expanding from the original hedge fund strategy in a diversified manner is to use a factor model. A factor model analyzes the relationship between the returns for a particular hedge fund strategy and a list of (typically macro) variables that likely impact a fund's returns. A study by Schneeweis, Kazemi, and Martin (2001) analyzed the relationship between nine macro variables and hedge fund returns for the following categories:

- Equity Hedge
- Relative Value Arbitrage
- Global Macro
- Equity Market Neutral
- Convertible Arbitrage
- Fixed Income Arbitrage

The nine macroeconomic variables in their model include the shape / movement of the yield curve, credit risk premium, short-term interest rate, long-term interest rate, intramonth volatility for the S&P 500, implied volatility for the S&P 500, intramonth volatility for bonds, large cap stock returns, and small cap stock returns. **Table 4** summarizes the results. It shows for each hedge fund strategy the scenarios, corresponding to the values of the nine macroeconomic factors, where it performs the best. For example, the Equity Hedge group of funds (which most closely maps into our discussion of Long / Short) performs best when the yield curve is moderately upward slowing, the credit risk premium is declining, long-term interest rates are moderate, volatility is moderate, and stock returns are strong.

Table 4: Strategy Performs Above Its Historical Average When …

HF Strategy → Macro Factor ↓	Equity Hedge	Relative Value Arbitrage	Global Macro	Equity Market Neutral	Convertible Arbitrage	Fixed Income Arbitrage
Yield Curve	Moderately upward sloping with no substantial change	Moderately upward sloping with no substantial change	Upward sloping and declining	Moderately upward sloping and declining	Slope is not changing	Upward sloping and increasing
Credit Risk Premium	Declining	Declining	Declining	High	Moderate	High and declining
Short-Term Rate	No substantial changes	Low and not changing	Low and not increasing	N/M	N/M	N/M
Long-Term Rate	Moderate and not increasing	Moderate and not changing	Moderate or high levels and not increasing	Declining	Low or moderate and not changing	High or is not decreasing
S&P Intra-Month Vol.	Moderate levels and not increasing	Moderate or low levels and not increasing	Low and not increasing	N/M	Moderate levels and not increasing	Not high and not changing
S&P 500 Implied Vol.	Moderate levels and not increasing	Moderate or low levels and not increasing	Low and not increasing	Moderate levels and not changing	Moderate levels and not increasing	Not high and not changing
Bond Intra-Month Vol.	Declining	Moderate	Low to moderate and not changing	Low	Not increasing	Moderate and not changing
Large Cap Stock Ret.	High	High	High	High	High	Moderate
Small Cap Stock Ret.	High	High	High	High	High	N/M

Source: Adapted from Schneeweis, Kazemi, and Martin (2001)

Based on the information in the table, a Fixed Income Arbitrage hedge fund strategy may be the next logical candidate for expansion, if the fund principals wanted to branch out from their original Long / Short strategy in a diversified manner. The Fixed Income Arbitrage strategy is less dependent on stock market returns and generally performs best when long-term interest rates are high or not decreasing — essentially the opposite of the Equity Hedge case.

3. Multistrategy Hedge Fund vs. Multiple Hedge Funds

Once a decision has been made to expand beyond a single strategy fund, the next crucial decision is to decide between a multistrategy fund and multiple funds. Each has its advantages and disadvantages. Millennium Partners is one of the best-known multistrategy funds with all of its $12 billion assets in a single fund, albeit with domestic and offshore permutations. SAC Capital has the bulk of its assets in a multistrategy fund, although in recent years it has branched out into additional funds. Conversely, Goldman Sachs has several multi-billion dollar hedge funds, such as Global Alpha and Global Equity Opportunities.

Perhaps the greatest weakness of the multistrategy fund is its limited number of investor slots: 99 for a 3c1 fund and 500 for a 3c7 fund. On the other hand, opening five separate hedge funds would result in a total of 495 to 2500 slots. Another weakness, or perhaps strength if returns are outstanding, is that a single number measures its performance. If the number is not good, substantial outflows may occur and the viability of the firm can be threatened.

One strength of the multistrategy fund is that management's attention is focused on a single fund, albeit with multiple strategies under the surface. The multistrategy fund also has lower expense ratios, for a given asset amount, since it requires only one audit, administrator, and legal advisor.

Arguably the most important attribute of a multistrategy fund is that it is more appealing to large fund of funds that may be concerned with the look-through rule. The look-through rule states that if a single investor accounts for more than 10% of a fund's assets, then the number of investors from the larger fund must count in the limited number of slots for the smaller fund. For example, if the original fund has 50 investors and $250 million under management in a 3c1 fund structure and the fund of fund has 75 investors in its fund and wishes to make an investment of $50 million in the smaller fund, it would not be possible since it would fail the look-through test. Fund of funds account for approximately 43% of hedge fund assets under management, so their importance cannot be minimized.[3]

Pension funds are not subject to the look-through rule, but are often uncomfortable accounting for a large percentage of a fund's assets. Although there is virtually unlimited capacity in a multistrategy fund and series of individual funds, pension funds often prefer to make a limited number of investments with a particular investment manager. They often do not want to run the risk of having a single fund close due to capacity constraints.

On the contrary, the weaknesses of the multistrategy fund are the strengths of the multiple funds approach and visa versa. Namely, the multiple funds approach has a virtually unlimited number of slots and its performance is not dependent on a single number. Among several funds, it is likely that at least one is performing well, resulting in a more continuous marketing operation for the fund management company. The multiple funds approach may be a better approach for attracting and retaining talent, since star performers can be given their own fund to manage. It is not as attractive for employees to run a part of a multistrategy fund, since the track record is technically created by a team and therefore generally not portable to new ventures. **Table 5** succinctly summarizes some of the key differences between the multistrategy fund and series of fund approaches.

Table 5: Comparison of Attributes of Multistrategy Funds vs. Multiple Hedge Funds

Attribute	Multistrategy	Multiple Funds
Fund of Fund Capacity	Greater	Lesser
Total Capacity	Slightly Lesser	Greater
Ability to Retain Talent	Worse	Better
Number of Fund Slots	Less	More
Pension Fund Interest	Greater	Lesser
Expense Ratio	Lower	Higher
Look-through Issues	Better	Worse
Performance Risk *	Greater	Lesser
Business Diversification	Worse	Better
Management Attention	Lesser	Greater

* Performance risk refers to the notion that the multistrategy fund has a single number that is reported to investors and databases, while under the multiple funds approach there may be several funds that are performing well despite a poor overall average for the parent investment management company.

5. Acquiring In House Talent vs. Deploying Capital In Outside Funds

An important issue related to the growth of the hedge fund management company is to deploy excess capital, beyond the initial hedge fund strategy, to external managers or to identify talent that could manage the funds in house. At first glance, it may appear that it would be more profitable to keep everything in-house. There is certainly greater control and oversight with an in-house operation.

However, there are many cases of extremely successful hedge fund companies that have outsourced a material percentage of their capital to outside funds. For example, S. Donald Sussman of Paloma Partners was one of the earliest investors in D. E. Shaw, a firm ranked as the sixth largest hedge fund company in the world by *Alpha* in 2008 with over $32 billion in assets. Lehman Brothers bought a 20% stake in D. E. Shaw in March 2007. Paloma was also one of the seed investors for Alpha Simplex, a firm founded by MIT Professor Andrew Lo.

Natixis Global Asset Management agreed to acquire Alpha Simplex in September 2007.

Julian Robertson, a member of *Alpha's* "Hedge Fund Hall of Fame," is perhaps the best-known investor in external funds. Robertson's Tiger Management was among the most successful fund groups ever, with total firm assets peaking at nearly $22 billion in the late 1990s. However, Robertson shut down his hedge fund in March 2000 after it dropped 40% in a little over two years during the height of the Internet Bubble. Although the hedge funds Tiger managed on behalf of investors shut down, Robertson continued to manage his own sizeable portfolio and seeded many of his former analysts, popularly known as "Tiger Cubs."

According to Taub (2008), Robertson earned over $1 billion in 2007 and earned a 75% rate of return on his own personal portfolio. The 28 "Tiger Cubs" funds that he seeded earned an average of 56% in 2007, before fees, and collectively manage more than $30 billion, which would make it the seventh largest hedge fund in the country if housed under one firm. Taub also notes that eight of the fiftieth highest paid hedge fund managers in the world, as measured by *Alpha*, are "Tiger Cubs" — although Robertson did not seed every Tiger alumnus on the *Alpha* list.

The profit sharing arrangements for seed capital investments vary widely, but one rule of thumb is that the seeder receives a 1% ownership stake in the new fund for each million dollars of capital contributed. For example, a $20 million contribution would entitle the seeder to a 20% stake in the new startup hedge fund. The seeder would earn two revenue streams: 1) the profits from the new fund management company; 2) the return on the $20 million in contributed capital, which typically flows into the seeder's initial fund.

Providing seed capital to outside funds may enable them to thrive in a more entrepreneurial environment, akin to a biotechnology firm in a joint venture relationship with a "Big Pharma" firm. It is certainly possible, but usually less profitable, to contribute capital to outside hedge funds, without obtaining equity ownership. The benefit of not owning a piece of the external fund is greater flexibility. With ownership often comes a lockup requirement (generally of two to five years) that could potentially impair the returns and reputation of the original fund if the new fund has poor performance. As with our discussion of multistrategy versus multiple funds, the principals of the hedge fund management company will ultimately know if an outsourcing solution is best in their particular case.

Hedge Fund Alpha Tear Sheet — Chapter 9

- Although the best path for some funds may be to stick to their particular niche within a single strategy hedge fund format, many firms have the desire to expand via a multistrategy hedge fund or through multiple separate hedge funds.
- Two common approaches for expanding beyond the initial fund's core strategy are:
  1. Expand to other strategies related to the initial fund's core competence.
  2. Expand to other strategies uncorrelated to the firm's initial strategy.
- The hedge fund management company is less likely to make a mistake by expanding into other areas related to their core competence, but it runs the increased risk of having their entire business being out of favor at the same point in time.
- Expanding to new, uncorrelated areas will likely maximize the risk adjusted returns of the overall hedge fund management company, but the principals of the original hedge fund strategy are more likely to make mistakes in areas that they do not fully understand.
- Many hedge fund management companies may choose to grow by seeding or deploying capital to outside hedge funds, typically in return for partial ownership of the newly seeded fund.
  - Ownership provides an extra revenue stream that may become substantial if the seeded firm grows into a star (e.g. Paloma Partners' seeding of D. E. Shaw).
  - One important disadvantage of owning a piece of an external hedge fund is the typical lockup period of two to five years that might detract from the performance and reputation of the parent fund in the event that the seeded fund falters.

End Notes

[1] Statement of the Financial Economists Roundtable on Hedge Funds, Financial Economists Roundtable, Stanford Graduate School of Business, July 10–11, 2005.

[2] In Chapter 10 we examine the separate issue of the pros and cons of managing or investing in a multistrategy fund versus a fund of funds.

[3] The 43% figure is cited by Balter (2008).

References

Balter, Brad, "Change In The Air For Fund Of Funds Fee Structures," FIN*alternatives*, August 15, 2008. http://www.finalternatives.com/node/5243

Markowitz, Harry, *Portfolio Theory: Efficient Diversification of Investments*, Yale University Press, 1959.

Naik, Narayan, Tarun Ramadorai and Maria Strömqvist, "Capacity Constraints and Hedge Fund Strategy Returns," *European Financial Management*, Vol. 13, No. 2, pp. 239–256, March 2007.

Schneeweis, Thomas, Hossein Kazemi, and George Martin, "Understanding Hedge Fund Performance: Research Results and Rules of Thumb for the Institutional Investor," Center for International Securities and Derivatives Markets, November 2001.

Statement of the Financial Economists Roundtable on Hedge Funds, Financial Economists Roundtable, Stanford Graduate School of Business, July 10–11, 2005.

Taub, Steven, "Tiger, Tiger Burning Bright," *Alpha*, April 2008, p. 38.

10

FUND OF HEDGE FUNDS

Jeffrey Glattfelder, CFA, CAIA, John Longo PhD, CFA,
and Stephen Spence, CFA, CAIA

*Citi Alternative Investments; Rutgers Business School & The MDE Group;
Terrapin Partners*

1. History of Fund of Funds (FoF)

It is believed that the first fund of hedge funds, Leveraged Capital Holdings, was started in Switzerland in 1969, by George Coulon Karlweis[1]. Shortly thereafter, in 1971, Grosvenor Capital Management started the first fund of hedge funds (FoF) in the United States. While these are recognized as the first formal fund of hedge fund structures, efforts to create diversified portfolios of hedge funds date back to 1954, when Alfred Jones changed the structure of his partnership to allow for allocation to multiple hedge fund managers.[2]

Like many developments in the capital markets, the creation of the first hedge fund of funds coincided with other developments in the investment markets. In this case, the growth in the number of hedge funds, which was estimated by the SEC in 1968 to be 1,403, created the opportunity for investment managers that could source, gain access to, and manage an investment in hedge funds.

From this simple beginning, hedge fund of funds has become a significant force in the alternative investment industry. Eurekahedge estimates that at the end of 2007, there were over 3,000 funds with assets of $747 billion accounting for over 35% of global hedge fund assets.

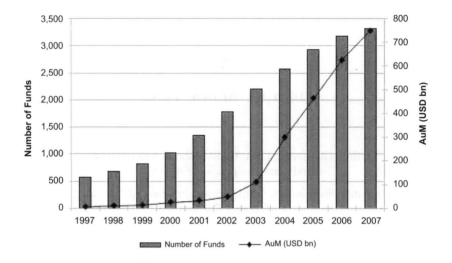

Figure 1: Number of Fund of Funds and Assets Under Management

Source: Eurekahedge

2. Objective of Fund of Funds

The primary objective of fund of funds is to deliver attractive risk adjusted returns, as measured by Sharpe Ratio, Sortino Ratio, or other metric. Most fund of funds aim to deliver annual returns, net of fees, in the high single digit to low double-digit range. Risk management is crucial since many investors choose to invest in fund of funds to avoid the risk of the large drawdowns that occur more frequently in individual hedge funds. The "tail risk" of a fund of funds losing all of its capital is far less than that of an individual fund due to the extra diversification provided by holding a basket of hedge funds.

Fund of funds provide "instant diversification," giving investors a diversified portfolio of hedge funds for a capital commitment typically on the order of $500,000 to $1 million. Conversely, it would cost an investor perhaps $20 million for a diversified portfolio of high quality hedge funds, since top performing funds often have minimum investments of a million dollars and up. Clearly, a portfolio investment of this magnitude is out of reach of the "mass affluent" hedge fund investor and falls within the realm of institutional or ultra high net worth investors.

3. Advantages and Disadvantages of Fund of Funds

As noted above, as an advantage, fund of funds provide investors with a diversified portfolio of hedge funds for a capital commitment of $1 million or less. Another advantage is that investors may have partial access to closed hedge fund managers, since these managers are often willing to give one of their limited slots to a fund of funds. The investment commitment of most fund of funds to a top-performing fund is usually larger than that of the typical individual investor. For example, a fund of funds managing $500 million, equally spread across 25 funds, would result in an investment of $20 million to each external manager. Hedge fund managers running a 3c1 fund are limited to 99 slots, while those operating a 3c7 fund have a larger, but still limited, 500 slots. Other things equal, the limit on the number of investors in a fund inclines hedge funds to have a strong preference for those, such as fund of funds, which can make large capital commitments.

The organization managing the fund of funds provides services, which an individual investor would be hard pressed to replicate. The due diligence process of most fund of funds is quite substantial. Most funds of funds perform extensive quantitative and qualitative analyses before selecting a portfolio of funds. After the initial fund of funds portfolio is created, there is ongoing monitoring, asset allocation, and hiring / firing decisions. Chapter 13 focuses on due diligence procedures for investing in single hedge funds and fund of funds.

The main disadvantage of the fund of funds is the additional layer of fees. The typical fund of funds charges a 1% annual asset management fee and a 10% incentive fee. However, fees can vary widely, as with single strategy hedge funds. Other common fee structures include a higher asset management fee, such as 1.5%, and no incentive fee, or an incentive fee that is realized after a risk free rate of return is surpassed.

Another disadvantage is that fund of funds investors almost always have to file for a tax extension. Many investors are uncomfortable having to wait until late summer or early fall to "close the books" on the prior tax year. Fund of funds cannot complete their K-1 partnership forms until they receive the tax information from each of their underlying funds. Typically, the fund of funds will receive K-1s from their underlying funds in late March or early April of each year, making it virtually impossible to provide their investors with completed tax forms by the usual April 15th deadline.

Fund of funds, due to its diversified nature, is unlikely to deliver the "blowout" returns that are possible with investments in single funds. For example, Paulson & Co's Credit Opportunities LP Fund returned a reported 590% in 2007, using derivatives to take a short position in the subprime mortgage market. A fund of funds return of 20% in a single year would be considered "off the charts."

4. Taxation of Fund of Funds

Fund of funds are generally tax inefficient, since its underlying holdings often exhibit high turnover. They are taxed on a pass through basis, with the taxes of the underlying strategy passing through to the holders of the fund of funds. Accordingly, many fund of funds are held in retirement vehicles, such as pension funds and qualified retirement accounts and managed through the offshore counterpart of a domestic fund or through a master feeder relationship. To use a trivial example, if a fund of funds held by a high net worth domestic investor provides a gross return of 10% (assume all short-term gains) and an investor is in a 40% marginal tax bracket, the after-tax return would only amount to 6%. The inefficient nature of most individual and fund of funds have led to the development of derivative or structured products on hedge funds, a trend discussed later in this chapter.

5.1 Fund of Funds vs. Direct Investment

As discussed previously, the main advantage of a direct investment in a portfolio of hedge funds, versus a single investment in a fund of funds, is to avoid a layer of fees. **Table 1** shows the extra loss in returns, or alternatively the extra alpha that needs to be earned, in order to overcome the fees charged by the typical fund of funds. For example, if an investor selected a portfolio of hedge funds that returned 10% after fees, a fund of funds selecting the same funds would provide a net return to its

Table 1: Returns for Fund of Funds vs. Direct Investment in Hedge Funds

Net Return of Portfolio of Individual Hedge Funds	Net Return of Fund of Funds	Absolute Difference
-20.0%	-21.2%	-1.2%
-18.0%	-19.2%	-1.2%
-16.0%	-17.3%	-1.3%
-14.0%	-15.3%	-1.3%
-12.0%	-13.3%	-1.3%
-10.0%	-11.4%	-1.4%
-8.0%	-9.4%	-1.4%
-6.0%	-7.4%	-1.4%
-4.0%	-5.4%	-1.4%
-2.0%	-3.5%	-1.5%
0.0%	-1.5%	-1.5%
2.0%	0.5%	-1.5%
4.0%	2.2%	-1.8%
6.0%	4.0%	-2.0%
8.0%	5.7%	-2.3%
10.0%	7.5%	-2.5%
12.0%	9.3%	-2.7%
14.0%	11.1%	-2.9%
16.0%	12.8%	-3.2%

Note: The calculation assumes the Fund of Fund (FoF) charges an annual asset management fee of 1%, has annual operating expenses of 0.5%, and charges a 10% incentive fee for all positive returns.

investors of 7.5% after the additional layer of expenses. This example assumes an annual asset based fee for the fund of funds of 1%, annual operating expenses of 0.5%, and a 10% incentive fee. It may be unrealistic to assume that the investor creating a "do it yourself" fund of funds has no expenses, but they are likely to be less than the 2.5% lost in fees to the conventional fund of funds discussed in our example. The higher the returns of the underlying portfolio, the greater the costs due to the 10% incentive fee kicking in when positive returns are achieved.

5.2 Fund of Funds vs. Multistrategy Funds

Multistrategy funds, as discussed in Chapter 1, deploy capital across a number of investment strategies. They provide additional diversification, relative to a single strategy fund, and in some cases, comparable diversification to a fund of funds. Since the multistrategy fund is housed in a single partnership structure, it consists of only one layer of fees. Conversely, fund of funds include a second layer of fees. On the surface, multistrategy funds seem to dominate the fund of funds approach due to their lower fee structures. However, multistrategy funds have the same management, operations and risk management processes, providing a lack of diversification on these key non-security selection areas. The blowup of Amaranth Advisors in 2007 has cast fresh doubt about the superiority of a multistrategy approach vis-a-vis a fund of funds in the minds of many investors. In Chapter 9 we discuss evolving from a single strategy fund to a multistrategy fund or series of funds.

5.3 Fund of Funds vs. Portfolio of Managed Accounts

In managed account structures, hedge fund managers replicate their strategies in separate accounts that are titled in an investor's name. The account is run in a largely identical manner to the individual fund, with the same holdings, weights, trading activity and so forth. In some cases, managed accounts place restrictions on the holdings and impose additional risk management mandates. But for all intensive purposes, the managed account is run *pari passu* to the manager's hedge fund.[3] The minimum investment to have a manager run a separately managed account is close to $5 million for startup funds to $50 million or more for established funds. In short, owning a managed account is like having a fund manager run a separate hedge fund for you.

From an investor's perspective, there are several benefits to having a separately managed account in lieu of an investment in the hedge fund limited partnership or limited liability company. The most important is a dramatically reduced risk of fraud. Although quite rare, fraud occasionally does occur in the hedge fund space. Recent examples include improprieties related to funds, such as those run by Bernard Madoff, Bayou Fund, KL Financial, and International Management Associates. It would be very difficult for an unscrupulous manager to make off with your money if it were held in an account in your name, relative to you sending a check or wire transfer to an account controlled by a hedge fund.

Transparency is another important benefit derived from owning a separate account rather than a slot in an individual fund. Owners of a managed account typically receive monthly statements showing the account's holdings and trades. This knowledge often provides investors with greater insight and comfort related to the hedge fund manager's strategy. Of course, many hedge fund managers will refuse to run a separately managed account for fear of divulging their investment strategy and holdings, since it can often be "reverse engineered" by an analysis of the monthly financial statements. In addition, there is an extra administrative burden on the manager to run separate accounts. Accordingly, there is often a selection bias, with managed accounts run by managers without the best performance.

Many high quality managers will run separate accounts if their strategy is long-term or if they have a strong trust factor, supplemented by a non-disclosure agreement (NDA) with the client. Long-term strategies can often be uncovered by reviewing a fund's 13F holdings, so there is not much incremental risk to the manager to "show their hand" in a separately managed account format. The importance of a trust or strong relationship between the manager and investor allays the manager's fears that their strategy will be misappropriated in any way.

For example, the family office of a billionaire is unlikely to start his or her own hedge fund by copying the strategy utilized in a managed account.

As noted previously, managed accounts also allow for greater customization, by placing restrictions on the portfolio, such as avoiding "hot issues" and limiting leverage and concentration. In addition, tax loss selling trades can be mandated if necessary. In many cases, liquidity provisions are often better with the managed account, relative to the 1+ year lockup period required by most hedge funds. In sum, separately managed accounts are generally in the best interests of investors, but often not desirable to hedge fund managers, so their use varies widely.

6. Historical Performance of Fund of Funds

To assess the historical performance of fund of funds, we have chosen to utilize the Hedge Fund Research (HFR) Fund of Funds Composite Index, an equal-weighted index of the monthly performance of currently over 800 fund of funds. Although it is not an investable index, the historical returns of new funds added to the index are not utilized, reducing backfill bias; and survivorship bias has been reduced by maintaining the historical performance of funds that have closed or stopped reporting to the HFR database. The monthly returns of the fund of funds that are included in the index are driven by the performance of their individual hedge funds and are not subject to database reporting biases.

In **Table 2** on the following page, we compare the performance of the HFRI FoF Composite to the total return of the S&P 500. We show summary statistics over two consecutive, nearly decade long periods, one with high equity returns and one with low equity returns, and the combined period. The returns of the two indices over the combined period are equal, although the volatilities of the paths traveled were widely different. The volatility of the FoF Composite was 60% less as measured by standard deviation (5.5% versus 13.9%) and 70% less as measured by maximum drawdown (13.1% versus 44.7%).

Table 2: Hedge Fund Performance

Performance Measure	Strong Equity Markets Jan 1990 – Feb 1999		"The Lost Decade"[4] Mar 1999 – Jun 2008		Combined Jan 1990 – Jun 2008	
	HFRI Fund of Funds Composite	S&P 500 Total Return	HFRI Fund of Funds Composite	S&P 500 Total Return	HFRI Fund of Funds Composite	S&P 500 Total Return
Annualized Return	11.0%	17.7%	8.0%	2.0%	9.5%	9.5%
Ann. Std. Deviation	5.7%	13.5%	5.3%	14.0%	5.5%	13.9%
Max Drawdown	(13.1%)	(15.4%)	(5.3%)	(44.7%)	(13.1%)	(44.7%)
Sharpe Index (5%)	1.01	0.92	0.56	(0.14)	0.79	0.37
% Positive Monthly Returns	77%	70%	69%	58%	73%	64%
Correlation	0.40		0.50		0.45	
Number of Months	110		112		222	

To highlight the differences in the distributions of the returns, histograms of the monthly returns of the two indices are shown in **Figure 2**, on the next page, for the same periods. In each histogram, the light and dark colored bars represent positive and negative monthly returns, respectively. The mean return is indicated by the vertical line. The shape of a smoothed distribution is estimated using a kernel density function and is indicated by the thin, curved line. The FoF index has had fewer and much less severe losses. This ability to reduce the downside and preserve capital has attracted high net worth investors to fund of funds.

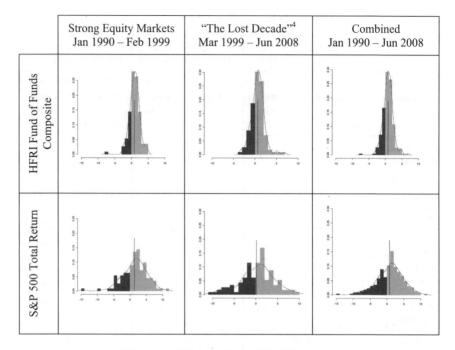

Figure 2: Distribution of FoF Returns

The correlation between the two indices is 0.40 in the first period and 0.50 in the second period and is 0.60 over the last three years ending in June 2008, indicating a potential increase in correlation over time.

7. Investment Process

7.1 Strategy Allocation

As discussed above, the diversification provided by a fund of funds is one of its primary benefits to investors. One of the most important drivers of this diversification is how a fund of funds portfolio is allocated among the various hedge fund strategies available. **Figure 3** outlines assets under management by investment strategy.

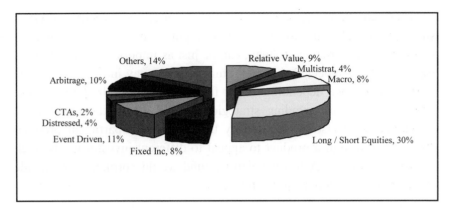

Figure 3: Proportion of Hedge Fund Assets By Strategy

Source: Eurekahedge

While the chart above is illustrative of the general investment strategies used by fund of funds managers, there are many sub-strategies within these broad categories that need to be evaluated when constructing portfolios. For instance, in the largest category, Long / Short Equities, there may exist sub-strategies focusing on directional equity exposure, emerging markets, market neutral, statistical arbitrage, and sector specific or short biased strategies. Ongoing developments in the capital markets also present managers with an ever-changing menu of strategies to choose from. Strategies will typically go in and out of favor with investors as the opportunity set for that strategy changes over time.

Fund of funds managers also have the ability to work with underlying hedge fund managers to "create" exposures that may be unavailable elsewhere, or not available on a consistent basis. Dedicated short equity portfolios are a good example of one of these types of strategies. In the process of evaluating and monitoring an underlying hedge fund manager, a fund of funds manager may uncover that the hedge fund manager has a robust short selling strategy that is a component of their long / short portfolio. The fund of funds manager may ask the hedge fund manager to carve out this short portfolio to provide a defensive strategy for the fund of funds to allocate to.

There are numerous processes used by managers to decide on which strategies to allocate to. Qualitative inputs, such as experience in investing in a particular strategy, can be just as important as quantitative inputs, such as expected risk and return. A firm may include or exclude various strategies depending on a firm's overall guiding investment principles, such as avoiding strategies that rely on leverage. Strategy allocations may also be dictated by the design of a particular product. Firms often design a product to appeal to different investor needs, such as lower volatility. A lower volatility fund would normally not include exposure to directional equity strategies.

7.2 Fund Sourcing

Manager sourcing is another area of significant focus by fund of funds managers. Before any allocation decisions can be made among strategies, hedge fund managers must be sourced and evaluated. Finding unique and talented managers is extremely challenging, but can often be a differentiating factor among firms. There are three primary methods for sourcing hedge fund managers: databases, capital introduction meetings, and referrals.

There are a number of organizations that offer databases of hedge funds that a fund of funds manager could use to identify potential investments. Firms such as Lipper Tass, Eurekahedge, and Hedge Fund Research all offer products, which allow for the scanning of their database for hedge fund managers that meet various criteria. A great deal of academic and practitioner research has been written on the potential limitations of hedge fund databases when examining historical returns. Like many quantitative investment tools, hedge fund databases should be used in conjunction with the other quantitative and qualitative tools at the managers' disposal.

Many firms also maintain their own database of hedge fund managers that they have been introduced to. As the number of hedge fund managers that ultimately receive an investment allocation is a small percentage of the managers that a firm may review or follow, these private databases can be quite robust. In addition, the data collection is controlled by the firm and would include elements that the fund of funds manager deems important, which may not be reflected in public databases.

Capital introduction meetings are another way for fund of funds managers to meet hedge fund managers. These meetings are typically organized by a prime broker or third party marketing firm for the purpose of introducing hedge fund managers to potential investors. Along with hedge fund of funds managers, other institutional investors such as family offices, pension and endowment funds and investment consultants, often attend these types of meetings. The goal of the organizer of the meeting is to get as many investors to hear the manager's presentation as possible, which is counter to the goal of the fund of funds manager, i.e., trying to uncover unique managers. For this reason, capital introduction meetings are the least important sources of new manager introductions for fund of funds managers.

The most important source of new hedge fund managers is by referrals from existing managers that the firm has investments with, or from the firm's professional network. Hedge fund firms are often closely associated with the founder or founders of the firm. Often the firm's investment edge is driven primarily by the skill set of these founders. It is critically important when evaluating these types of investment organizations, that you are able to gain insight into these key personnel through your network. It is also important to have a well-developed referral network, because at times certain new hedge fund organizations may open for investment for very short periods of time. The ability to evaluate, and more importantly, to get access to these types of managers, will depend upon your referral network.

7.3 Fund of Funds Portfolio Construction and Rebalancing

Fund of funds often construct their portfolios with a combination of a "top-down" and "bottom-up" approach. The top-down approach develops forward-looking estimates of the relative or absolute performance of strategies based on views of the expected economic and market environment. Specific targets for strategy allocations or looser overweight / underweight guidelines are then developed. The bottom-up process is continuously seeking to identify the "best of breed" managers within each strategy group to fill each strategy bucket.

Fund of funds must carefully manage their overall liquidity to ensure their portfolio provides for the liquidity they offer to their investors. This has become increasingly challenging due to the longer lock-ups instituted by individual funds. While longer lock-ups are justified by the nature of the holdings of many funds, some funds instituted lock-ups longer than 2 years to avoid the SEC registration rule that *was* in effect and other funds have increased lock-ups simply because they have strong investor demand. In addition to lock-ups, many funds impose various gate structures that give the fund the right to limit the percentage of assets that can be redeemed in a specific period, commonly 25% per quarter for a fund with quarterly redemptions. Furthermore, funds often have the right to suspend redemptions all together to protect the fund and its investors and to ensure that all investors are treated equally. Fund of funds maintains a liquidity calendar that shows overall portfolio liquidity and the next liquidity opportunity for each fund. This is driven off a schedule, that shows for each tranche of investment in a fund, its liquidity terms including lock-up, redemption notification period and frequency, and early redemption fees.

In constructing a portfolio of a fund of funds, the key objectives are to diversify risk and deliver a high risk adjusted return to the fund's investors. Techniques utilized in the long-only world, but often with some modifications, can be applied to this task, and include correlation and beta analysis to help ensure diversification. Because of the non-normality of many hedge fund distributions, downside correlation and tail beta can be used to focus on the downside. Most hedge funds have an exposure or beta to one or more factors or market indices, and the fund's alpha, or residual return can be determined once the beta effects are removed. Some funds invest thematically, and if those themes overlap across funds, an undesirably large exposure may result. In addition, there is a sharing of ideas in the hedge fund community and "piggy-backing" on investment ideas. One of the primary goals in portfolio construction is to eliminate the excessive exposures and to create a portfolio with low correlations across funds.

Each fund must not only be evaluated on a stand-alone basis but also in a portfolio context. Specifically, each fund's expected level of return must be evaluated relative to its marginal contribution to the overall portfolio risk. Risk budgeting techniques can be utilized to ensure that the portfolio is well constructed to deliver a high return for a given level of risk. Risk may be measured by many different metrics such as standard deviation; downside deviation; value-at-risk (VaR), the maximum expected loss over a period of time with a specified probability; or conditional value-at-risk (CVaR), the expected loss given the loss exceeds the VaR. CVaR takes into account the entire tail structure beyond the VaR which is unaffected by the size of the potential losses beyond its value. Optimization procedures such as the maximization of return for the level of the conditional value at risk can be used, as discussed in Rockafellar and Uryasev (2000), and FinAnalytica's Cognity and AlternativeSoft are commercial software programs quite strong in this area. Given the other constraints in constructing the portfolio and the tendency of optimizers to maximize data and model error, optimization might best be used as a check to portfolios constructed with a more manual risk budgeting procedure.

7.4 Risk Management of Fund of Funds

A quantitative analysis of a historical track record of a fund is challenging due to the short history of many funds and the low monthly frequency of the reporting of returns. Many funds will provide weekly or daily returns upon request, and analysis of higher frequency data may uncover issues that are hidden in the monthly returns. For example, the fund's volatility calculated using daily data might be significantly higher than that of monthly. Backfilling returns using statistical models based on economic factors, hedge fund indices or similar funds is one alternative to dealing with short return histories.

Individual funds provide a wide range of transparency or look through to their holdings to potential and existing investors. Only a small minority of funds provides total transparency to their holdings on a frequent basis. Often times, only the largest positions are identified.

Some funds are willing to reveal their entire book only during on-site visits, increasing the importance of regular meetings with the manager in their offices.

Just as in the long-only world, the primary characteristics of fund portfolios that add considerable risk are concentration, leverage, illiquidity, and poor quality. The vast majority of funds that have gotten into significant trouble have had very concentrated and leveraged portfolios and have suffered from reduced liquidity as they attempt to deleverage their portfolios. From an operational point of view, the biggest risk is fraud.

An array of performance measures has been developed to assess and rank the relative performance of hedge funds. Since many funds are not normally distributed, some of the standard measures utilized in the long-only world, such as standard deviation and Sharpe Index, are less useful. A number of measures have been developed that focus on the downside risk or tail risk and do not penalize a fund for upside volatility. In general, it is useful to use a mosaic of measures as no one single measure provides all the information necessary. A very useful starting point is to plot the histogram of the distribution of returns and assess the degree of normality by creating a quantile-quantile plot and calculating both the skewness and kurtosis. Funds with a negative skew (leftward tilt or long negative tail) and positive excess kurtosis (fat tails) are least attractive, but again the histogram should effectively convey these features. Funds that require excessive leverage to generate attractive returns should be approached with caution or avoided altogether. Certain strategies and funds may generate attractive returns most of the time, but have a small probability of generating very large losses. These funds may appear quite attractive based on their historical performance if the large losses have yet to occur, but can be very unattractive when their true downsize risk is taken into account.

The compensation structure of hedge funds with an asymmetric pay-off and a high water mark can encourage funds to increase risk or "swing for the fences" if they are in a significant drawdown. Continuous monitoring of each fund's leverage and exposures is critical. This tendency is reduced if the portfolio managers have a significant percentage of their net worth invested in the fund and is one of the advantages of selecting funds where the portfolio managers are "eating their own cooking." Chapter 12 discusses hedge fund risk management in more detail.

8. Recent Developments

8.1 Registered Fund of Funds

The minimum investment required to invest in most fund of funds is beyond the reach of the vast majority of investors. For example, if a fund of funds has a minimum investment of $1 million, an investor would need a net worth of at least $5 million in order to not put more than 20% of their wealth in a single investment. Several large investment managers, such as Lazard, now offer registered fund of funds investments to investors. The minimum investment in registered vehicles is typically much lower (i.e., $50,000) and by being registered they avoid the limited number of slots required of 3c1 and 3c7 funds. The fees of these funds are generally 0.5% per year or more higher than unregistered funds, and they represent an additional revenue stream for asset managers.

8.2 Impact of Longer Individual Manager Lockups on Fund of Funds

A recent trend for individual funds has been to increase their lockup periods from one year to two years or more. The increase in lockups was due in part to the desire of many hedge funds to avoid mandatory registration by the SEC. The mandatory registration process went into effect in February of 2006, but was repealed less than six months later, after a series of appeals by hedge funds and court rulings that struck down the rules as "arbitrary."

In Chapter 15 we suggest that over the long-term, lockups will *decrease*. However, at present they have been increasing and have implications for managing fund of funds. Some fund of funds are increasing their lockup to two years or more. Others simply avoid individual funds with long-term lockups, eliminating a material percentage of top performers from the universe of investment managers. The majority of fund of funds still accepts and seeks out top performers, despite their longer lockups, and accordingly has had to develop the skills necessary to manage a portfolio with illiquid assets.

If the underlying fund of funds has a portion of its assets locked up, dynamic asset allocation can often be accomplished through an overlay manager. Overlay managers typically trade in derivative products, using the underlying assets of the fund of funds as collateral. For example, if a fund of funds is locked into a Short Biased manager and wants to alter its asset allocation to a neutral position, the overlay manager could go long in equity index futures, reducing the impact of the Short Biased fund in the event of a rise in the market.

8.3 Theme Oriented Fund of Funds

In Chapter 1 we briefly discussed sector-oriented hedge funds. These hedge funds focus almost exclusively on a specific sector, such as Financials, and their managers often articulate that their singular focus gives them a greater chance of earning alpha. Some investors also like targeting specific themes such as "Clean Energy." Given the proliferation in fund of funds, many have tried to distinguish themselves in some capacity. Just as individual hedge funds have specific categories, some funds of funds have chosen to differentiate themselves by following a certain theme. For example, some fund of funds are focused exclusively on the funds that invest primarily in Brazil, Russia, India, and China (BRIC). Other fund of funds focus exclusively on hedge funds managed by women. There is no limit to the themes that may be created as long as sufficient demand exists.

8.4 Leveraged Fund of Funds

Most fund of funds invest in single hedge funds that employ some degree of leverage. The amount of leverage of each underlying manager varies widely, with those following Arbitrage and Global Macro strategies generally employing the most leverage, while Long / Short and Emerging Market managers are typically on the lower end of the leverage spectrum. Fund of funds investors should carefully analyze the risk, or ask questions pertaining to the true leverage their fund of funds vehicle.

Given the inherent tax inefficient nature of most hedge funds, various techniques have been used to increase after tax returns. Perhaps the two most common techniques are the use of leverage (through borrowing) and the use of derivative products that aim to convert short-term gains and losses to long-term. Many prime brokers are willing to provide financing at reasonably attractive rates, due to the relatively low volatility of fund of funds returns.

Leverage is not tax efficient per se, but if the returns of the fund of funds are higher than its cost of capital, it will result in a higher net return to the investor. **Table 3** shows returns for a fund with various combinations of borrowing costs and unleveraged returns for the

Table 3: Net Returns for Fund of Funds with 2x and 3x Leverage

Fund of Fund Net Returns With 2x Leverage						Fund of Fund Net Returns With 3x Leverage					
FoF Return	Cost of Borrowing in %					FoF Return	Cost of Borrowing in %				
	4.0%	5.0%	6.0%	7.0%	8.0%		4.0%	5.0%	6.0%	7.0%	8.0%
-8.0%	-20.0%	-21.0%	-22.0%	-23.0%	-24.0%	-8.0%	-32.0%	-34.0%	-36.0%	-38.0%	-40.0%
-5.0%	-14.0%	-15.0%	-16.0%	-17.0%	-18.0%	-5.0%	-23.0%	-25.0%	-27.0%	-29.0%	-31.0%
-2.0%	-8.0%	-9.0%	-10.0%	-11.0%	-12.0%	-2.0%	-14.0%	-16.0%	-18.0%	-20.0%	-22.0%
1.0%	-2.0%	-3.0%	-4.0%	-5.0%	-6.0%	1.0%	-5.0%	-7.0%	-9.0%	-11.0%	-13.0%
4.0%	4.0%	3.0%	2.0%	1.0%	0.0%	4.0%	4.0%	2.0%	0.0%	-2.0%	-4.0%
7.0%	10.0%	9.0%	8.0%	7.0%	6.0%	7.0%	13.0%	11.0%	9.0%	7.0%	5.0%
10.0%	16.0%	15.0%	14.0%	13.0%	12.0%	10.0%	22.0%	20.0%	18.0%	16.0%	14.0%
13.0%	22.0%	21.0%	20.0%	19.0%	18.0%	13.0%	31.0%	29.0%	27.0%	25.0%	23.0%
16.0%	28.0%	27.0%	26.0%	25.0%	24.0%	16.0%	40.0%	38.0%	36.0%	34.0%	32.0%

Note: The left hand column refers to the gross return of the unleveraged FoF. The figures on the uppermost row refer to the borrowing cost of using leverage. The leveraged FoF returns in the middle of the table, correspond to the appropriate pair wise combination of the FoF unlevered return and its borrowing cost. The table on the left is for the case of 2x leverage, while the table on the right pertains to the case of 3x leverage.

underlying fund of funds. Nearly any magnitude of leverage is possible, but the table examines the most common approaches, 2x and 3x the amount of the fund of funds capital. Leverage cuts both ways making the good times better and bad times worse. For example, a fund of funds utilizing 2x leverage, with a 10% unlevered return and cost of capital of 6%, provides a pre-tax return to the investor of 14%. Conversely, if the fund of funds generates a 5% loss on an unlevered basis, with the same 6% cost of capital, its pre-tax return is a loss of 16%.

8.5 Derivatives on Fund of Funds

One way of making fund of funds more tax efficient is to convert its short-term gains and losses to long-term. Reducing federal taxes from 35% to 15% is a substantial boon to the taxable hedge fund investor. The most common way of achieving such a transformation is to hold a call option on a hedge fund or fund of funds. These options are nearly always over the counter transactions written by the trading desks of investment banks, often in concert with their prime brokerage units. Accordingly, they entail credit risk in the event of a default by the issuer. These options fall under the general term of structured products. According to the Structured Products Association (SPA) nearly $100 billion of structured products were issued in 2007.[5]

The call option is held generally for at least one year and as long as 5 to 7 years if a principal protection feature is desired. Principal protection, if desired, does not mean the absence of risk. If the option expires out of the money, the investor may get their principal back, but they have also missed out on the opportunity cost of 5+ years of gains that may have been achieved by investing in another security or portfolio.

Other structured products enable the investor to earn a multiple of the underlying fund of funds return, without traditional borrowing techniques. For example, it may be possible to create a structured product on a fund of funds that has the first 10% of losses protected, but caps out at a maximum return of 15% on the upside. The price of an option is the function of many factors, but the current level of interest rates and volatility of the underlying investment play critical roles. There are virtually an infinite number of permutations of structured products on fund of funds, so the end user should have a clear understanding of their desired risk return tradeoff before entering into a transaction.

Hedge Fund Alpha Tear Sheet — Chapter 10

- Under some interpretations, the first fund of funds was started by A. W. Jones in 1954 after he restructured his original investment partnership, allowing for external management of capital.
- George Coulon Karlweis of Leveraged Capital Holdings in Switzerland, managed the first formal fund of funds in 1969.
- Grosvenor Capital Management managed the first fund of funds in the United States, starting in 1971.
- Fund of funds have the following advantages:
  - A diversified portfolio of hedge funds for a capital commitment of $1 million or less.
  - Greater access to closed hedge fund managers.
  - Fewer and much less severe losses relative to individual funds.
  - Reduced operational, management, and other risks, relative to a multistrategy fund.
- Fund of funds have the following disadvantages:
  - The main disadvantage of the fund of funds is the additional layer of fees.
  - Investors almost always have to file for a tax extension.
  - Fund of funds, due to their diversified nature, are unlikely to deliver the "blowout" returns that are possible with investments in single funds.
- There are three primary methods for sourcing hedge fund managers: databases, capital introduction meetings, and referrals.
- Fund of funds often construct their portfolios with a combination of a "top-down" and "bottom-up" approaches.
- Primary risk characteristics of fund of funds portfolios include concentration, leverage, illiquidity, and poor quality.
- The following trends have impacted the fund of funds market in recent years:
  - Growth in registered fund of funds.
  - Longer individual fund manager lockups.
  - Increase in theme oriented fund of funds.
  - Growth in leveraged fund of funds.
  - Development of derivatives or structured products on fund of funds.

End Notes

[1] Iniechen (2004) states Leveraged Capital Holdings was the first fund of fund.

[2] Lookout Mountain Capital (1995) discusses the evolution of A.W. Jones' original hedge fund.

[3] *Pari passu* is a Latin phrase meaning "in equal step."

[4] Browning (2008) labels the March 1999–June 2008 period "the lost decade" since annual returns were nominally positive during this time frame.

[5] Growth in structured products issuance and other details may be found on the Structured Products Association (SPA) website at http://www.structuredproducts.org/

References

Browning, E.S., "Stocks Tarnished by 'Lost Decade'", *Wall Street Journal*, March 26, 2008.

Ineichen, Alexander M., UBS Investment Research, AIS Report, European Rainmakers, April 2004.

Lookout Mountain Capital, "A Primer on Hedge Funds", 1995.

Report of the President's Working Group on Financial Markets, April 1999.

Rockafellar, R. Tyrrell and Stanislav Uryasev, S, "Optimization of Conditional Value-at-Risk", *Journal of Risk*, Vol. 2, No. 3, Spring, 2000, pp. 21–41.

PART II

UNDERSTANDING PERFORMANCE

11

THE PSYCHOLOGY OF HEDGE FUND MANAGERS

John M. Longo, PhD, CFA

Rutgers Business School & The MDE Group, Inc.

1. Introduction

The role of psychology in the financial markets has been discussed almost since the beginning of time. John Maynard Keynes (1936) referred to the "animal spirits" embedded in humans that drive stock market prices. Benjamin Graham (1949) used the effective "Mr. Market" analogy, comparing the oscillating behavior of the financial markets to that of a schizophrenic business partner. David Dreman (1977), a highly regarded Value manager, who also runs a hedge fund, has discussed the relationship between Finance and Psychology for decades.

In recent years, Behavioral Finance has emerged as a legitimate school of thought within Financial Economics, as evidenced by Daniel Kahneman and Vernon Smith's co-sharing of the Nobel Memorial Prize in Economics in 2002. Despite the mushrooming literature on the link between markets and psychology, I have seen little mention of relevant psychological principles applied specifically to the hedge fund industry. Any understanding of the actions and behaviors of hedge fund managers can help us glean insight into how alpha is generated or lost.

Hedge funds are a diverse group and are unlikely to move in a monolithic manner. Spectacular hedge fund blow-ups, such as those experienced by Long Term Capital Management, Amaranth, and Bear Stearns Asset Management, garner much of the industry headlines and represent fascinating, if not morbid, case studies. On the positive side, articles describing the investment practices of highly successful hedge fund managers, such as Steve Cohen, often refer to their intense focus on cutting losses quickly.[1]

2. The Relationship Between Hedge Fund Manager Investment Performance and Emotions

The desire for money, the thrill of competition, and the intellectual challenge of outperforming the market are among the driving forces behind hedge fund manager behavior. Some of these factors, such as intellectual challenge, are difficult to quantify, so economists who seek to model behavior often have to make simplifying assumptions.

A reasonable place to start an inquiry into the dynamics of hedge fund manager behavior would be with the assumption that hedge fund managers seek to maximize their happiness, or utility, in economic terms. Utility is not only a function of returns, which directly translates into near term money, but also performance relative to industry benchmarks. The latter point may relate to the long-term ability to earn money and increase the sustainability of the fund management company. **Table 1** posits the relationship between hedge fund manager investment performance and their utility or state of happiness for a given return. The

Table 1: Hedge Fund Manager Investment Performance and Emotions

Performance Scenario	Emotional State
Fund Up X%, Benchmark Down	Happiest
Fund Up X%, Benchmark Up, Fund Up More Than Benchmark	Very Happy
Fund Up X%, Benchmark Up, Fund Up Less Than Benchmark	Happy
Fund Down X%, Benchmark Down, Fund Down Less Than Benchmark	Somewhat Sad
Fund Down X%, Benchmark Down, Fund Down More Than Benchmark	Sad
Fund Down X%, Benchmark Up	Saddest

Note: The absolute value of x% is the *same* in each scenario to allow for greater comparability.

implications of the table may help explain some elements of hedge fund investment behavior.

Table 1 implies that *alpha is not the sole determinant of fund manager happiness.* For example, under the classification scheme presented above, a manager would be happier with a negative alpha and positive return, than with a positive alpha and negative return. Quite simply, the manager earns an incentive fee under the first scenario, while he does not in the second scenario. Of course, in the long run, positive alpha might result in increased assets for the fund. However, the perception still exists that most hedge funds should not lose money, not to mention the high watermark that typically must be surpassed in order to continue earning incentive fees.

The table provides some interesting implications. Risk averse fund managers will generally avoid large bets that could result in the last scenario, often dubbed as being "wrong and alone." Aggressive managers, on the other hand, will often attempt to stand out from their peers by taking outsized bets or by making investments far outside their conventional investment universe. A fund's levels of leverage, concentration, and liquidity are often telltale signs of the risk tolerance of its fund manager. A one sentence summary of **Table 1** might be, the first priority of hedge fund managers is to put up positive returns, closely followed by a desire to outperform their peers or investment benchmark.

3. The Importance of Positive Monthly Returns

During the course of my due diligence trips to meet with hedge fund managers as part of my job responsibilities with The MDE Group, I was surprised to learn of a somewhat common practice among hedge funds: several funds convert their portfolios to Cash or significantly hedge their strategies if they have earned an intramonth positive return. The goal of this behavior, of course, is to show a positive return for the month. Why is this important to hedge fund managers?

The vast majority of hedge funds place the monthly returns of their funds in databases that are used for screening by investors and consultants. Many hedge fund managers are discovered by these screens, or placed on a short list as a result of these screens. The databases typically include a table of a fund's monthly returns since inception. These monthly returns are used as the basis for many popular performance statistics, such as Sharpe Ratio, Sortino Ratio, and Percentage of Positive Monthly Returns. The latter two statistics are directly improved by having a lower amount of months with negative returns. One takeaway from this discussion is that one should be skeptical of the results of illiquid funds, since there is a strong incentive to smooth the returns.

In fact, a study by Getmanksky, Lo, and Makarov (2004) find that hedge fund returns are perhaps too good to be true and are partially the result of data smoothing of illiquid securities. They go on to show that the smoother the return pattern, the greater the ex-ante risk for a correction in the market or fund strategy. They state, "For portfolios of illiquid securities, reported returns will tend to be smoother than true economic returns, which will understate volatility and increase risk-adjusted performance measures such as the Sharpe ratio."

A specific example of illiquid securities may clarify the smoothing issue. In my view, the returns of illiquid private equity funds are not directly comparable to the returns of hedge funds investing in liquid assets. For example, the returns of private equity funds often exhibit a smooth J Curve, where early years result in negative returns as capital is put to work, while later years often show sharply rising internal rates of return (IRR). For example, the returns of publicly traded stocks are quite volatile. Yet the returns from most LBO funds exhibit far less volatility, due to their infrequent marking to market valuation procedures. As such, the underlying fundamentals of most LBO firms are similar to those trading in the public equity markets, since they are part of the same economy. Indeed, the underlying fundamentals of most LBO firms may be more volatile due to the extensive leverage employed in most LBO funds. A well known relationship in finance is that beta, or market sensitivity, increases, as a firm adds leverage since stockholders have to wait at the end of a longer line before receiving any payments. A common expression to describe this relationship would be, "Debt makes the good times better and bad times worse."

The results of this section suggest the need for greater emphasis on intramonth or daily performance measures and that one needs to be extra skeptical or conservative when dealing with funds that have illiquid securities.

4. The Call Option Nature of Hedge Fund Compensation

The call option nature of hedge fund compensation has been well documented, but it bears repeating. It results in a "Heads I win, tails you lose" game whereby a hedge fund manager earns incentive fees in the event of a positive return (assuming no highwater mark needs to be surpassed), but never has to return money if the fund experiences a loss. Most funds have a highwater mark, but if the losses are more than double digits, many funds shut down and amazingly, often start another fund. The most notorious example is Long Term Capital Management, which is expertly chronicled in Roger Lowenstein's book *When Genius Failed: The Rise and Fall of Long-term Capital Management*. The firm was run by a "dream team" of Wall Street professionals and academics and lost nearly all of their capital in the aftermath of the Russian Ruble Crisis. The fund had to be bailed out by a consortium of Wall Street firms in order to stave off potential disaster for the global financial markets due to the possibility of the rapid unwinding of a multi-billion dollar highly leveraged portfolio. Several of the principals of Long Term Capital resurfaced with a new bond arbitrage hedge fund. A recent *Bloomberg* article (2008) finds that the new fund has run into serious, although not quite as disastrous, trouble, falling 24% over the first quarter of 2008.

The call option problem can be mitigated to a significant extent by having managers invest a significant part of their liquid net worth in the funds that they manage. However, this principal (limited partners)- agent (fund manager) problem cannot be fully eliminated, as demonstrated in the Long Term Capital case. Risk monitoring procedures should be put in place to ensure that fund managers are not increasing risk as they generate negative returns or fall far behind industry benchmarks.

5. Behavioral Finance and Hedge Fund Managers

The behavioral finance or investor psychology literature has grown quite rapidly in recent years. Dozens of investor biases have been documented. A useful list of many of these biases, with links in some cases directly to source articles, may be found at www.behaviouralfinance.net. Using this website as a resource, several behavioral biases have been listed which, in my view, are most relevant to the hedge fund industry. There is often some overlap among the biases, so the list is not meant to be mutually exclusive or exhaustive. Hedge fund analysts and managers should ask themselves if they are susceptible to these biases. Individuals or institutions investing in hedge funds should assess if their managers suffer from these biases and if they are likely to have an impact on the fund's performance.

The tendency of individuals to base decisions on information that is readily available, as opposed to conducting more rigorous research that may ultimately result in a different investment decision, is referred to as "*Availability Heuristic.*" A common example could be the practice of some managers to rely on third party research instead of conducting primary research. Kahneman and Tversky (1974) state, "Availability is a useful clue for assessing frequency or probability, because instances of large classes are usually reached better and faster than instances of less frequent classes. However, availability is affected by factors other than frequency and probability. Consequently, the reliance on availability leads to predictable biases…"

Confirmation Bias refers to the occasions whereby one notices or looks for information that confirms their preexisting beliefs, while ignoring evidence that contradicts them. It is likely to occur more often at hedge fund firms dominated by a single individual rather than organizations where the power is shared among several people.

Conservatism Bias results in a situation where investors are too slow in updating their beliefs in response to recent information. Phillips and Edwards (1966) note, "To make matters worse, once people have formed a probability estimate, they are often quite slow to change the estimate when presented with new information. This slowness to revise prior probability estimates is known as 'conservatism'. "

For example, because of its stellar long-term history, investors might have initially underreacted to information that Bear Stearns was in the midst of a liquidity crisis, thereby resulting in a catastrophic loss until it was purchased by J. P. Morgan. Less dramatic examples, such as the slow but steady multi-decade decline in former corporate icons, such as General Motors, Ford, and Eastman Kodak may also indicate a conservatism bias on the part of many investors.

Disposition Effect is described as the tendency of individuals to hold losing investments too long and to sell their winning investments too soon. The term was coined by Shefrin and Statman (1985) and is more colorfully known as "get-evenitis." Amateur investors or relatively new hedge fund managers are more likely to suffer from this bias, since nearly all seasoned professionals have probably heard many times the advice of "sell your losers and let your winners run."

Endowment Effect refers to the behavior where people value an asset more highly once they own it, in relation to the value of a similar object held by a third party. For example, owners often get attached to their cars or homes and are often unwilling to sell these assets at market values. Some fund managers have the tendency to "fall in love" with their investments and often continue to hold even in the presence of deteriorating fundamentals. Thaler (1980) is credited with naming this effect.

Hubris Hypothesis was developed by Roll (1986) in the context of corporate takeovers and it helps explain why bidding firms often overpay for target firms. According to Roll, hubris or excessive pride and arrogance are often major culprits in the failure of many mergers. It is not a stretch to extend the Hubris Hypothesis to the hedge fund industry, whereby certain managers fail to adequately plan for the possibility that their strategy may stop adding alpha or will be unable to add alpha as their fund grows larger. It may also result in managers extending the risk parameters of their fund beyond prudent levels.

Law of Small Numbers refers to the common behavior where people make inferences from small sample sizes even though they may have no statistical validity. For example, if a fund manager outperforms his benchmark two years in a row, it often results in strong inflows to the fund. However, it could take several years, maybe decades, to accurately assess the skill of a long-term fund manager. Kahneman and Tversky (1971) were among the first to recognize this bias.

Illusion of Control is, according to Langer and Roth (1975), "the tendency for human beings to believe they can control or at least influence outcomes which they clearly cannot." Arguably, this bias affects larger and more successful investors to a greater extent than emerging managers. For example, British Billionaire Joseph Lewis may have experienced an illusion of control in his initial and subsequent investments in Bear Stearns as it spiraled towards bankruptcy and its "shotgun wedding" with J. P. Morgan. Despite impending litigation, it appears that the world-renowned trader has lost more than a billion dollars on his Bear position.

Illusion of Knowledge, as stated by Barber and Odean (2001), is the tendency of investors to make a stronger inference than is warranted by the data. In a world of Regulation Fair Disclosure (FD), ubiquitous Internet and Bloomberg machines, managers should carefully ask themselves if the information they are acting upon has any unique value.

Overconfidence refers to a stronger belief that an investment thesis is correct than would be warranted by an objective assessment of the facts. Plous (1993) stated, "No problem in judgment and decision making is more prevalent and more potentially catastrophic than overconfidence." Overconfidence often results in a manager taking concentrated, illiquid, and leveraged positions more than would be prudent. Foreshadowing the Long Term Capital Management saga years before it occurred, Plous also finds that the discrepancy between accuracy and confidence is not related to a decision maker's intelligence. In short, all hedge fund managers need to be wary of overconfidence in their investments.

The tendency of people to place more weight on recent events and less weight on events in the distant path is known as *Overreaction.* For example, during the late 1990s investors had an insatiable appetite for Internet stocks. However, by the time the 2000–2002 equity bear market in the United States got into full swing, most Internet firms — even strongly profitable ones — were left for near dead. A similar cycle appears to be unfolding with many financial firms, with former market leaders such as Goldman Sachs and Morgan Stanley now trading near multiyear lows.

Recognition Effect refers to the tendency of people to place greater value on a known item relative to an unknown one. For example, people tend to vote more often for candidates they have heard of prior to elections, as opposed to candidates that they have no information about. The recognition effect may also partially explain why well known growth firms such as Google and Apple are often bid up to levels higher than those suggested by conventional discounted cash flow models. Goldstein and Gigerenzer (1999) are credited with formalizing this behavioral bias.

Self-Attribution Bias occurs when people attribute successful investment outcomes due to their skillful analysis, while blaming negative outcomes on bad luck. For example, many hedge fund managers engaged in the carry trade often refer to shocks in the market as the result of a "hundred year flood" rather than owning up to the inherent riskiness in a long term strategy of borrowing short and investing long. Hundred year events seem to happen every five years or so in the hedge fund industry.

Sunk Cost Fallacy is related to the *disposition effect* and refers to the tendency of investors to continue holding a stock after money, time, and effort have been expended more than an objective assessment of the fundamentals would suggest is warranted. Arkes and Blumer (1985) suggest that the "psychological justification for this behavior is predicated on the desire not to appear wasteful..."

The *Value or Asymmetry of Gains and Losses Function* finds that losing a dollar hurts an average person two times as much as gaining a dollar helps.[2] Hedge fund managers should be cognizant of this relationship when establishing risk management procedures and dealing with clients.

In sum, there are many psychological biases that fund managers and their investors should take into account before putting capital at risk. At a minimum, awareness of the major documented biases in the behavioral finance literature may prevent fund manager and investors from "shooting themselves in the foot." At best it may be possible to design strategies based on investor psychology that earn alpha. David Dreman's success was briefly noted at the top of this chapter, but other hedge funds such as J. P. Morgan Highbridge and Baupost Group also use psychology as a key input to their investment processes. Seth Klarman, founder and managing partner of Baupost said, "... rather than buy from smart, informed sellers, we want to buy from urgent, distressed or emotional sellers. This concept applies to just about any asset class: debt, real estate, private equity, as well as public equities," Great advice from an investor with a stellar track record for those seeking attractive returns with a margin of safety.

Hedge Fund Alpha Tear Sheet — Chapter 11

- The role of psychology in the financial markets has been discussed almost since the beginning of time, but in recent years Behavioral Finance has emerged as a legitimate school of thought within Financial Economics.
- Despite the mushrooming literature on the link between markets and psychology, there has been relatively little discussion of relevant psychological principles applied specifically to the hedge fund industry.
- Hedge fund managers may be especially susceptible to the following behavioral biases:
  o Availability Heuristic
  o Confirmation Bias
  o Conservatism Bias
  o Disposition Effect
  o Endowment Effect
  o Hubris Hypothesis
  o Law of Small Numbers
  o Illusion of Control
  o Illusion of Knowledge
  o Overconfidence
  o Overreaction
  o Recognition Effect
  o Self-Attribution Bias
  o Sunk Cost Fallacy
  o Value or Asymmetry of Gains and Losses Function
- At a minimum, awareness of the major documented biases in the behavioral finance literature may prevent fund managers and investors from "shooting themselves in the foot."
- At best it may be possible to design strategies based on investor psychology that earn alpha.

End Notes

[1] See Vickers (2003) for an article on Cohen's strategy and his practice of cutting losers quickly.

[2] See Kahneman and Riepe (1998) for a discussion of the utility placed on gains and losses for the typical investor.

References

Arkes, Hal and Catherine Blumer, Catherine, "The Psychology of Sunk Cost," *Organizational Behavior and Human Decision Process*, Vol. 35, pp. 124–140, 1985.

Barber, Brad and Terrance Odean, "The Internet and the Investor," *Journal of Economic Perspectives*, Vol. 15, No. 1, pp. 41–54, Winter, 2001.

Burton, Katherine, and Sajel Kisan, "John Meriwether's Bond Fund Loses 24% on Credit Market Plunge," *Bloomberg*, March 19, 2008.

Getmansky, Mila, Andrew W. Lo and Igor Makarov, "An Econometric Model Of Serial Correlation And Illiquidity In Hedge Fund Returns," *Journal of Financial Economics*, Vol. 74, pp. 529–609, 2004.

Goldstein, Daniel and Gerd Gigerenzer, "The Recognition Heuristic: How Ignorance Makes Us Smart," Chapter 2 in Gigerenzer, Gerd, Peter Todd, and the ABC Research Group, *Simple Heuristics That Make Us Smart*, Oxford University Press, 1999.

Graham, Benjamin, *The Intelligent Investor*, HarperCollins, 1949.

Kahneman, Daniel and Mark Riepe, "Aspects of Investor Psychology," *The Journal of Portfolio Management*, pp. 52–64, Summer 1998.

Keynes, John M., *The General Theory of Employment, Interest and Money*, Macmillan Cambridge University Press, 1936.

Langer, Ellen and Jane Roth, "Heads I Win, Tails It's Chance: The Illusion of Control as a Function of the Sequence of Outcomes in a Purely Chance Task," *Journal of Personality and Social Psychology*, Vol. 32, No. 6, pp. 951–955, 1975.

Lowenstein, Roger, *When Genius Failed: The Rise and Fall of Long-Term Capital Management*, Fourth Estate, 2001.

Phillips, Lawrence and Ward Edwards, "Conservatism in a Simple Probability Inference Task," *Journal of Experimental Psychology*, Vol. 72, pp. 346–55, 1966.

Plous, Scott, *The Psychology of Judgment and Decision Making*, McGraw-Hill, 1993.

Roll, Richard, "The Hubris Hypothesis of Corporate Takeovers," *Journal of Business*, Vol. 59, pp. 197–216, 1986.

Seeking Alpha website, "Seth Klarman: Second Coming of Benjamin Graham?" June 5, 2008.
http://seekingalpha.com/article/80180-seth-klarman-second-coming-of-benjamin-graham

Shefrin, Hersh and Meir Statman, "The Disposition to Sell Winners Too Early and Ride Losers Too Long: Theory and Evidence", *Journal of Finance*, Vol. XL, No. 3, 1985.

Thaler, R., "Toward a Positive Theory of Consumer Choice," *Journal of Economic Behavior and Organization*, Vol. 1, pp. 39–60, 1980.

Tversky, Amos and Daniel Kahneman, "Belief in the Law of Small Numbers," *Psychological Bulletin*, Vol. 76, pp. 105–110, 1971.

Tversky, Amos and Daniel Kahneman, "Judgment Under Uncertainty: Heuristics and Biases," *Science*, Vol. 185, pp. 1124–1131, 1974.

Vickers, Marica, "The Most Powerful Trader on Wall Street You've Never Heard Of," *Business Week*, July 21, 2003.
www.behaviouralfinance.net

12

RISK MANAGEMENT FOR HEDGE FUNDS

Saad Rathore

Algorithmic Capital Markets

1. Overview

Financial markets, over the last few years, have become extremely competitive, innovative and complex. Short-term profit opportunities immediately disappear. In the long run, capital flows fluidly, at the pressing of a keystroke, towards entities that exhibit superior nominal and risk adjusted returns. On top of this competitive environment, advancements in financial and mathematical theories continue to occur at a rapid rate, resulting in a very complex market system in which managers are trying to generate alpha. Financial organizations, in many instances, have had to increase leverage in order to generate competitive returns.

Advancements in financial theory have resulted in several new investment products that may aid the portfolio manager in generating alpha. Hedge fund portfolios are becoming increasingly complex and require multifaceted monitoring. Investment management as a science continues to evolve and a trend towards absolute return strategies continues to gain momentum. In light of these advancements, portfolio creation and holding has generally become a complex and dynamic exercise. Risk management as a practice is designed to aid in effectively wading through this environment. At the heart of it, risk management is at first knowing the portfolio composition and then understanding the pitfalls in the portfolio. Lastly, a good risk manager supports the investment function by suggesting effective hedging options.

Any student of financial markets can immediately recall spectacular and unexpected losses, such as those realized in the cases of Long Term Capital Management, Bear Stearns, Lehman Brothers, AIG, Washington Mutual, and Wachovia. Once the dust settles, the usual suspects are rogue traders, bad reporting, inappropriate acquisitions, statistical outliers, and human greed. It would be virtually impossible to ensure that large portfolio losses never occur, but an effective risk management plan can go a long way towards limiting the possibility of catastrophic losses. Good traders, managers and organizations understand this concept and, as a result, the role of effective risk management has increased to near the top of organizational priorities.

2. Risk Management as a Source of Superior Returns

Superior risk management may increase investment performance in a number of ways. For example, risk managers may suggest periods where it is prudent to increase or decrease portfolio beta, resulting in increased returns or lesser losses if the assessment is correct. More specifically, it may make economic sense *in the short-run* to increase beta when credit spreads are slim, or to reduce beta when credit spreads spike. Effective risk management may determine when it is the most opportune time to use leverage via a carry trade. Proper risk management may provide a better way of sizing individual trades. Additionally, proper risk management may aid in most efficiently allocating capital across a number of strategies within a multistrategy fund or across several funds. In this chapter, we will discuss specific techniques, such as the Impact Ratio, Kelly Formula, and Sortino Ratio as a way of measuring portfolio risk and calibrating it for a specific portfolio.

3. Distinction Between Trading and Investing

We will segment our investment process into pre-trade, post-trade period and interim-trade periods. Moreover, we will further divide our study of risk management between shorter horizon (trading) and longer horizon (investing) points of view. Of course, there may be some overlap between these two classes, but the mindset and investment processes often differ markedly. We conclude the chapter with a discussion of operational risk, an important but not closely followed element of effective risk management practice.

    Risk management is as much art as science, since there is no uniformly agreed upon definition of risk. We define risk management as the process of understanding portfolio return drivers with the simultaneous goals of maximizing risk adjusted returns and minimizing the chance of financial ruin. In other words, we wish to achieve the commonly stated goal of maximizing return for a given level of risk, but also desire to limit to a great extent the chance of a catastrophic loss. The aftermath of the credit market bubble in 2007–2008 has demonstrated that the long-term definition of risk is not sufficient, as evidenced by the actual or near bankruptcies of Bear Stearns, Countrywide, Lehman Brothers, Washington Mutual, Wachovia, Bradford & Bing, and Hypo Real Estate.

4. Trading Risk Management

Trading strategies are geared towards generating returns within a shorter time horizon and often include technical or quantitative analysis driven approaches, an analysis of market sentiment, and trader instinct. Conversely, fundamental and macro-oriented trades, which comprise the bulk of traditional investment and hedge fund strategies, generally rely on accounting data, industry analysis, and economic oriented variables.

4.1 Risk Management and Conventional Wall Street Wisdom

Some of the essentials of managing risk have become almost axiomatic in the marketplace. It is worthwhile to list some of this conventional "Wall Street wisdom."

1) Cut your losses short and let your winners run.
2) Gain more on your winners and lose less on your losers.
3) Have more winners than losers.
4) Reduce exposures in positions that go against you and increase exposures in bets that are working to your advantage.
5) Never overexpose your capital on a single trade.
6) Gain statistical advantage by generating a higher number of trades within a trade cycle.
7) If you must trade different strategies, try to allocate capital such that overall correlation is reduced to an index or any other performance benchmark.
8) Never fight the tape.
9) If you have been wrong about the trade repeatedly, don't fight the market.
10) Use Stop Losses and, if possible, trailing stop losses.
11) Understand your financial environment.
12) Bet bigger if more trades are going in your favor, if it is otherwise, bet lesser amounts of capital.
13) Never second-guess the market.
14) Analyze execution costs and reduce trading friction.
15) Stay away from "hot" issues.
16) Liquidity is as important as price.
17) Understand your fundamental capital base; bet larger only on gains but not on the underlying capital base. If your capital base is cut, decrease the size of your bet.
18) Always have a plan for selling as well as buying.
19) Don't let pride get in your way.
20) Try to be greedy when others are fearful, be fearful when others are greedy. *(Attributed to Warren Buffett)*
21) When in doubt, stay out.

22) Never lose on a winner or let a small loss on a trade become a big loser.
23) Don't overpredict the market; follow the market.
24) Don't be afraid of taking profits.
25) Markets have no fundamental and fair values.
26) Mean reversion has empirical basis but determining how long it takes the trade to revert to mean is impossible.
27) Liquidity is not a static phenomenon.
28) Remember, the trend is your friend.

We will now look at the quantitative aspects of these "adages" as to how we can employ a framework to manage our risk with trading. We will also include some metrics that help traders evaluate the efficiency of their strategies and improve those consequently.

4.2 Risk Management and Profit and Loss (P&L) Analysis

Profit and Loss (P&L) is the money made or lost by the trader over a specific time interval, such as hourly, daily, weekly, monthly or yearly. For the sake of simplicity, we will use daily profit and loss in our example.

The profit and loss number is expressed in currency as well as percentage terms. For example, if a trader managing $1 million has made $25,000 on a given day he or she will have profit and loss of $25,000 or 2.5%. A time series of profit and loss can easily be computed on a daily and cumulative basis, as shown in **Table 1**.

The return and risk of the strategy are of prime importance. Standard deviation is a common measure of volatility and is used in the calculation of the Sharpe Ratio, which is widely utilized in the hedge fund industry and discussed later in this chapter. **Table 2** shows the standard deviation of the trader's account value (AUM) and daily profit and loss. If the trader is taking on too much volatility, there is a higher likelihood of hitting stop losses, getting out of trades too early, and being whipsawed. Furthermore, high volatility of a strategy increases stress on both traders and clients. Volatility calculations are generally backward looking, but they do play an important role in evaluating the effectiveness of a strategy.

Table 1: Sample Profit and Loss (P&L) Analysis

DATE	AUM	P&L (daily)	P&L (%)	Cumulative P&L %
1/2/2007	$ 5,000,000	$ 56,941	1.14%	1.14%
1/3/2007	$ 5,056,941	$ (887)	-0.02%	1.12%
1/4/2007	$ 5,056,054	$(104,808)	-2.07%	-0.98%
1/5/2007	$ 4,951,246	$ 27,966	0.56%	-0.42%
1/8/2007	$ 4,979,212	$ (297)	-0.01%	-0.42%
1/9/2007	$ 4,978,915	$ 385	0.01%	-0.41%
1/10/2007	$ 4,979,300	$ 7,293	0.15%	-0.27%
1/11/2007	$ 4,986,593	$ 9,791	0.20%	-0.07%

Table 2: Time Series Analysis of Profit and Loss (P&L)

DATE	AUM	P&L (daily)	P&L (%)	Cumulative P&L %
1/2/2007	$ 5,000,000	$ 56,941	1.14%	1.14%
1/3/2007	$ 5,056,941	$ (887)	-0.02%	1.12%
1/4/2007	$ 5,056,054	$(104,808)	-2.07%	-0.98%
1/5/2007	$ 4,951,246	$ 27,966	0.56%	-0.42%
1/8/2007	$ 4,979,212	$ (297)	-0.01%	-0.42%
1/9/2007	$ 4,978,915	$ 385	0.01%	-0.41%
1/10/2007	$ 4,979,300	$ 7,293	0.15%	-0.27%
1/11/2007	$ 4,986,593	$ 9,791	0.20%	-0.07%
Volatility	$ 35,758		0.86%	
Formula	STDDEV(B2:B9)		STDDEV(D2:D9)	

The consistency of winning trades is another important metric that can be obtained from a P&L analysis. Most firms and hedge funds try to avoid horizontal inequality strategies, or those whose profits are driven by a small number of positive days. A simple batting average can be computed that divides the number of periods with positive P&L by the total number of trades. Ideally, this ratio should be 60% or better, but some strategies may be viable with ratios on the order of 50%. In our example, the trader has made money 5 days out of 8 days and possesses a winning percentage or batting average of 5/8, or 62.5%.

4.3 Impact Ratio

The Impact Ratio is another important statistic for evaluating the effectiveness of trading strategies. It measures the ratio of gains to losses and is computed as follows.

Impact ratio = average gain on positive days / absolute value of average loss on negative days.

An impact ratio greater than 1 indicates that the trader is making more on his winners than he is losing on his losing trades. **Table 3** shows the impact ratio calculation for our example that was introduced in the prior section. Our trader's Impact Ratio is 0.58. This value indicates that the trader is not quick to realize losses or has allowed losses on losing trades to grow. The Impact Ratio measures the trader's adherence to the classic trading adage — let your winners run and cut short your losses.

Table 3: Sample Impact Ratio Analysis

Down Days

1/3/2007	$ (887)		Average Loss	$ (35,331)
1/4/2007	(104,808)		Average Gain	$ 20,475
1/8/2007	$ (297)		Impact Ratio	0.58

Up Days

1/2/2007	$ 56,941
1/5/2007	$ 27,966
1/9/2007	$ 385
1/10/2007	$ 7,293
1/11/2007	$ 9,791

4.4 Kelly Formula for Position Sizing

The concept of position sizing is central to an effective risk management process. The Kelly Formula or Kelly Criterion, introduced by Kelly (1956) of Bell Labs, builds on the foundation of the Impact Ratio. Its main purpose is to help traders gauge the appropriate size of a particular trade. Assume the following inputs and notation:

- o   Kelly Formula for position size = KF
- o   Win ratio = pW = 70%
- o   Loss ratio = pL or (1 – pW) = 30%
- o · Average Loser in $ terms = aL = $1,000
- o   Average Winner in $ terms = aW = $1,500

The Kelly Formula (KF) is computed as follows:

- o   KF = pW – pL(aW/aL)
- o   KF = 70% – 30%($1500/$1000) = 25%

Accordingly, traders would be directed to commit 25% of their capital to such a trade. The trade is worth making as long as the Kelly Formula remains in positive territory. The expected return on a single outcome is computed as follows:

- o   ($1,500*70%)-($1,000*30%) = $750

The trader faced with the good problem of having too many profitable trading opportunities should balance high expected returns with the risk corresponding to each trade. Position limits at the firmwide level may also be set allowing for a maximum of x% in any particular trade.

4.5 Drawdown Analysis

Maximum Drawdown (MD) analysis is the quantification of Murphy's Law and assumes that an investor enters a strategy at its peak and sells at its trough. It can be computed as follows:

o **MD = (Minimum Price – Maximum Price) / Maximum Price**

Notice that if your portfolio is not at an all time high, then it will show a drawdown. This dynamic is often discomforting for "perfectionist" traders, since their portfolios will rarely be trading at a peak. Good risk management technique allocates more capital to strategies that exhibit lower drawdown values and quick recovery times.

Once a drawdown occurs, risk managers should carefully analyze that a trader or hedge fund manager does not attempt to make the lost capital back by increasing risk. In fact, risk managers should generally advise firms to cut exposure if there is the existence of a material drawdown.

The existence of a drawdown could simply be due to profit taking by the market as a whole or that the strategy is losing its effectiveness. The difference between the two can only be determined when the sample size is large enough. Hence, it is easier to determine if a trader's strategy is "broken" relative to an intermediate or long-term investor.

It is important for risk managers to limit drawdowns to manageable levels (e.g. no more than 10% to 20%). For example, if a strategy or fund loses 50% of its value from a peak, it would require a 100% return to breakeven. After a large initial drawdown, the viability of the firm itself would be in question due to the highwater mark that must be surpassed in order to earn profit sharing fees. This issue is discussed further in Chapter 14.

4.6 Correlation Analysis

Correlation is a measure of the strength and direction of the relationship between two variables. Traders often compute the correlation of their strategy with a particular benchmark, such as the S&P 500, or to a corresponding hedge fund index. It is easy to compute correlation in Excel by using the CORREL function.

Correlation ranges in value from −1 to +1. The lower the value, the greater the diversification benefits of the strategy, relative to a benchmark. A correlation value of 1 implies that the two variables move in perfect lockstep together. Conversely, a correlation value of −1 will mean that the two variables move in opposite direction. If the variables are independent, then the correlation is 0. For example, many gold stocks have a negative correlation with the stock market, rising when the market falls and visa versa. Most equities have a positive correlation since they are all part of the same economy. In practice, traders and hedge fund managers find investments that are negatively correlated with the stock market by short selling, purchasing put options, selling short futures and using other hedging techniques.

Many calculations are skewed by the staring and stopping points, so it is often more effective from a risk management perspective to computing rolling correlations. This approach looks at correlation over a specific time period, such as three years, and analyzes how its value changes over time. The rolling correlation approach often enables risk managers to uncover if traders or hedge fund managers have changed their strategies.

It is also worth noting that correlation does not imply causation. Two variables can show a relationship merely by chance. Perhaps the best-known example is the Superbowl Indicator, which has correctly predicted the direction of the U.S. stock market approximately 90% of the time. Of course, football has nothing to do with stock prices; therefore its relationship to the stock market is random or spurious, despite its terrific batting average.

5. Investment Risk Management

The risk manager of a longer-term oriented hedge fund often focuses on different techniques relative to those utilized in the trading arena. In this section we focus on the most common metrics for longer-term oriented funds. Some measures focus on return relative to total risk, while others focus only on losses below a certain threshold.

5.1 Sharpe Ratio

The Sharpe Ratio, developed by Nobel Prize Winner William Sharpe (1966), is one of the most commonly used measures of investment performance in the hedge fund industry. It measures excess return per unit of risk, where risk is determined by standard deviation. It can be computed as follows:

- o **Sharpe Ratio = (Average Return of the Fund – Risk Free Rate of Interest) / Standard Deviation of the Fund's Return**

The higher the value, the better the performance generated by the manager. The Sharpe Ratio focuses on excess returns since any hedge fund strategy worth its salt should provide a higher return over time than the risk free rate of interest. One criticism of the Sharpe Ratio is that it unfairly penalizes high volatility due to *positive* returns. For example, if Fund A had returns of +20% and +10% and Fund B had returns of 9% and 9.1%, Fund B would have the better Sharpe Ratio. Most rational investors would prefer Fund A due to its higher positive returns. The Sharpe Ratio remains widely deployed since it was one of the very first techniques used to measure investment performance.

5.2 Treynor Measure

The Treynor Measure, developed by Jack Treynor in 1966, is similar to the Sharpe Ratio in that it measures excess return per unit of risk. However, the Treynor Measure uses beta, or market volatility as its measure of risk, while the Sharpe Ratio employs standard deviation, or total risk. The Treynor Measure is computed as follows:

o **Treynor Measure = (Return of Portfolio - Risk Free Rate) /
   Portfolio Beta**

Most traditionalists believe the Sharpe Ratio works best for well
diversified portfolios, while the Treynor Measure works for both
diversified and undiversified portfolios. The Treynor Measure has fallen
out of favor in recent years due to the doubt cast upon the validity of the
simple Capital Asset Pricing Model (CAPM). Many analysts today
believe that the CAPM adds some value, but that multifactor approaches
do a better job explaining the risk-return relationship.

5.3 Jensen's Alpha

Jensen's Alpha, developed by Michael Jensen in 1968, measures the
difference between a portfolio's actual return and its expected return
according to the CAPM. The term alpha, as indicated in the title of this
book, was popularized after the Jensen paper. Today alpha refers to
excess risk adjusted returns and is not tied as closely to the CAPM as in
the Jensen Model. Jensen's Alpha differs from the Sharpe Ratio and
Treynor Measure in that it attempts to measure performance not simply
in excess of the risk free rate of interest, but also with respect to portfolio
risk, as measured by the CAPM.

o **Jensen's Alpha = Portfolio Return - (Risk Free Rate +
   Portfolio Beta * (Market Return - Risk Free Rate))**

Of course the term alpha is widely used in the hedge fund
community, hence the title of this book. However, as noted above, in
recent years doubt has been cast upon the validity of the CAPM, thereby
reducing its effectiveness.

5.4 Sortino Ratio

The Sortino Ratio, discussed in Sortino and van der Meer (1991), is a modification of the Sharpe Ratio, where risk is not measured by standard deviation, but downside deviation. Semi-deviation, which examines returns below a certain threshold (e.g. zero or the rate of inflation), is the most common statistic used in Sortino calculations. The Sortino Ratio is computed as follows:

o **Sortino Ratio = (Return of the Portfolio – Riskfree Return) / Downside Deviation**

The Sortino Ratio has the appealing feature of not penalizing a fund that has high volatility due to strongly positive returns. Only negative returns, or returns below a certain threshold, contribute towards its risk calculation. The best hedge fund managers do have the skill to outperform during both up and down markets and often exhibit outstanding Sortino Ratios, while their Sharpe Ratios may label them as average.

5.5 Omega Ratio

The Omega Ratio, introduced by Keating and Shadwick (2002), uses all the information in a return series, not simply its mean and variance. Its computation is quite advanced, but its intuition can be clearly communicated. For a given target return, R, the Omega Ratio is the weighted gain to loss ratio. The weights refer to the probabilities of gains or losses corresponding to each return.

Its chief benefit is that it provides a ranking of portfolios that is more consistent with investors' intuition. Its rankings rely simply upon the belief that investors prefer more wealth to less, rather than assuming that standard deviation, or some other metric, best characterizes their risk preferences.

5.6 Downside Risk Measurement

Downside risk can be measured by taking the standard deviation of data points that fall below a certain predefined level. Its focus is strictly on risk, not excess returns per unit of risk. For example, we may choose to measure downside risk as all the returns that are below zero in a P&L time series. The downside risk measures indicate that when we are wrong, how wrong are we? Its weakness, of course, is that it does not give "credit" for positive returns, or returns above the target threshold.

5.7 Exposures

A risk manager must be able to manage extensive amounts of data. Many modern hedge funds have complex portfolios consisting of domestic equities, options, futures, foreign equities and swaps / forward contracts. Pricing data is relatively easy to obtain for exchange traded instruments. However, the risk manager must often estimate prices for illiquid or over the counter (OTC) instruments, such as credit default swaps. Overall portfolio risk calculations can be quite complex, given the difficulty in accurately estimating correlations among various financial instruments. However, as a first line estimate, many risk managers compute portfolio exposures. In essence, exposure analysis places securities in specific buckets (e.g. Long or Short, Region, Security Type, etc.) and sometimes nets them out to get a top level look at a portfolio's characteristics. We list the most common exposure statistics below.

5.7.1 Long Market Value (LMV)

Long market value (LMV) is the aggregate dollar investment of securites that are purchased long. On the surface its calculation is simple, but it has become more complex in recent years due to the proliferation of inverse exchange traded funds (ETFs). For example, the purchase of an inverse ETF that moves in the opposite direction of the S&P 500 would increase the LMV of the portfolio, but reduce overall portfolio risk or beta.

5.7.2 Short Market Value

Short market value (SMV) is the aggregate dollar investment of securites that are sold short. Theoretically, short positions rise in value when the market goes down. As with LMV, caution must be used when dealing with securities that have atypical market movements. For example, selling a put option may increase a portfolio's SMV but will generally rise in value when the market goes up. Several software vendors provide programs that aggregate risk exposures. A sample exposure analysis is shown in **Figure 1**.

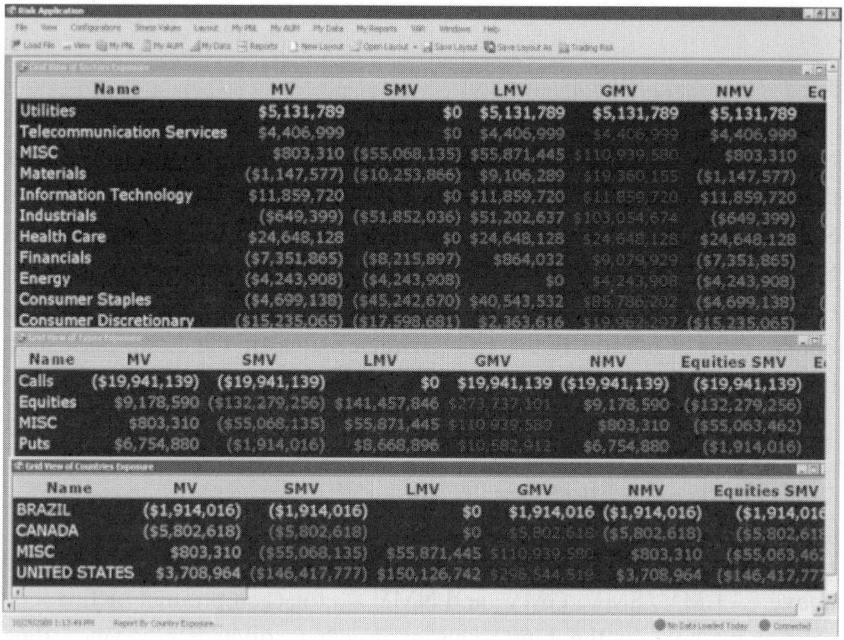

Name	MV	SMV	LMV	GMV	NMV
Utilities	$5,131,789	$0	$5,131,789	$5,131,789	$5,131,789
Telecommunication Services	$4,406,999	$0	$4,406,999	$4,406,999	$4,406,999
MISC	$803,310	($55,068,135)	$55,871,445	$110,939,580	$803,310
Materials	($1,147,577)	($10,253,866)	$9,106,289	$19,360,155	($1,147,577)
Information Technology	$11,859,720	$0	$11,859,720	$11,859,720	$11,859,720
Industrials	($649,399)	($51,852,036)	$51,202,637	$103,054,674	($649,399)
Health Care	$24,648,128	$0	$24,648,128	$24,648,128	$24,648,128
Financials	($7,351,865)	($8,215,897)	$864,032	$9,079,929	($7,351,865)
Energy	($4,243,908)	($4,243,908)	$0	$4,243,908	($4,243,908)
Consumer Staples	($4,699,138)	($45,242,670)	$40,543,532	$85,786,202	($4,699,138)
Consumer Discretionary	($15,235,065)	($17,598,681)	$2,363,616	[illegible]	($15,235,065)

Name	MV	SMV	LMV	GMV	NMV	Equities SMV
Calls	($19,941,139)	($19,941,139)	$0	$19,941,139	($19,941,139)	($19,941,139)
Equities	$9,178,590	($132,279,256)	$141,457,846	$273,737,101	$9,178,590	($132,279,256)
MISC	$803,310	($55,068,135)	$55,871,445	$110,939,580	$803,310	($55,063,462)
Puts	$6,754,880	($1,914,016)	$8,668,896	$10,582,912	$6,754,880	($1,914,016)

Name	MV	SMV	LMV	GMV	NMV	Equities SMV
BRAZIL	($1,914,016)	($1,914,016)	$0	$1,914,016	($1,914,016)	($1,914,01
CANADA	($5,802,618)	($5,802,618)	$0	$5,802,618	($5,802,618)	($5,802,61
MISC	$803,310	($55,068,135)	$55,871,445	$110,939,580	$803,310	($55,063,46
UNITED STATES	$3,708,964	($146,417,777)	$150,126,742	$296,544,519	$3,708,964	($146,417,77

Figure 1: Sample Exposure Analysis

Source: RiskApplication.com

5.7.3 Gross Market Value

Gross Market Value (GMV) is a measure of total capital exposure and simply adds Long Market Value (LMV) to the absolute value of Short Market Value (SMV). GMV is one measure of a fund's leverage. For example, if a fund has $100 million in investors' capital, $200 million in LMV and $200 SMV its GMV would be $400 million. Leverage is simply GMV divided by investor capital, or:

- o **Leverage Ratio = Gross Market Value of the Portfolio / Capital.**

In our example, the fund's leverage would be:

- o $400 million / $100 million = 4 to 1.

5.7.4 Net Market Value

Net Market Value (NMV) often provides a better measure of risk than the Levarge ratio and is simply the difference between LMV and SMV. In our example, our Long Market Value is $200 million and our Short Market Value is $200 MM. Therefore, the NMV of the fund is (200 – 200) 0. This particular portfolio would be dollar neutral, but may not be market neutral if the risk characteristics of the Long and Short books substantially differed.

5.7.5 Product Exposures

Product exposure analysis computes each of the statistics discussed above — LMV, SMV, GMV, and NMV — for each product or financial instrument held in the fund. This approach is often handy since fund management duties are often partitioned by financial instrument. For example, one team might work on the equity book, while another will trade derivatives and so forth. The risk manager will then create an overall picture of the fund's assets and suggest appropriate hedging vehicles as warranted.

5.7.6 Sector and Industry Exposures

The market as a whole can be partitioned into broad economic sectors, such as Financials, Energy, and Utilities. Securities within a specific sector often move in tandem, since they are influenced by the same economic factors. Sector currents are often so strong that they override market movements. For example, most Energy stocks around the world were in positive territory in 2007 while most Financial stocks were down across the globe over the same period. Industries provide further subdetail than sector analysis and exhibit even higher volatility. For example, industries within the Healthcare sector include Pharmaceuticals, Biotechs, Medical Devices, and Managed Care Providers.

Risk managers will often map securities into specific industries and market sectors in order to obtain an overall assessment of the portfolio's risk. The risk manager may use this information to see if the fund is sensitive to certain macroeconomic variables, such as interest rates, oil prices, and gold. Overconcentration in a particular sector or industry is clearly a risk. For example, the SEC instituted a temporary ban on the short sales in a broad array of Financial securities during the fall of 2008. Financial oriented hedge funds may have had a difficult time executing their strategies during this period.

5.7.7 Country Exposures

Country Exposure is an additional risk factor that risk managers often monitor separately. For example, most Russian and Chinese stocks, regardless of industry, were down in excess of 60% over the 2008 calendar year. Macroeconomic forces, such as GDP, interest rates, and exchange rates generally affect most firms in a country in a similar directional manner. Of course the biggest risk, expropriation or nationalization of foreign assets, is political and has occurred in Iran, Russia, Venezuela, and several other countries over the past century.

5.7.8 Liquidity Exposures

Hedge funds will often build up positions that go in their favor but when they have to close those positions, they find the act of their trading moves prices. In other words, their trades have market impact. The tagline from Black Flag's popular Roach Motel commercial comes to mind — "Roaches check in, but they don't check out." That is, trying to exit an illiquid position often turns a winning position into a losing one. Accordingly, risk managers should keep close tabs on, and limit to a reasonable extent, illiquid positions. Illiquid positions do not have to be necessarily completely avoided, since they may often be a source of alpha.

One simple measure of liquidity is the number of days it would take to exit a position, at the security's Average Daily Trading Volume. For example, assume our hedge fund manager holds 1 million shares of stock in ABC Inc. Suppose, ABC Inc. has an average daily volume of 750,000 shares per day. The Head Trader at the fund may state that he can offload 20% of the Average Daily Volume per day without "giving his hand" or having the trading activity result in significant market impact. Now we can calculate Days to Liquidate as:

- o   Days to Liquidate = Number of Shares / (Average Daily Volume * Percentage of Volume to Trade)

- o   = 1,000,0000 / (750,000 * 20%)

- o   = 1,000,0000 / 150,000 or 6 2/3 days.

Our risk manager may conduct a Days to Liquidate analysis for each position in the portfolio. If there are some highly illiquid positions, the fund manager may either initiate a position where they can offload those positions earlier than their initial target or talk to institutional trading desks about a block transaction. A highly illiquid portfolio can be disastrous during times of market distress, as holders of subprime securities have found out over the 2007–2008 time period. Good risk managers will ensure that their hedge funds never have the bulk of their portfolio subject to a liquidity crunch.

5.7.9 Portfolio Quality Exposure

Hedge fund portfolios may also be partitioned by quality as a further risk management technique. The high quality vs. low quality partition is fairly natural in the fixed income market with the well known distinction between investment grade and high yield or "junk" bonds. Standard and Poor's also produces Quality Ratings for equities. High quality companies generally have consistent earnings and stable dividends. Value Line has a similar ranking for equities. Some derivatives also partition securities into tranches, with the top tranches offering the best quality and lowest risk. An effective risk manager can tell portfolio managers when it pays to own low quality instruments (e.g. when credit spreads are low) or anticipate or speedily react to "flight to quality" crowd behavior.

5.8 Beta Adjusting the Portfolio

Let's go back to our earlier example of a fund with $100 MM in Capital. The fund is Long $200 million and Short $200 million. This fund is dollar neutral and has a Net Market Value of $0. On the surface this fund has no risk, but if the market factor or beta or industry compositions of the Long and Short sides differ significantly, the portfolio may be quite risky. For example, a dollar invested in Google (a hypergrowth technology company) is not the same as a dollar invested in a conservative utility, such as Public Service Enterprise Group.

Beta Adjusting a portfolio helps calibrate portfolio risk in a manner beyond simple gross or net exposures. The process multiplies the dollar value of part or all of the portfolio by its corresponding beta value, as shown in the equation below:

- o **Beta Adjusted Value of a Position = Market Value of the Position * Beta**

Let's continue with our Google example. Assume you own 1000 shares of Google, with a beta value of 2, and it is trading at $500 per share. The Beta Adjusted Value of Google is given as;

- o **= 1,000 * $500 * 2 = $1,000,000**

Notice this figure differs substantially from the non beta adjusted market value of $500,000 (i.e. 1,000 * $500)

Beta adjusting a position measures risk exposure, rather than dollar exposure. Risk managers conducting this process on the entire portfolio of a hedge fund may uncover, for example, that a "safe" dollar neutral fund may actually be Short low beta and Long high beta securities. This portfolio would likely incur substantial losses in the event of a bear market.

5.9 Delta Adjusting the Portfolio

Option positions in a fund should be Delta Adjusted and then, as a further step, Beta Adjusted due to their nonlinear payoffs. Delta is a measure of the change in the price of an option due to a change in the price of the underlying instrument. Let's illustrate the concept of Delta Adjusting with an example. Suppose we purchase 5 Call Options on Research in Motion (RIMM) with a Strike Price of $124 for a Cost or Premium of $7. Assume the current price in the market of RIMM is $130 and we estimate its Delta to be 0.67. The following equation uses Delta Adjustment to the position.

- o **Delta Adjusted Option Position = Number of Contracts * Contract Multiplier * Underlying Value * Delta.**

Now, plugging in the appropriate values, we get:

- o **Delta Adjusted Position = 5 * 100 * 130 * 0.67 = \$43,550**

It is helpful to combine the previously mentioned Beta Adjusted Position with the Delta Adjusted Position. The benefit of performing this procedure is to get a more precise estimate of the change in the value of our fund, due to a change in market movements. Let's continue with our RIMM example and assume that its stock has a Beta value of 2.0. Our Delta-Beta Adjusted equation multiplies the Delta Adjusted Value by the Beta of the security and is given by the following equation:

- o **Delta-Beta Adjustment = Delta Adjusted Value * Beta**

- o **= \$43,550 * 2.0 = \$ 87,100.**

This figure differs substantially from the \$3,500 in premium we paid and the \$43,550 option delta adjusted exposure we calculated. In short, hedge funds with option-like securities that do not perform this calculation may be substantially underestimating the risk they are taking.

5.10 Value at Risk (VAR)

The Value at Risk (VAR) framework to risk management was developed by a number of Wall Street firms, including Bankers Trust and J. P. Morgan. VAR focuses on the likelihood of losing a specified dollar amount over a certain time interval. For example, if a portfolio of stocks has a one-month 5% VaR of \$10 million, there is a 5% probability that the portfolio will decline in value by more than \$10 million over the next month. Its widespread use remains controversial since it did not help prevent the failures of Bear Stearns, Lehman Brothers, AIG, Wachovia, Washington Mutual, and many others in the credit crisis that unfolded in 2008. However, no widely agreed upon successor to VAR exists today so its widespread use will likely continue, despite its shortcomings.

The popularity of VAR is partially attributed to the fact that it condenses risk to a single number that can easily be comprehended by management. The following information is needed to calculate VAR:

- o   Time Series of P&L Data
- o   Confidence Level
  - –   The most commonly used confidence levels are 95% and 99%.
- o   Unit of Value (such as percentage or Dollar amount)

We will briefly discuss several methods for computing VAR. Risk managers will have to use judgment to determine the method that applies best to their particular fund.

5.10.1 Variance-Covariance Value at Risk (VCV VAR)

The Variance-Covariance (VCV) VAR model, also known as the Delta Model, was popularized by J. P. Morgan. The model is based on the assumption that security risk and return metrics are normally distributed. It also relies to a great extent on historical correlation numbers.

In practice, market stresses occur more often than predicted by the normal distribution. In statistical terms, the tails in reality are "fatter" than those shown in the normal distribution. Furthermore, correlations often approach 1 during times of market distress. The calculation of VCV method VAR is somewhat complex. Most practitioners use third party tools, such as those provided by RiskMetrics, to estimate VCV VAR.

5.10.2 Historical Simulation Method of VAR

The Historical Simulation Method assumes that the past is prologue to the future and is perhaps the simplest way to calculate VAR. It sorts past returns from lowest to highest and places them in a histogram. **Figure 2** shows the histogram of daily returns for the Nasdaq 100 ETF, whose symbol was once QQQ but is today QQQQ.

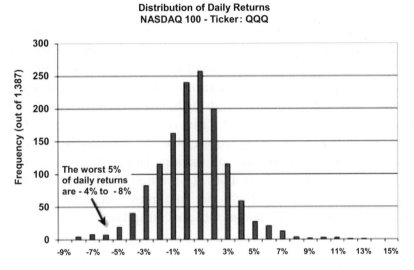

Figure 2: Distribution of Daily Returns

Source: Investopedia

Through interpreting this figure we can state, based on historical evidence, with 95% confidence, that our worst daily loss will not exceed 4%. If our hedge fund was $100 million in size, we could state we are 95% confident that our loss would not exceed $4 million ($100 million * −4%) over the course of one day. Of course, our primary focus in risk management is what happens during the 5% of days where losses are greater than 4%. Hence, Historical VAR often performs poorly when events unfold that are different than those in the historical database (e.g. Travel Stocks post 9/11).

5.10.3 Monte Carlo Simulation Method of VAR

The Historical VAR method suffers from a relatively small amount of independent data points. The Monte Carlo Simulation Method of VAR uses thousands (or more) of hypothetical scenarios and estimates how the portfolio would have performed under each scenario. It requires the risk manager to specify structural relationships among the variables that drive portfolio returns. The computer simulation would output hypothetical returns for the portfolio and these returns can be placed in a histogram. Similar inferences can be made with the Monte Carlo VAR as with those discussed with Historical VAR. The strength of the Monte Carlo approach is that nearly every conceivable scenario can be tested. Its weaknesses include its reliance on (perhaps faulty) structural financial models and intensive computations. In practice, Monte Carlo VAR is used most often for hedge funds that hold many securities that exhibit nonlinear returns, such as mortgage-backed securities.

5.11 Other Risks

Effective risk managers will also focus on several other factors that can have a material impact on the hedge fund. We briefly discuss some of these factors below and expand on these and other topics in Chapter 13 on Hedge Fund Due Diligence

5.11.1 Counterparty Risk

Counterparty risk refers to the chance that the entity on the other side of the trade from you will fail to meet their obligations. It may also refer to the risk that your service providers (e.g. Prime Broker, Administrators, etc) fail to operate as promised. Generally, counterparty risk is remote for exchange traded contracts, since the clearinghouse often settles "broken" trades. However, counterparty risk can be quite severe for over the counter (OTC) instruments such as swaps. The bankruptcies of Enron and Lehman Brothers resulted in substantial losses for counterparties to these two institutions after their respective Chapter 11 filings. Furthermore, hedge funds, who prime brokered at Lehman had substantial delay in accessing their funds, resulting in non-performance related problems for the hedge fund management company. Counterparty risk should be continually assessed regardless of the reputation of the counterparty. If Bear Stearns, Lehman Brothers, and AIG can go under, so can virtually any other counterparty.

5.11.2 *Currency or Exchange Rate Risk*

Most hedge funds report returns in the unit of their home currency, such as U.S. Dollars. If the hedge fund invests in international securities, unless specifically hedged, exchange rate risk will be incurred. This risk is perhaps best exemplified by the "carry trade" employed by many hedge funds, whose goal is to borrow money where it is cheap and deploy it in the areas returns appear to be the greatest. Currency movements can be quite volatile and should be closely monitored by risk managers.

5.11.3 *Legal & Regulatory Risk*

The absence of uniform legal, accounting and financial reporting and disclosure standards across the globe means that risk management has to ensure that there are no "toxic" elements in the portfolio. Although risk managers are generally not compliance officers per se, they should be conversant in the rules of regulations of the markets where the hedge fund is engaged in trading activity. Questionable activities should be discussed with the appropriate compliance personnel or fund principals.

Hedge Fund Alpha Tear Sheet — Chapter 12

- Risk management is as much art as science, since there is no uniformly agreed upon definition of risk.
- We define risk management as the process of understanding portfolio return drivers with the simultaneous goals of maximizing risk adjusted returns and minimizing the chance of financial ruin.
- Superior risk management may increase investment performance in a number of ways, such as the following:
  - o Risk managers may suggest periods where it is prudent to increase or decrease portfolio beta, resulting in increased returns or lesser losses if the assessment is correct.
  - o Effective risk management may determine when it is the most opportune time to use leverage via a carry trade.
  - o Proper risk management may provide a better way of sizing individual trades.
  - o Good risk management may aid in most efficiently allocating capital across a number of strategies within a multistrategy fund or across several funds.
- Effective techniques for the risk management of trading oriented hedge funds include the utilization of Profit and Loss (P&L) Analysis, Impact Ratio, Kelly Formula for Position Sizing, Drawdown Analysis, and Correlation Analysis.
- Effective techniques for the risk management of investment oriented hedge funds include the utilization of the Sharpe Ratio, Treynor Measure, Jensen's Alpha, Sortino Ratio, Omega Ratio, Downside Risk Measurement, Exposure Analysis, Beta and Delta Analysis, and Value at Risk (VAR).
- Other risks for hedge funds include Counterparty Risk, Currency or Exchange Rate Risk, and Legal & Regulatory Risk.

References

Harper, David, "Introduction to Value At Risk (VAR) — Part 1," Investopedia. http://www.investopedia.com/articles/04/092904.asp

Jensen, Michael, "The Performance of Mutual Funds in the Period 1945-1964," *The Journal of Finance*, Vol. 23, No. 2, 1968, pp. 389–416.

Keating, Kon and William Shadwick, *A Universal Performance Measure*, The Finance Development Centre, 2002.

Kelly, John Jr., "A New Interpretation of Information Rate," *Bell System Technical Journal*, Vol. 35, 1956, pp. 917–926.

Sharpe, William F. "Mutual Fund Performance," *Journal of Business*, January 1966, pp. 119–138.

Sortino, Frank A. and Robert van der Meer, "Downside Risk," *The Journal of Portfolio Management*, Vol. 17, No. 4, 1991, pp. 27–31.

Treynor, Jack, "How to Rate Management of Investment Funds," *Harvard Business Review*, Vol. 43, No. 1, 1966, pp. 63–75.

13

HEDGE FUND DUE DILIGENCE

Erman Civelek

The MDE Group

1. Introduction

The number of hedge funds has skyrocketed in the last few years to more than 15,000, and their assets under management have ballooned to almost $2 trillion as of late 2008. With this growth came more complex trading strategies that resulted from hedge funds' need to differentiate themselves against the intense competition. Despite this growth, the process of conducting due diligence on hedge funds is quite similar to performing due diligence on traditional equity, fixed income, and commodity strategies. The goal of the due diligence process ultimately is to separate skill from luck, true alpha from market beta, and manager talent from market timing.

2. Sourcing

The hedge fund due diligence process starts with the sourcing of managers. Most consultants use internal or external manager databases as a start. While it's possible to construct an internal database of hedge fund managers, the sheer size of the universe makes it more convenient to subscribe to external databases. The largest databases include Hedge Fund Research, Hedgefund.net, Barclay Hedge, Morningstar Altvest, MSCI, and Cogent Hedge. **Table 1** lists most of the hedge fund databases available for subscription. Annual subscription fees range from $2,000 to $7,000.

Table 1: Alternative Investment Databases

Barclay Hedge	Hedge Fund Intelligence
Barclay Hedge Database (HF+FOF)	AsiaHedge Database (Asian HF)
Barclay Fund of Funds Database	EuroHedge Database (European HF)
Barclay CTA Database	InvestHedge Database (FOF)
Barclay Global Database (HF+FOF+CTA)	Absolute Return Database (US HF)
Barclay Graveyard Database	South AfricaHedge Database (S. African HF)
CISDM (HF+FOF+CTA)	Hedge Fund Research
CogentHedge (HF+FOF+CTA)	HFR Database (HF+FOF+CTA)
Daniel B. Stark (CTA)	HFR FOF Database
Eurekahedge	HedgeFund.net
Global Hedge Fund Database	Global Database (HF+FOF+CTA)
Asian Hedge Fund Database	Global Database Quarterly (HF+FOF+CTA)
Emerging Markets Hedge Fund Database	Asia Database (HF+FOF+CTA)
European Hedge Fund Database	Europe Database (HF+FOF+CTA)
North American Hedge Fund Database	International Traders Research (CTA)
Latin American Hedge Fund Database	MondoHedge (Italian HF)
Global Fund of Funds Database	Morningstar Altvest (HF+FOF+CTA)
Global Absolute Return Fund Database	MSCI Hedge Fund Database (HF)
CTA Fund Database	Lipper TASS (HF+FOF+CTA)

The hedge fund database industry is quite fragmented, with different hedge fund managers choosing to report to certain database(s), but not others. Hence, due diligence firms find it most convenient to subscribe to several databases, and aggregate the data using reporting and analytical software. Pertrac, one of such analytical platforms, features information management, statistical analysis, investment searches, reporting studio, asset allocation, portfolio construction, peer group analysis, style analysis, and Monte Carlo simulations. **Figure 1** on the following page displays a sample screenshot from Pertrac.

In addition to the statistical sources, managers can be identified through industry contacts and peer referrals. In fact, the referral networks account for a large percentage of how blue chip fund of funds identify star hedge fund managers. Managers without track records and managers with capacity concerns often do not report to hedge fund databases, making the database method of sourcing managers somewhat ineffective.

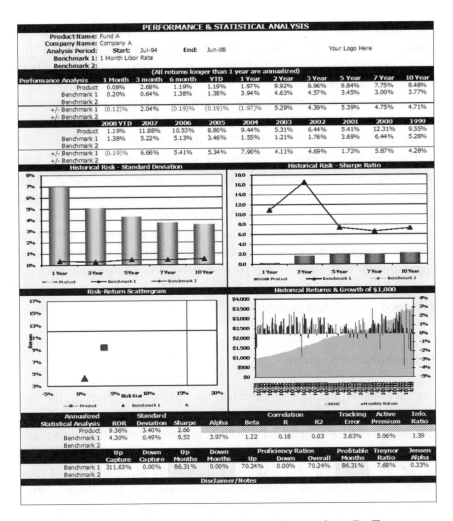

Figure 1: Sample Hedge Fund Manager Report from PerTrac

Talking to a former co-worker, boss, or supervisor can reveal many valuable insights about an individual who is spinning off to start his own hedge fund. One can assess how the manager thinks about investment risk, portfolio management, and teamwork through a first-hand account of his past experience. Talking to current or past investors of a hedge fund manager can expose unique personal and professional traits about the hedge fund manager as well. Even though past success is no guarantee of future performance, ultimately, peer rankings is one of the most important valuation techniques in manager evaluation, both statistically and qualitatively.

Industry events, conferences, and prime brokerage events also offer introductions to different hedge fund managers. Unfortunately, there is a negative selection bias with these "cap intro" events, as most managers that attend these types of events are eager to spend a lot of time marketing their funds and raising assets, not dedicating their precious time to managing portfolios. However, there are some quality managers that can be identified from industry events. Attending an event with 10 managers and listening to the standard 10-minute pitch by each manager can cut down a lot of unnecessary time and resources to set up individual appointments with each of the 10 managers. The due diligence person can quickly identify if the team, strategy, and investment process would be a good fit for future exploration.

3. Quantitative Analysis

Once a potential manager is identified for further due diligence, the first step that most investors look at is past track record. Too many people rely heavily on past numbers, which is unfortunate. It is extremely important to discount past numbers and extract out the true value. This is not an easy step. How can one judge the sustainability of past performance? What was the underlying environment that existed during which the past returns were generated? How much risk was taken to produce the past results?

Evaluating risk-adjusted results, not just the absolute results, can put various investment alternatives on a level basis. Comparing a hedge fund manager with 200% historical gross exposure to a non-leveraged index, or comparing two market-neutral funds with discrepant risk limits does not serve full justice to either one. Once the returns are adjusted for risk, then comparing the risk-adjusted returns of different funds to one another and/or to different indices can be accomplished in a fair fashion.

It is important to look at return not only through the standard (but arbitrary) periods of 3yr, 5yr, 10yr, etc., but also to establish rolling time periods for performance evaluation. A manager can have a great track record as of an artificial end-date, but become a bottom performer in the period to follow. Therefore, rolling time period analysis is more advantageous than a static period analysis.

It is useful to divide the past track record into up periods and down periods and analyze how a strategy performed on a relative basis during each period. There are lots of risky hedge fund managers that do quite well in up markets, as there are defensive hedge fund managers that produce good alpha in down markets. The challenge is to find managers that have optimized returns and can capture a good portion of the upside without exposing themselves to much of the downside. After all, hedge funds are designed to generate absolute returns, regardless of the market direction. For an investor with medium risk tolerance, finding strategies with 70-80% upside capture and 20-30% downside capture can offer a good risk/return payoff. A sample upside/downside analysis can be found in **Figure 2**.

High peer ranking is always a desired goal. In order for peer ranking analysis to work, the hedge fund strategy must be compared to the right peer group. Finding a universe of hedge fund strategies that invests in similar markets with similar exposures is the key. No manager can always stay in the top quartile consistently year in year out; therefore, the search criteria should not be overly restrictive, as it will limit the results to a sub-optimum number of managers. Observing the rankings of the hedge fund managers over different periods (relative to peers and indices) can reveal interesting patterns about the consistency and volatility of the manager. Ideally, one would like to select managers with consistent performance, which can show talent rather than luck.

There is a long list of risk factors that can impact a hedge fund: market risk, credit risk, interest rate risk, inflation risk, business risk, event risk, and political risk. While some of these are hard to measure statistically (i.e., business risk, political risk), and others can be measured based on simulation methods (i.e., interest rate risk, event risk), the main risk factors that most investors are primarily concerned about are the market risk (for equity investors) and the credit risk (for fixed income

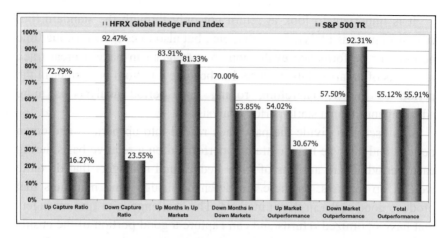

Figure 2: Sample Upside / Downside Analysis

investors). Market risk can be easily identified through portfolio beta, or sensitivity to market moves, while the credit risk can be obtained through a detailed analysis of the credit rating of the individual names and portfolio as a whole.

Different portfolio risk measures can reveal important channels to look through and identify contribution to portfolio risk from various equity, fixed income, and commodity exposures. The most frequently used risk measure is standard deviation, which measures the total risk inherent in the past returns. One reason not to rely too heavily on standard deviation is because it incorporates both the good risk (upside risk) and bad risk (downside risk). It is more appropriate to look at semi deviation, which is a standard measure for downside risk. The natural derivates for total risk (standard deviation) and downside risk (semi deviation) are the Sharpe and the Sortino ratios, which are risk-adjusted return calculations. As stated previously, evaluating managers based on these risk-adjusted measures is a better way to evaluate performance than just performance alone.

VaR, or Value at Risk, is another common risk measure. It is defined as the maximum loss not exceeded with a given probability. It can be calculated using three different methods: variance-covariance, historical simulation, and Monte Carlo simulation. The caveat of this measure is that it requires a vast history of past data and that it has a normal distribution assumption that is often violated.

Monitoring current and past exposures (security, market, industry, sector, country, geography) is a key risk mitigation tool. It can warn investors if excessive risk is taken with respect to the investments. Many hedge fund blow-ups occur because of concentration or heavy leverage. Understanding how a manager sets, monitors, and adjusts the gross exposure, the net exposure, and the portfolio leverage is extremely important to making a judgment about the fund's effectiveness in managing the portfolio risk. The investor should receive monthly data of exposures and leverage and understand the typical and maximum weights in each category. The most effective risk management method is diversification, but not at the expense of mediocrity; hence the right balance has to be achieved between diversification and over-diversification.

Hedge funds are marketed as low correlation vehicles, thus investors have to measure and evaluate correlation matrixes against various market indices. It also pays to check correlations against existing investments, as adding a manager with good performance expectations to a portfolio of strategies that it is not correlated to can bring down the portfolio risk. Not unlike volatility, correlations can change over time, therefore, observing rolling correlations, and most importantly observing correlations during stress periods are often warranted (**Figure 3**).

Many hedge fund allocators use stress tests to shock the current portfolio against past exogenous events (LTCM, 9/11, Asian currency crises, etc.) and calculate the potential sensitivity to past stress event. I find this approach quite weak. There is no assurance that the current portfolio of the hedge fund manager used to stress test would be the same portfolio the manager would have had in the past periods. The availability of investment vehicles today is also quite different from what was available in past periods (ETFs, derivatives, etc.). Backtested and simulated performance results often used in marketing pitches also need to be discounted and discarded for the same reason; they often have very little predictive value.

The longer the track record of real investments, the higher the potential value it can add to the due diligence process with respect to the

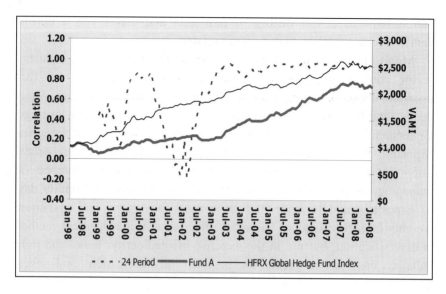

Figure 3: Rolling Correlation Analysis

talent of the manager navigating tough investment markets. The investors should also keep a close eye on the monthly AUM of the fund and compare the returns generated to the AUM. Many hedge fund managers generate spectacular returns with low risk in the first few years of their hedge funds and, as money chases performance, they become too large to sustain their early success. Performance deterioration and alpha decay are two important concepts that have to be monitored in evaluating hedge fund managers. This topic is further discussed in Chapter 14.

A related concept is the monthly return distribution pattern (**Figure 4**), skewness, and kurtosis of a hedge fund manager. Unlike traditional investments, most of the alternative strategies have non-normal return distributions and, as such, are subject to fat tail risk. One should seek out managers with a positive skew to their returns and limited downside risk. Getting caught in a 5 standard deviation event can erase all (or more) of the portfolio gains in a heartbeat. However, just because the past performances do not show a large negative skew does not mean that the managers do not have the potential to lose a lot of money in a short period of time. Monthly return distribution analysis is just a single tool

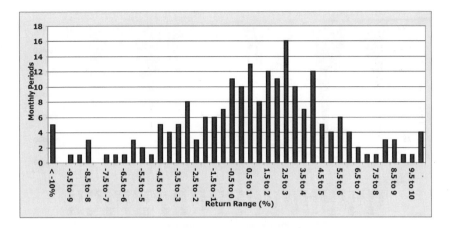

Figure 4: Histogram of Hedge Fund Returns

among hundreds of quantitative and qualitative tools that have to be combined in a delicate fashion in order to make a judgment about a manager.

Drawdown analysis is another tool used to evaluate the probability, magnitude, and recovery of portfolio losses. There is no free lunch in the investment world, and there is no such thing as riskless return (other than Treasury bonds). All money making managers are expected to lose money from time to time. The drawdown analysis can shed important light on whether a manager tends to lose a lot of money frequently and take a long time to recover the losses, or is one that has limited losses infrequently and easily recoups them. Ideally, one would like to go with the latter manager. A sample drawdown analysis can be found in **Figure 5**.

One of the most revealing quantitative analyses that comes quite handy in analyzing a hedge fund is performance attribution analysis (**Figure 6**). To make a judgment about the sustainability of good absolute and relative performance, one has to see signs of widespread and consistent performance attribution, not just a few good past home runs. Hedge funds often list the weights of their top 5 and top 10 names in the portfolio for portfolio concentration purposes. This analysis should be extended to include the percentage of the fund returns attributable to any

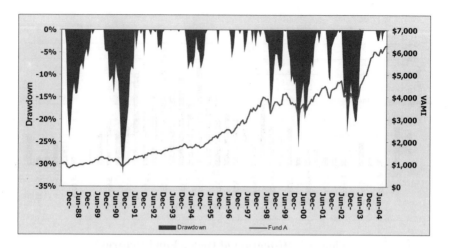

Figure 5: Sample Drawdown Analysis

given number of securities. The goal of this exercise is to see to it that the manager is capable of generating positive returns across many securities and sectors, not just a few. Diversification of the attribution leads to lower risk for the future returns, as long as the manager sticks to his or her investment discipline. Understanding the number of positions held in the portfolio over rolling periods and turnover can uncover hidden risks in the portfolio. If the number is too low, it can increase the risk of a large negative attribution from a single name. If the number is too high, institutional mediocrity can come into play. A right balance needs to be achieved for optimum results. Turnover is also important for tax sensitivity of the portfolio. A high turnover indicates a lot of short-term holdings, which are taxed at the higher short-term capital gain tax rates.

The liquidity profile of the strategy is also a significant risk factor that needs to be monitored. One of the ways hedge funds are able to generate good absolute performance is by going into illiquid securities. Such investments need to be monitored closely to make sure that the liquidity provisions of the portfolio match the liquidity rights offered to investors, and that the manager can get out of certain investments if the investment rationale no longer holds. Understanding the amount of time

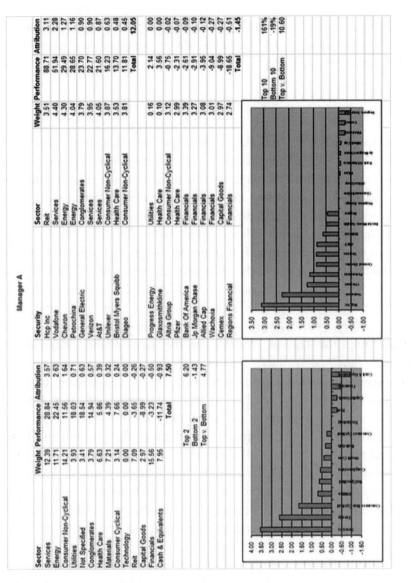

Figure 6: Manager Performance Attribution

it would take to get out of 90%, 95%, and 100% of the portfolio holdings are important data points to know in evaluating the liquidity profile of a fund. It makes sense to be conservative and increase the time periods to account for a liquidity dry-up during down periods when everybody wants to exit crowded trades.

4. Qualitative Analysis

Quantitative analysis is limited in its scope. Its reliance on past data decreases its predictive value for the future. Investors need to spend more time analyzing the firm, the fund, and the manager qualitatively, through a Socratic way of questioning and drilling down to get the answers they need to make a professional assessment about a manager.

The qualitative review should start with the firm history and history of the key individuals. It is important to search for good pedigree in evaluating the backgrounds of managers. One should look for a reputable school, and preferably the MBA/CFA designation in the educational backgrounds. It is also important that the managers have relevant professional backgrounds with experience in managing and implementing the current strategy in the past. Many hedge fund managers have good track records running traditional investments (long-only), but lack shorting experience. It is challenging to find managers that can consistently add alpha through their short books, as markets go up over time and a majority of the securities rise in price. However, a skilled manager can make money in both the long book and the short book in all markets. Hedge fund managers require extra resources to manage their funds than long-only investors due to higher exposures, higher turnover, and a higher demand to keep the volatility and correlations low; hence it is extremely valuable to find a manager who has a deep experience in running a successful hedge fund in his resume.

The ownership and compensation structures should be evaluated to make sure that the key employees are incentivized for long-term strategic contribution and success. It is vital that everybody has a vested interest (i.e. equity) in the success of the firm and that the interests of the firm are aligned with interests of the individuals working for the firm.

The succession process is equally important. To achieve a continuity of the firm, succession plans have to be evaluated. This is a challenge for most hedge funds, as most of them rely on one or two key individuals. Nonetheless, larger institutions with larger infrastructures can offer depth and breadth at the firm to accomplish a smooth transition if a key individual were no longer associated with the firm. On a related topic, it is quite valuable to assign ownership to the track record (individual vs. team) that was generated at the firm and compare it to the current management team at the firm. Stability of the business model must be evaluated before delving into the investment strategy.

If the management team truly believes in the attractiveness and soundness of the strategy, it invests a large portion of its liquid net worth in its own fund. This is always a good sign, although not an easy one to verify independently.

Summary of all assets under management by fund and strategy (since inception, taxable and non-taxable) is a good starting point in understanding the size and focus of the firm. One should look for a diverse group of investors, not just a few anchor investors that can cause instability if they are not satisfied with the investment results and/or have to pull money out for exogenous reasons.

The hedge fund universe, despite being a tiny fraction of the capital markets, is still capacity constrained, since most hedge funds seek to generate alpha through chasing after the short-term anomalies and inefficiencies that can exist in the markets for a short period of time. Hence, capacity analysis is a significant concern in evaluating hedge funds. Investors should seek and independently verify the capacity of each unique strategy. Hedge funds' closing their doors to outside (and sometimes existing) investors is often a positive sign that they would like to preserve the integrity of the strategy and returns. Discussing the past and current soft or hard closings of the fund can reveal important signals as to the willingness of the management to serve in the best interest of current investors by aligning the capacity in the fund with the capacity required to generate consistent absolute returns. If a manager is on a capital maximization routine, he or she can jeopardize the returns delivered to current investors. This is especially more applicable for the arbitrage strategies (i.e., convertible arbitrage) with higher capacity constraints. As a result, a careful evaluation of the marketing and business development goals is required.

The most important part of hedge fund due diligence pertains to the investment strategy. Investors must make sure that the strategy is clear, consistent, rational, repeatable, and disciplined. Many hedge fund blow-ups occur when portfolio managers stray off the reservation to areas that they are not perfectly familiar with, in an attempt to generate higher returns. This often leads to mistakes and portfolio losses. The investment strategy has to be one that is proven and durable, and accompanied by deep research.

The manager needs to be articulate in explaining the portfolio positions from sourcing to final implementation. Having same or similar sources to everybody else's can lead to market-like returns. Likewise, if the process is the same top-down or bottom-up process that everybody else uses, mediocrity is unavoidable. The manager needs to possess unique insights in finding, vetting, and implementing investment ideas.

If the investment strategy is dictated by an individual, it can be more efficient to implement the investment insights, but at the same time it can lack the benefits of team management when it comes to playing off certain ideas across a group or carving out the portfolio to different individuals. There is no consensus view as to whether the star hedge fund manager system or the multi-manager approach is superior. Having multiple offices as opposed to a single office containing all of the portfolio managers and the analysts is also important to evaluate in terms of the efficiency of communication between the investment professionals.

After the evaluation of the investment strategy, one must evaluate whether the strategy makes sense in the current environment. Investment styles can go in and out of favor. By way of example, market neutral managers thrive on volatility, hence a low volatility environment does not bode well for the market neutral space. Likewise, global macro strategies struggle in directionless markets. The team and the process could be outstanding, but the wind also has to be blowing in the right direction to achieve good hedge fund performance. All economic environments need to be evaluated to assess how the strategy would perform under various scenarios, and an assessment needs to be made to assign probability-based outcomes to each scenario. An essential element of the market environment analysis is to judge how the manager would act and react if the current thesis is wrong and certain exogenous events shock the system to create market stress. The manager's responses to the stress period questions are much more important than any quantitative analysis that can stress test the portfolio for past events.

If the strategy is a fundamentally driven one, valuation techniques used to calculate intrinsic value of a company or a security is of high essence. Most analysts use (in one shape or form) the same discounted cash flow (DCF) or relative valuation (P/E) model. Having good modeling skills with the ability to adjust the model for an infinite number of exceptions is required. Hedge fund managers are often viewed as information processing units, and need to hold an edge in obtaining and processing data accurately and efficiently before the competition and the media jumps on the same bandwagon. This is how true alpha can be generated.

Trade examples often provide a distinctive angle into understanding how a manager thinks. Discussions surrounding dozens of long and short ideas can provide immense benefits in the due diligence process. One must look for a consistent, rational, and convincing investment thesis on each and every portfolio holding examined. One must not get too carried away with the manager's intimate knowledge base into a company or a sector though, as it can lead to overconfidence, which is one of the primary psychological biases in the investment world.

The risk management process is as important as the investment process. Hedge funds are not return maximization vehicles, they are risk optimization vehicles. As such, risk management carries a heavier weight for hedge fund managers than the traditional equity or fixed income managers. Investors should go through the list of quantitative risk measures discussed previously, in a qualitative fashion. For example, ask a manager to define, measure, and evaluate risk. Make sure that he thinks of risk in the same terms that you do. Go through all of the past examples of significant drawdowns, evaluate the macro environment that existed in each of the periods, what the investment rationale was, how the risk was mitigated, and whether there is a high likelihood of a repeat scenario. Watch for signs of excessive risk taking (relative to expectations) and style drift. If the statistical measures show a high fat tail risk (high negative skew), ask the manager why that is, and assess whether the data point is an outlier and should be thrown out, or a red flag for future losses that should be examined more closely.

Sell discipline is as important as the buy discipline. Most investment mistakes are committed not because a bad buy decision was made, but rather the winners were kept in the portfolio for too long. Past investors often reap the benefits of the past gains, but the current investors who may have chased those great past results can get stuck with the past winners turning into current losers. The manager has to have a sell discipline that makes sense and is applied consistently. Unfortunately, the hedge fund world is an opaque one with lack of transparency. Investors should ask and receive independent portfolio reports directly from the prime brokers, as most reports provided by the managers will be biased, showing only the positive results.

Another area where the quantitative process has to be evaluated in conjunction with the qualitative process is portfolio concentration. A Socratic questioning method could reveal a love for a certain sector or industry that can lead to a large concentration in the area, even though past concentration is not evident in the statistics. This may be okay with certain investors that seek outsized returns, but not so much with others who look for absolute and consistent returns with low volatility and low beta. Willingness to time the market and raise cash levels can also raise a risk factor; the number of managers that can time the markets consistently is extremely small. Global macro managers can move from one bet on an asset class (long or short) to another fairly quickly, but market timing is almost impossible to achieve. Therefore, close attention has to be paid to the ability of the manager to drive value from market and sector bets. Hedge fund managers are heavy users of derivatives (i.e., options and futures) to hedge the portfolio against market, sector, and industry risk. The evaluation for portfolio construction has to net out the derivative position against the portfolio positions to reveal the true exposures in the portfolio.

Hedge funds are leveraged vehicles. The leveraging and the de-leveraging processes must be assessed qualitatively to test its soundness and proven quantitatively. Leverage is not a static figure; it changes daily as the underlying value of the portfolio securities move with the markets. A skilled manager should be able to add leverage dynamically in up trends and scale it down as a risk management function during market corrections.

The same performance analysis and performance evaluation analyses evaluated during the quantitative analysis should be reviewed with the manager qualitatively to verify the facts and get a sense as to the ability of the manager to spread the bets across many sectors. I would again assign a heavier weight on the future expected tendencies of the manager rather than the past success. Constantly challenging the portfolio manager and reviewing his thinking can expose reason for future success or grounds to be concerned.

Lastly, the qualitative process can uncover several conflicts of interest, actual or potential, that could conceivably affect the investors adversely. Existence of an internal broker-dealer, an auditor that is a related party, self administration of the fund, certain Wall Street relationships, and engagement in an unrelated business are all valid reasons not to invest in a hedge fund manager. Scrupulous operational due diligence meetings can help uncover some of these red flags.

Key findings of the qualitative due diligence process can be summarized in a table format based on a relative scoring system for an easy review, and updated periodically (**Table 2**).

Table 2: Qualitative Due Diligence Analysis

Factor Evaluation Model

(5-best, 1-worst)	Fund A	Fund B	Fund C	Fund D	Fund E	Fund F	Fund G	Fund H	Fund I
Qualitative - Part I									
Pedigree	4	5	3	4	3	3	3	4	3
Investment Process	4	4	4	4	3	3	4	4	4
Research	3	5	3	4	3	4	4	4	3
Risk Management	2	4	3	4	3	2	3	3	3
Trading	3	4	3	3	3	4	4	4	4
Infrastructure	4	5	4	4	3	3	5	4	3
Fat-tail Risk	3	5	4	3	4	3	3	2	4
Current Appeal	3	5	5	3	4	3	4	4	4
Capacity	3	5	4	3	3	3	5	4	4
Business Model	2	4	4	3	5	4	4	4	4
Conflicts of Interest	5	5	5	4	5	5	5	4	5

5. Operational Review

It is commonly reported that more than half of the hedge fund failures occur due to non-investment reasons, hence operational due diligence takes on great importance. The operational evaluation starts with a review of the operational team, compliance team, processes in place, and key responsibilities. The goal is to assess whether the hedge fund has adequate infrastructure to support the execution of the investment strategy accurately, successfully and consistently. A thorough review of the independent compliance procedures and the firm's adherence to them is also important. A close examination of the systems used for accounting, portfolio management, trading, compliance and risk management is warranted. The quality of the service providers needs to be studied for any potential weak links as well (**Table 3**). Ideally, one

Table 3: Sample Hedge Fund Service Providers

Fund name	SMA/ HF	Prime Broker	Administrator	Auditor	Accountant	Legal Counsel
Fund A	SMA	UBS Securities	Rothstein, Kass & Co.	Rothstein, Kass & Co.	Rothstein, Kass & Co.	Cobb & Eisenberg
Fund B	SMA	Morgan Stanley	CACEIS	Deloitte & Touche	BDO Seidman	Shartsis, Freise, & Ginsburg
Fund C	SMA	Deutsche Bank	HSBC	PriceWaterhouseCoopers	BDO Seidman	Shartsis, Freise, & Ginsburg
Fund D	HF	Goldman Sachs	Bisys	BDO Seidman	BDO Seidman	Kramer Levin Naftalis & Frankel
Fund E	SMA	Deutsche Bank	Insinger de Beaufort	PriceWaterhouseCoopers	Anchin, Block & Anchin	Cadwalader, Wickersham & Taft
Fund F	HF	BNP Paribas	SS&C	KPMG	Weinick Sanders Leventhal	Dennis Rooker
Fund G	HF	Bank of America	Fortis	Eisner LLP	Owens & Peeler	Dennis Rooker
Fund H	SMA	JP Morgan	Cogent	Rothstein, Kass & Co.	Rothstein, Kass & Co.	Seward & Kissel
Fund I	HF	Goldman Sachs	Cohen & Assoc.	KPMG	BDO Seidman	Seward & Kissel
Fund J	HF	Goldman/ Morgan	Eisner LLP	Eisner LLP	Eisner LLP	Seward & Kissel
Fund K	SMA	Morgan Stanley	Citco	Rothstein, Kass & Co.	Rothstein, Kass & Co.	Cadwalader, Wickersham & Taft
Fund L	SMA	Goldman Sachs	IFS	Ernst & Young	Rothstein, Kass & Co.	Cadwalader, Wickersham & Taft

would like to see a service provider list containing experienced and resourceful firms. Selecting the largest provider does not always lead to the best results though, as smaller hedge funds can receive lackluster service from the big firms. Quality of service, timeliness of service, and accuracy of service, all need to be evaluated in parallel to find a provider that can provide the right level of services demanded by the unique needs of each manager.

Understanding how a hedge fund initiates money transfers is critical. The due diligence person needs to understand exactly how the money transfers occur. One must see to it that there are at least two independent sources at the hedge fund administrator that have to sign off on any money transfers into and out of the master hedge fund account. Hedge fund fraud, unfortunately, is a somewhat common phenomenon. Much of the fraud can be avoided if one can track how money transfers occur closely and make sure that there are several levels of independent checks and authorizations before any money can be transferred across accounts. The investigation needs to be much deeper if the hedge fund manager has accounts with several prime brokers.

One of the most important aspects of operational due diligence is a review of the execution efficiency and minimization of transaction costs. Hedge funds usually have high turnover, which leads to higher fees that must be taken out of potential gains before the gains can be passed on to the investors. One must look for a cost ratio that is below average for the strategy. The following questions can help address the execution efficiency:

- *What is the time of day that trades are generally executed?*
- *What are the slippage costs?*
- *What are the interest costs?*
- *What are the clearing costs (ticket charges, etc.)?*
- *What are the annual commission costs as a percentage of assets?*
- *What are the all-in trading costs as a percentage of assets?*
- *What is the execution method associated with your strategy (floor, electronic)?*
- *Who executes the trades (portfolio manager, broker order desk)?*
- *Do you place limit or market orders (or both)?*

Most hedge fund managers (as well as long-only managers) receive investment research from various 3rd party providers, paid with soft dollars. There has been a tendency to begin to pay for research with hard dollars, but it is far from becoming a major trend. Until that time, the due diligence process needs to uncover the ability of each hedge fund manager to meet both the requirements and recommendations of the CFA Institute's Soft Dollar Standards.

The ability to deal with dramatic inflows and outflows is also critical to the implementation of the strategy. If the new money is invested too fast, it can lead to unnecessary risk, but if it is invested too slowly, it can become a drag on performance. Staging in and phasing out is often the preferred method. Investors need to receive frequent communication from the hedge fund managers regarding any significant capital contributions or redemptions, as it may impact the ability of the manager to run the business and the strategy successfully.

If the manager runs several funds and separately managed accounts (SMAs), the allocation policies are important to review for fairness purposes. No investor should be rewarded or penalized for someone else's actions. All investors should receive simultaneous and pro-rata allocations for all investments. I am not a big fan of side pocket arrangements, where illiquid investments are hidden in secret buckets. I am all for complete transparency.

Many institutional investors have been demanding separately managed accounts (SMAs) from the hedge fund managers for transparency reasons, which may put resource pressures on the firm. If the manager is willing to entertain SMAs, the firm must also have matching resources to accommodate additional needs of running and maintaining an SMA. Every hedge fund needs accurate and timely recording and reconciliation of trades. Proxy votes have to be completed in a timely fashion and voted in the best interest of shareholders. Company reorganizations and other corporate actions have to be appropriately reflected in the financial books and records. Participation in class action lawsuits (when needed) also consume resources of hedge funds. If these services are not outsourced, the operational team needs to dedicate enough resources to assure that the manager acts in the best interest of the investors. If a mistake is discovered, the client should be made whole, and the financial loss should be covered by the management company.

A potential investor should learn the standard terms for all classes of the hedge fund (minimum investment size, lock-up, redemption rights, flood gates, management fee, incentive fee, operating fees, penalties, etc.), as well as the best terms offered to any investor, including the separately managed accounts. Every investor should understand the exact terms and how they are applied before making an investment into the fund. If special terms are offered to certain investor(s), it should be made available to all investors. Most hedge fund managers try to avoid cannibalizing their business by offering advantageous terms to certain investors, as it would force them to violate a potential Most Favored Nation (MFN) clause in future prospects who may demand to receive most favored terms. However, as it is often the case, early seed investors who provide venture capital can get better terms than the investors that come in after the development phase of the hedge fund. Again, complete transparency is warranted.

The frequency and the form of portfolio transparency provided to investors is also of high importance. Managers unequivocally will publish only the good trades, reasonable exposures, and strong risk management characteristics in the standard pitch books. However, one should ask for and obtain full transparency to prove that the marketing materials match the reality. Granted, the best managers with the highest returns will not provide transparency (even after a non-disclosure agreement), as they would want to stay exclusive and not reveal their trade secrets. This may cause a negative selection bias when selecting hedge fund managers. It is also debatable that the investors know how to effectively analyze complex trade books. Nonetheless, more transparency is always better than less transparency and therefore the right balance has to be achieved for optimum results.

A good understanding of the pricing policies and valuation techniques used by hedge funds and their administrators are vital in putting the monthly returns into perspective. A perfectly smooth month-to-month return distribution for a fixed income arbitrage hedge fund manager may indicate that certain investments are carried at cost and/or only the interest portion of the total return is reflected. An independent verification of the portfolio values needs to be conducted as a check of the pricing policies used by hedge fund managers. Many administrators give the hedge fund managers leeway in pricing certain illiquid securities that do not have a public price (in Bloomberg, Reuters, IDC/FT Interactive, and other price vendors) at a price that is subjective and open to manipulation. Self-pricing of securities and funds is a major compromise of independence and objectivity. One should examine and test the prices used to calculate the net asset value (NAV) for the fund vigilantly. Special attention needs to be paid to IPOs, hot issues, and restricted securities, if the fund invests in such securities, for a consistent and logical pricing method.

Service requirements should be evaluated to make sure that the hedge fund is willing and capable of meeting the expectations. A timely and proactive client service always achieves a high score among investors. Providing prompt performance reporting and thoughtful investment letters is an absolute minimum. Look for consistency in performance reporting (i.e., past revisions) and dig deeper into performance deviations that are beyond the historical averages or beyond the expected range of returns. Read the investment letters carefully to analyze the thought process and investment rationale behind the portfolio positioning. Evaluate whether the frequency and the depth of the client mailings are sufficient to meet your unique needs. Too frequent, or infrequent mailings, are both suspects. Too much detail and too little detail can also be suspicious, as they could be signs for hiding certain information from investors.

Hedge funds are known to have delayed tax reporting (K-1s) due to the esoteric nature of the portfolio securities. Observation of a timely and accurate tax report (as well as a final audit) is also a big plus in the due diligence process. The hedge fund must be willing and capable of responding to special requests demanded by investors, as unique needs can differ from investor to investor. By way of example, an evaluation of how a hedge fund manager can respond to a change of entity request, a change of Tax ID request, or an evaluation of the delivery method of the Form ADV can lead to a good understanding of the manager's ability to meet unique needs of an investor.

Internal policies with respect to employees' trading for their own account should also be examined on fairness grounds. Front running trades (filling in orders for own account before clients' accounts) is not legal and should not be allowed under any circumstance, as it can lead to price manipulation.

Disaster preparedness is another hot topic that is covered under the operational due diligence. Not only do the managers need to have a comprehensive plan in place to guard against disasters, but it also has to be tested periodically to make sure that it can be implemented in case of a disaster. Back-up procedures, remote office locations, and sharing of all critical contact information across all employees are all critical elements of the disaster preparedness program.

Finally, any complaints, litigations, or enforcement actions outstanding against the firm, affiliates, or investment professionals (current and past five years) need to be investigated to reveal insights about the character of each manager. Investors often use an outside third-party firm to help with the background investigations.

6. Background And Reference Checks

Kroll, First Advantage-Backtrack Reports, and CheckFundManager are three of an increasing number of firms that provide background checks on hedge fund managers. The items that are researched include:

- *Corporate Records*
- *Bankruptcy Records*
- *Criminal History (Federal, state, county)*
- *Civil Litigation History (Federal, county)*
- *Financial Institutions Sanctions (SEC, NASD, NFA, DOL)*
- *Education Verification*
- *Media Sources (Newspaper, Periodical, Online)*
- *Online Public Records*
- *Professional License Verification*
- *Social Security Number Trace*
- *Federal and State Tax Liens*

Several databases and data sources are checked to obtain any and all information about the firm and the key professionals working at the firm. The cost of a full background report can range anywhere from a couple of thousand dollars to ten-fifteen thousand dollars, depending on the depth of the research and how many human hours go into searching, processing, and reporting the data. There are certain red flags to look for in the background reports: lack of verification of educational and professional experience, gaps in the resume, regulatory violations or censures. It is necessary to update the background reports at least annually to capture any changes in the facts surrounding a firm or an individual. A sample background check report can be found in **Appendix 3**.

Equally important are reference checks. The investors should talk to former co-workers, former supervisors, former business partners, former and current investors, former and current service providers and former college professors. It is important to note that the reference lists provided by the hedge fund managers are heavily biased to include only those individuals who are likely to say only positive things about the manager. Therefore, it is critical to identify references independently through professional networks. While the background check can be more efficiently and accurately accomplished through an outside party, it is valuable to conduct the reference checks internally to draw connections to the quantitative and qualitative due diligence that have been conducted prior to reference checks. Sample questions to ask references include:

- *What is your current and former relationship to the manager?*
- *Do you currently have any financial or non-financial arrange-ments with the manager?*
- *How long have you known the manager?*
- *Could you describe the manager's positive and negative attributes?*
- *What are some of the areas that (s)he can improve upon?*
- *What are your expectations from the manager? Did (s)he meet those expectations?*
- *How closely do you monitor the manager's strategy and per-formance results? How do they compare to your expectations?*

- *What can you tell me about his/her business management, portfolio management, and risk management skills?*
- *How would you rank the manager on a relative basis, compared to other hedge fund managers that run similar strategies?*
- *How risk averse do you think is the manager? How does (s)he manage the investment and operational risks?*
- *If you had two recommendations for the manager, what would they be?*

Although not frequently used, a credit report can also reveal noteworthy information about the firm and the managers. A small sized firm needs enough capital resources to sustain the day to day running of the firm; a credit report would provide details about the finances of a firm, albeit on a limited scale. One would need a signed release form in order to obtain a credit report.

7. Ongoing Due Diligence

After an overview of all of the facts and analyses conducted on a hedge fund manager, a judgment needs to be made on the manager. As stated in the very first paragraph of this chapter, the ultimate goal of the due diligence process is to separate skill from luck, true alpha from market beta, and manager talent from market timing. If a decision is made to hire the manager, the due diligence process does not stop there. In fact, ongoing due diligence is as important as the initial due diligence.

All of the quantitative and qualitative processes need to be updated and examined frequently as market conditions change on a daily basis. One cannot sit back comfortably with a false assumption that the homework is done and the manager is approved indefinitely. Several important factors need to be monitored very closely. On a quantitative basis, changing correlations to equity, fixed income, and alternative markets, consistency of returns, and attribution of performance should be tracked and analyzed to re-assure that the initial reasons for the hire are still intact. On a qualitative basis, capacity to grow, personnel turnover, and service quality are important factors to keep a close eye on. Daily trade activities, monthly strategy reviews, frequent conference calls and on-site visits to review firm level, investment-related, and operational concerns are highlights of ongoing due diligence.

Hedge fund due diligence is more of an art than a science. There is no magical formula that can separate good managers from bad managers. Past success does not translate into future success. Through a comprehensive and exhaustive analysis of all of the information gathered during the due diligence process, one can minimize the chances of picking a rotten apple. Using quantitative information to verify qualitative information and vice versa, valuable judgment can be exercised on various managers. Hedge funds are risk reduction vehicles through execution of absolute-return oriented strategies, however, the inherent risk in the portfolio may not always be glaring at an investor through the standard risk measures reported on monthly statements. A proven track record of making money, capability to manage business, investment, and operational risk through different market environments, and maturity to grow the business successfully are key attributes to look for in successful hedge fund managers.

Hedge Fund Alpha Tear Sheet — Chapter 13

- The goal of the due diligence process ultimately is to separate skill from luck, true alpha from market beta, and manager talent from market timing.
- The hedge fund due diligence process starts with sourcing of managers.
  - Managers may be discovered through databases, industry contacts, and peer referrals.
- Rigorous quantitative due diligence includes an analysis of past risk adjusted returns on a rolling basis, upside to downside capture, stress testing, liquidity, rolling correlations, and peer group.
- Qualitative analysis is often conducted in Socratic fashion and should examine in detail, firm history, its key employees and their investment in the fund, succession planning, operations, compliance, and service providers.
- The most important part of hedge fund due diligence pertains to the investment strategy.
  - Investors must make sure that the strategy is clear, consistent, rational, repeatable, and disciplined with strong risk management controls.
- A potential investor should learn about the standard terms for all classes of the hedge fund (i.e. minimum investment size, lock-up, redemption rights, flood gates, management fee, incentive fee, operating fees, penalties, etc.), as well as the best terms offered to any investor, including for corresponding separately managed accounts.
- Background checks should include reference checks, credit reports, regulatory complaints, and litigation history against the firm, its affiliates, and investment professionals.
- Ongoing due diligence, like the initial process, should include both quantitative and qualitative analyses:
  - Performance attribution should be tracked and analyzed to re-assure that the initial reasons for the hire are still intact.
  - On a qualitative basis, capacity to grow, personnel turnover, and service quality should be emphasized.
  - Daily trade activities, monthly strategy reviews, frequent conference calls and on-site visits comprise additional ongoing due diligence techniques.

14

FROM BIRTH TO DEATH: THE LIFECYCLE OF A HEDGE FUND INVESTMENT STRATEGY

John M. Longo, PhD, CFA and Yaxuan Qi, PhD

Rutgers Business School & The MDE Group; Concordia University

1. Introduction

With the average length of a hedge fund lasting only three years, it is almost axiomatic that alpha is fleeting or unstable. Regardless of pedigree — new, old, high profile, low profile — many funds simply go out of business due to the failure of their ability to generate and sustain alpha.

The spectacular flameouts of Long Term Capital and Amaranth gain most of the popular press' attention, but the case of Ron Insana's fund of hedge funds is more typical. On the surface, his fund, Insana Capital Partners, had a number of advantages — a well-known principal, access to "closed" hedge funds run by star managers, and a strong corporate partner in Deutsche Bank. According to Ross Sorkin (2008), the fund shut down after one year of operation, losing five percent of its capital. A five percent loss is not a disaster, but also not sufficient to support the institutional-like infrastructure set up by the firm.

The purpose of this chapter is to analyze the sustainability of alpha in various well-known strategies, modified to generate hedge fund-like returns. It is problematic to obtain the returns of actual hedge funds, due to SEC anti-advertising laws, but we believe the discussion on the published strategies applies to the private strategies as well. The three well-known strategies that we will analyze are the Small Firm Anomaly, Momentum Anomaly and Accrual Anomaly. These strategies are adjusted to include a hedged component in order to make them better comparable to traditional hedge fund strategies.

Some hedge funds have no sustainable alpha from inception and will ultimately go out of business due to the lack of an effective investment strategy. However, many hedge funds have sound strategies but run the risk of going out of business due to the cyclical nature of the effectiveness of their strategies. In our view, this is the major factor resulting in the demise of hedge funds. Cycles are driven by a number of factors including increased competition, investor psychology, and economic fundamentals.

2. Theoretical Change in Alpha over Time

Alpha can be "born" in a number of ways. Often a trader will observe a particular investment pattern in the market and then incubate it with a small amount of capital, gradually scaled up over time. In other cases, quantitative traders will run a number of data mining algorithms and select those strategies that have superior historical risk adjusted returns *and* a logical explanation. Many positive alpha hedge funds are created by former analysts of successful funds who spin out to create their own funds, often with the insight that generated the alpha of the parent funds.

In theory, if a hedge fund does have a viable alpha generating strategy, its effectiveness should gradually diminish over time. The alpha opportunity can simply be arbitraged away due to the success of the fund's strategy or disappear due to competition following a similar strategy. **Figure 1** shows the theoretical change in alpha over time for a successful hedge fund, starting at a very high level (e.g. 20% per year) and then virtually disappearing over time, after the inclusion of fees and transaction costs. By year three, alpha is greatly diminished and by year ten, it is statistically insignificant, after deducting 2/20 fees and expenses. Combining this theoretical diminution of alpha for a strategy that actually works with one that never had any value, gets us in the ballpark of the three-year life span for the average hedge fund.

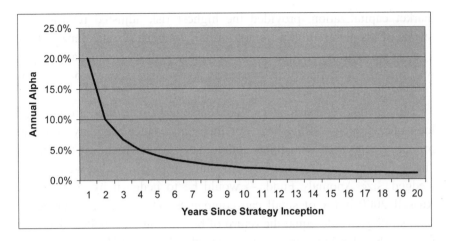

Figure 1: Theoretical Change in Alpha Over Time

In practice, the path of a strategy's alpha is rarely so smooth, resulting in difficulty in assessing the effectiveness of a hedge fund strategy. In other words, it is very difficult to answer the question that managers continually ask themselves, "Is my strategy no longer working or is it simply out of favor?" To better answer this question, it will help to analyze the performance of some actual investment strategies.

3. Alpha Behavior of the Size Anomaly

The Center for Research in Security Prices (CRSP) at the University of Chicago was created in 1960, with support from Merrill Lynch & Co, Inc. The center was directed by Professors James Lorie and Lawrence Fisher and produced the first comprehensive electronic database of stock prices. CRSP produces databases that contain monthly returns on NYSE stocks from 1926 and daily returns for most U.S. stocks since 1972. Accordingly, the CRSP databases have been the source of many doctoral dissertations worldwide.

One of the first significant stock market anomalies was uncovered in 1978 by Rolf Banz, fittingly then a doctoral student at the University of Chicago. Banz found that the decile of small stocks, as measured by market capitalization, provided the highest risk adjusted returns. The results of his dissertation were not formally published until Banz (1981). The excess returns, or alpha to this anomaly persists to this day, despite widespread knowledge of its existence. As we shall see, the path of this alpha is not continuous.

Most hedge fund managers would have a difficult time promoting a long only strategy as the basis for their fund, since their investors are primarily concerned with alpha, and not beta. An obvious way to create a "hedged" portfolio from the Size Anomaly strategy — what we term the Hedged Size Anomaly Fund — would be to hedge it by shorting the Russell 2000 index of small cap companies. The return for our hedge fund strategy would equal the return of being long the smallest decile of firms in the CRSP universe, selling short the Russell 2000 and adding the rebate from the short sales. We use the returns of the 30-Day Treasury Bill to approximate the rebate received from the short sales.

We begin the hypothetical Hedged Size Anomaly Fund in 1981, the year it was first published and end it in 2005, the last year we had readily available data. The hypothetical fund earned a compound 8.8% annual gross rate of return and a 4.6% return, net of 2/20 fees and expenses with a highwater mark. Since the portfolio has a beta close to zero, it is likely a hedge fund manager would utilize leverage to further enhance returns. For example, many fixed income arbitrage strategies employ leverage of more than 20:1 in order to monetize small spreads between two sets of bonds. Equity hedges, such as the one utilized in our example, are less precise in nature and typically employ leverage ratios of less than 10:1. The results of the Hedged Size Anomaly Fund are shown in **Table 1**.

The viability of most hedge funds is threatened if they have a single year of double-digit losses or two consecutive years of losses of any magnitude. A double-digit loss may signal the failure of the fund's risk management process. Two consecutive down years increase the likelihood of fund redemptions and may make any marketing efforts futile. Investor perception remains that hedge funds should earn positive returns regardless of the market environment. In **Table 1**, these "at risk" periods for the fund are highlighted. Therefore, even though the overall returns of the Hedged Size Anomaly Fund are reasonably good over the

Table 1: Performance of Hypothetical Hedged Size Anomaly Fund

Year	Gross %	Gross $	Net %	Net $
1981	11.79%	$ 1.12	7.65%	$ 1.08
1982	11.71%	$ 1.25	7.58%	$ 1.16
1983	22.69%	$ 1.53	16.19%	$ 1.35
1984	-1.63%	$ 1.51	-3.59%	$ 1.30
1985	-2.55%	$ 1.47	-4.50%	$ 1.24
1986	3.52%	$ 1.52	1.45%	$ 1.26
1987	0.92%	$ 1.53	-1.10%	$ 1.24
1988	-0.06%	$ 1.53	-2.06%	$ 1.22
1989	-2.01%	$ 1.50	-3.97%	$ 1.17
1990	-2.18%	$ 1.47	-4.14%	$ 1.12
1991	15.23%	$ 1.69	12.93%	$ 1.27
1992	24.56%	$ 2.11	12.59%	$ 1.42
1993	18.10%	$ 2.49	12.59%	$ 1.60
1994	0.10%	$ 2.49	-1.90%	$ 1.57
1995	7.68%	$ 2.69	4.42%	$ 1.64
1996	6.26%	$ 2.85	3.31%	$ 1.70
1997	0.97%	$ 2.88	-1.05%	$ 1.68
1998	-2.73%	$ 2.80	-4.68%	$ 1.60
1999	22.65%	$ 3.44	11.34%	$ 1.78
2000	-6.47%	$ 3.22	-8.34%	$ 1.63
2001	40.82%	$ 4.53	23.13%	$ 2.01
2002	23.15%	$ 5.58	16.55%	$ 2.35
2003	41.80%	$ 7.91	31.17%	$ 3.08
2004	6.55%	$ 8.42	3.53%	$ 3.18
2005	-1.77%	$ 8.27	-3.74%	$ 3.07
Average	9.56%		5.01%	
CAGR	8.82%		4.58%	

Note: We assume a starting investment value of $1. Portfolio returns are calculated as returns of the smallest decile size portfolio minus the returns of the Russell 2000 index plus the returns of the 30-Day T-Bill. Returns of the smallest decile portfolio are equal weighted and obtained from http://mba.tuck.dartmouth.edu/pages/faculty/ken.french/

entire length of the period, there are several periods that may have resulted in the "death" of the fund. Specifically, it experienced mediocre returns over the entire 1984-1990 period. The fund would surely have gone out of business during some point of this *seven-year* stretch, despite the absence of a double-digit loss in any single year. The cyclical nature of the alpha for the Hedged Size Anomaly Fund is shown in **Figure 2**.

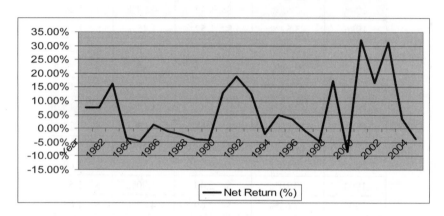

Figure 2: Return Over Time For Hedged Size Anomaly Fund

4. Alpha Behavior of the Momentum Anomaly

The momentum approach to investing is still widely utilized by many short-term traders across almost all hedge fund strategies. In brief, the strategy follows a "trend is your friend" philosophy, buying securities after they rise and shorting them after they fall. The strategy has been known on Wall Street since at least the early 1960s after the work of Donchian (1960) and Alexander (1961). Jegadeesh and Titman (1993) conducted one of the first comprehensive studies of the momentum strategy, using modern statistical techniques, and documented its superior risk adjusted returns.

As with the prior Size Anomaly, we will modify the long only momentum strategy to include a hedge. Since momentum securities are often affiliated with growth stocks, we will hedge it by shorting the

Russell 1000 Growth index. So the return for our newly created Hedged Momentum Anomaly Fund would be obtained from the return of being long the top decile momentum portfolio of the firms in the CRSP universe, selling short the Russell 1000 Growth index and adding the rebate from the short sales. Once again, we use the returns of the 30-Day T-Bill to approximate the rebate received from the short sales. The results of the Hedged Momentum Anomaly Fund are shown in **Table 2**.

Table 2: Performance of Hypothetical Hedged Momentum Anomaly Fund

Year	Gross %	Gross $	Net %	Net $
1993	41.81%	$ 1.42	31.18%	$ 1.31
1994	-2.93%	$ 1.38	-4.87%	$ 1.25
1995	13.02%	$ 1.56	8.61%	$ 1.36
1996	2.90%	$ 1.60	0.67%	$ 1.36
1997	1.48%	$ 1.62	-0.55%	$ 1.36
1998	-14.05%	$ 1.40	-15.76%	$ 1.14
1999	41.40%	$ 1.97	15.37%	$ 1.32
2000	27.55%	$ 2.52	20.00%	$ 1.58
2001	60.81%	$ 4.05	46.08%	$ 2.31
2002	22.69%	$ 4.97	16.19%	$ 2.69
2003	58.16%	$ 7.86	44.00%	$ 3.87
2004	18.27%	$ 9.30	12.72%	$ 4.36
2005	12.41%	$ 10.45	8.13%	$ 4.71
Average	21.81%		13.98%	
CAGR	19.78%		12.67%	

Note: We assume a starting investment value of $1. Portfolio returns are calculated as the returns of the momentum portfolio minus the returns of the Russell 1000 Growth index, plus the returns of the 30-Day T-Bill. Please refer to Jagadeesh and Titman (1993) for detailed methodology related to the construction of the momentum portfolio.

We begin the hypothetical Hedged Momentum Anomaly Fund in 1993, the publication year of Jegadeesh and Titman (1993), and end it in 2005, the last year we had readily available data. The hypothetical fund earned a compound 19.8% annual gross rate of return and a 14.0%

return, net of 2/20 fees and expenses with a highwater mark. Although the hedge is imprecise (i.e. value weighted Large Cap Growth vs. equal weighted momentum securities), a modest level of leverage would be used by most hedge fund managers running a similar strategy in order to further enhance returns.

The annual returns for the Momentum Anomaly are much larger than those of the Size Anomaly. As discussed previously, the viability of most hedge funds is threatened if they have a single year of double-digit losses or two consecutive years of losses of any magnitude. The shaded region of **Table 2** indicates a likely period of significant distress for the fund management company. Despite its very strong long-term performance, the Hedged Momentum Anomaly Fund experienced a double-digit loss of more than 14% in 1998. To make matters worse, the S&P 500 was up 28.6% and the Russell 1000 Growth was up 38.7% in the same year. The principals of this hypothetical fund would have had a lot of explaining to do in order to avoid having their business implode during this time period. The cyclical nature of the alpha for the Hedged Size Anomaly Fund is shown in **Figure 3**.

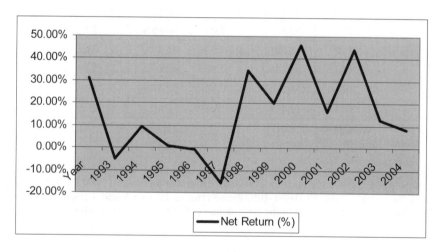

Figure 3: Return Over Time For Hedged Momentum Anomaly Fund

5. Alpha Behavior of the Accrual Anomaly

Hedge fund managers that rely on Fundamental Analysis often search for leading indicators of deteriorating earnings. Shorting a company after a poor earnings report is in many cases too late to earn substantial alpha. For many years analysts have looked at changes in balance sheet and income statement items as leading indicators of earnings quality. For example, if a firm has a sharp increase in inventory versus the same period the prior year, it may indicate that the company is having a problem selling its product and on the verge of an earnings warning. Similarly, if a company has a large rise in its allowance for doubtful accounts it may indicate a future earnings shortfall due to a weak customer base. The accrual anomaly, popularized by Sloan (1996), is one of the most common metrics on earnings quality and is widely followed by analysts today. Poor earnings quality often manifests itself in a divergence between earnings, an accounting construct, and actual cash flow generated by the business. High accruals often indicate that a company has to stretch to meet its earnings numbers at best, and playing games with the numbers at worst.

Following Sloan (1996), we create a hedged portfolio by buying a portfolio of low accrual firms and selling short a similar sized basket of high accruals firms. We begin the hypothetical Accrual Anomaly Fund in 1996, the publication year of Sloan (1996), and end it in 2005, the last year we had readily available data. The hypothetical fund earned a compound 12.9% annual gross rate of return and a 8.5% return, net of 2/20 fees and expenses with a highwater mark. The results are shown in **Table 3**.

As with the other two strategies we examined, the overall returns are strong, but there are periods of time that would result in significant distress for the hedge fund management company. These periods are highlighted with shading in **Table 3**. Leverage would likely be utilized in order to further enhance returns over the long-term. The cyclical nature of the alpha for the Accrual Anomaly Fund is shown in **Figure 4**.

Table 3: Performance of Hypothetical Accrual Anomaly Fund

2% / 20%

Year	Gross %	Gross $	Net %	Net $
1996	-1.55%	$ 0.98	-3.52%	$ 0.96
1997	-17.47%	$ 0.81	-19.12%	$ 0.78
1998	-20.24%	$ 0.65	-21.84%	$ 0.61
1999	88.13%	$ 1.22	80.29%	$ 1.10
2000	-21.92%	$ 0.95	-23.48%	$ 0.84
2001	72.89%	$ 1.65	59.32%	$ 1.34
2002	-4.60%	$ 1.57	-6.51%	$ 1.25
2003	124.00%	$ 3.52	97.01%	$ 2.47
2004	5.22%	$ 3.70	2.49%	$ 2.53
2005	-8.95%	$ 3.37	-10.77%	$ 2.26
Average	**21.55%**		**15.39%**	
CAGR	**12.92%**		**8.49%**	

Note: We assume a starting investment value of $1. Returns for the accrual portfolio are calculated as the returns of the lowest decile's accrual portfolio (i.e. the portfolio with the best accounting quality) minus the returns the largest decile accrual portfolio (i.e. the portfolio with the poorest accounting quality) plus the returns of the 30 Day T-Bill. For detailed methodology with respect to the construction accrual portfolios and the measure of accounting quality please refer to Francis, LaFond, Olsson, and Schipper (2005).

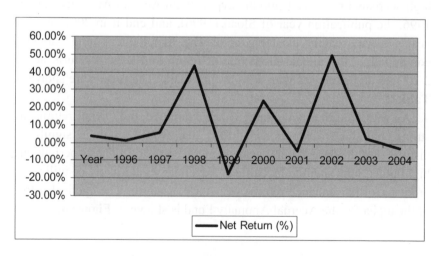

Figure 4: Return Over Time For Accrual Anomaly Fund

6. Extending The Lifecycle Through Diversification

Each of the three strategies that we examined had good long-term performance but had time periods when the viability of the fund would be seriously questioned. One way of extending the life cycle of the hedge fund management company is to diversify its overall performance through multiple funds or a single multistrategy fund. The pros and cons of each approach were discussed in Chapter 9.

Table 4 shows the results of an equally weighted portfolio of the three anomaly based funds that are the focus of this chapter — Hedged Size Anomaly Fund, Hedged Momentum Anomaly Fund, and the Accrual Anomaly Fund. For simplicity, we will call this aggregate portfolio the Multistrategy Anomaly Fund. As expected, the overall returns for this multistrategy fund are solid. The hypothetical fund earned a compound 15.8% annual gross rate of return and a 11.0% return, net of 2/20 fees and expenses with a highwater mark. The 1998 period remains the only period of notable distress, with a −4.4% net return, a

Table 4: Performance of Hypothetical Multistrategy Anomaly Fund

Year	Gross %	Gross $	Net %	Net $
1996	5.49%	$ 1.05	2.70%	$ 1.03
1997	2.01%	$ 1.08	-0.03%	$ 1.03
1998	-2.48%	$ 1.05	-4.43%	$ 0.98
1999	40.75%	$ 1.48	31.28%	$ 1.29
2000	1.79%	$ 1.50	-0.25%	$ 1.28
2001	43.06%	$ 2.15	32.21%	$ 1.70
2002	14.44%	$ 2.46	9.72%	$ 1.86
2003	54.75%	$ 3.81	41.32%	$ 2.63
2004	10.20%	$ 4.20	6.40%	$ 2.80
2005	3.32%	$ 4.34	1.00%	$ 2.83
Average	**17.33%**		**11.99%**	
CAGR	**15.80%**		**10.97%**	

Note: We assume a starting investment value of $1. Returns for the portfolio are an equal weighted average of the Hedged Size Anomaly Fund, Hedged Momentum Anomaly Fund, and Accrual Anomaly Fund.

significantly better value than the Hedged Momentum Anomaly Fund's return of −15.8% over this same period. More importantly, the overall Sortino Ratio, which measures excess return per unit of downside risk, is best for this diversified fund. Its Sortino Ratio (value of 4.4) is higher than those exhibited by the Hedged Size Anomaly Fund (1.3), Hedged Momentum Anomaly Fund (2.3), and the Accrual Anomaly Fund (0.9) over the same time period.[1]

7. Hedge Fund Lifecycle Checklist

If alpha is indeed cyclical, then there are two main takeaways from this chapter: 1) a multistrategy fund or multiple funds is likely needed in order to ensure the long-term viability of the hedge fund management company; 2) hedge fund companies should act in a similar manner to Pharmaceutical firms, creating a pipeline of products (i.e. hedge fund strategies) in the event that their primary product / strategy falters.

Since there are, and will continue to be, large numbers of single strategy firms, we suggest that the principals of these firms and their investors focus on answering (qualitatively and quantitatively) the following questions in order to arrive at a rough estimate of the remaining lifespan of the fund:

- Is there a logical reason why the investment approach of the fund makes sense?
- Has the number of funds following a similar investment strategy increased?
- Has the amount of capital following a similar investment strategy increased?
- Have regulations changed that may impact the performance of the strategy?
- To what extent is the alpha from this strategy generated from trading in illiquid securities?
- To what extend are the fund's returns driven by leverage?

By analyzing the path and characteristics of a fund's alpha, hedge fund principals and investors may avoid the fate of the well chronicled statistician who drowned in a river that was on average only three feet deep. In other words, average alpha is only one point of information in assessing the viability of a particular hedge fund strategy.

Hedge Fund Alpha Tear Sheet — Chapter 14

- With the average length of a hedge fund lasting only three years, it is almost axiomatic that alpha is fleeting or unstable.
- Some hedge funds have no sustainable alpha from inception and will ultimately go out of business due to the lack of an effective investment strategy.
- Most hedge funds have sound strategies but run the risk of going out of business due to the cyclical nature of the effectiveness of their strategies.
  o Cycles are driven by a number of factors including increased competition, investor psychology, and economic fundamentals.
- It is problematic to obtain the returns of actual hedge funds, due to SEC anti-advertising laws, so we analyzed the results of hedged versions of three well-known strategies — Small Firm Anomaly, Momentum Anomaly, and Accrual Anomaly.
  o In each case, we found good long-term results, but interim periods that threatened the viability of the strategy / fund.
- One way of extending the life cycle of the hedge fund management company is to diversify its overall performance through multiple funds or a single multistrategy fund.
  o This approach is likely to maximize the overall Sharpe Ratio or Sortino Ratio of the firm.
- Hedge fund companies should act in a similar manner to Pharmaceutical firms, creating a pipeline of products (i.e. hedge fund strategies) in the event that their primary product / strategy falters.

End Notes

[1] The Sortino statistic is discussed more fully in Chapter 12 on Risk Management. Sortino statistics for each of the strategies is not shown in their respective tables. The values were computed offline from data in Tables 1–4.

References

Alexander, Sidney, "Price Movements in Speculative Markets: Trends or Random Walk", *Industrial Management Review*, Vol. 2, May 1961, pp. 7–26.

Banz, Rolf, "The relationship between return and market value of common stocks", *Journal of Financial Economics*, Vol. 9, No. 1, March 1981, pp. 3–18.

Donchian, Richard, *Commodity Trend Timing* newsletter, first published in 1960 by Hayden Stone.

Francis, Jennifer, Ryan Lafond, Per Mikael Olsson, and Katherine Schipper, "The Market Pricing of Accruals Quality", *Journal of Accounting and Economics*, Vol. 29, June 2005, pp. 295–327.

Jegadeesh, Narasimhan, and Titman, Sheridan, 1993, "Returns to buying winners and selling losers: Implications for stock market efficiency", *Journal of Finance*, Vol. 48, March 1993, pp. 65–91.

Ross Sorkin, Andrew, "Running a Hedge Fund Is Harder Than It Looks on TV", *The New York Times*, August 18, 2008, pp. C1, C5.

Sloan, Richard, "Do Stock Prices Fully Reflect Information in Cash Flows and Accruals About Future Earnings?" *The Accounting Review*, Vol. 71, No. 3, July 1996, pp. 289–315.

http://mba.tuck.dartmouth.edu/pages/faculty/ken.french/

15

THE FUTURE OF HEDGE FUNDS:
SEVEN EMERGING TRENDS[1]

Mitchell D. Eichen, JD, LLM and John M. Longo, PhD, CFA

The MDE Group; Rutgers Business School & The MDE Group

1. Introduction

Hedge funds have become a global phenomenon with over 15,000 funds, managing \$2.1 trillion in assets.[2] Many observers, including Allan Greenspan, have called for a shakeout in the industry, while others, like Warren Buffett, have said fees are too high. Yet, few market analysts have offered any meaningful analysis or thoughtful insights into how this important industry may evolve. This chapter lists seven emerging trends in the hedge fund industry and discusses catalysts that may spur the realization of these trends.

Several reasons are responsible for the rapid growth of the hedge market:

- Cachet of exclusivity
- Strong relative outperformance during the 2000–2002 bear market for U.S. stocks
- Moderate historical correlation with standard equity and fixed income benchmarks
- High levels of fund manager compensation
- Fewer constraints on managers

While the hedge fund industry has grown enormously over the past several years, in our view, this still relatively young industry is about to embark upon an evolutionary phase. We believe the following factors will act as catalysts to activate this evolution in the industry:

- The current difficult investing environment
- Increased competition
- The prospect of new compliance regulations
- Increased institutional investor participation in the hedge fund asset class
- Fallout from the Bernard Madoff fraud scandal

The first point requires further expansion, while the others are more readily apparent and will be discussed in the rationale of our seven emerging trends.

2. A Difficult Investing Environment

Historically, inflation, interest rates, and taxes act as drags on the economy. The lower these elements, the more investors will pay for earnings per share on stocks, resulting in the market's higher P/E ratio. Since the start of the last great bull market in 1982, which lasted until March of 2000, inflation is 55% lower, short-term interest rates are 55% lower, capital gains tax rates are 25% lower. In contrast, the S&P 500 P/E multiple is 68% higher.

As **Figure 1** illustrates, P/E multiple expansion drove much of the stock market growth since 1982. If we assume no further multiple expansion, EPS growth consistent with its long-term historical average of 6% and a 2% return from dividends, over the long-term the stock market would be hard pressed to return in excess of 8% per annum. This anticipated return is a far cry from the routine double-digit returns we have experienced for much of the 1980s and the 1990s. Combining this muted U.S. stock market environment with a relatively flat bond yield curve that is starting from very low nominal levels, we have a recipe for muddling markets. They may not be as dim as those experienced over the

2000–2008 time period, but they are not likely to match the outstanding returns of the 1982–1999 period. Therefore, just as return expectations for the stock and bond markets must be lowered relative to their historical performance, so too must expected returns for hedge funds.

Not all hedge funds have material equity and fixed income beta exposure, but enough of the universe does, in order to crimp the returns of the overall hedge fund universe. To date, the aggregate hedge fund universe has experienced very disappointing returns for the bulk of 2008. For example, the HFRX Global Hedge Fund Index is down 19.6% from January–October 2008. In theory, since volatility was high over this limited time period, hedge fund returns should have been attractive. The global bear market of 2008 has revealed a dirty little secret of many hedge funds — they are often unhedged. With the notable exception of a few categories, such as Global Macro and Short Biased, returns have been largely negative across most hedge fund strategies in 2008. As such, we believe that the hedge fund industry must and will embark on an evolutionary path based on seven major thematic trends:

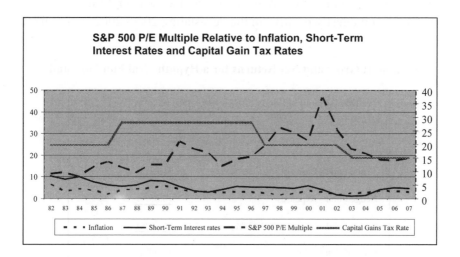

Figure 1

3. Seven Emerging Trends

Trend 1: Lower Fees

The standard hedge fund fee structure consists of a one to two percent asset based fee and a twenty percent profit participation or incentive fee. Many funds charge much higher rates and hedge fund of funds charge an additional layer of fees. For example, the financial press routinely reports that SAC Capital's Multistrategy Fund charges a 50% incentive fee (with no asset based fee) and Renaissance's Medallion Fund charges 5% of assets and a 44% incentive fee.

The typical Fund of Fund charges 1% of assets and 10% of profits. **Table 1** shows the gross return, typical fees, and net return for a hypothetical fund of fund. For example, a gross return of 10% shrinks to a net return of only 4.5% for the investor — pretax! Let's not even enter into a discussion about funds of funds of funds (3F), since the net return to the investor might be microscopic after accounting for three layers of fees. Hedge fund investors were glad to pay fees when returns were high, or even just modestly positive in the devastating 2000–2002 bear market.

Table 1: Gross and Net Returns for a Hypothetical Fund of Fund

Traditional Fund of Funds		
Hypothetical Gross Return		**10.00%**
Less:		
Hedge Fund - Base Fee	(1.00%)	
		9.00%
Hedge Fund - Expenses	(0.65%)	
		8.35%
Hedge Fund - Incentive Fee (20%)	(1.67%)	
		6.68%
Fund of Fund - Base Fee	(1.00%)	
		5.68%
Fund of Fund - Expenses	(0.65%)	
		5.03%
Fund of Fund - Incentive Fee (10%)	(0.50%)	
NET RETURN TO INVESTOR		**4.53%**

However, in a muddled market environment with more middling returns in the equity markets, these fees will simply generate too great a drag on, and become too large a percentage of, the total fund returns.

In addition, given the proliferation of new managers entering the space and intense competition that will ensue, it is inevitable that the average hedge fund fee will have to come down. Since institutional investors, who have more buying leverage and are not accustomed to paying rack retail rates, are contributing to hedge funds, it is hard to imagine that they will not demand fee concessions from many hedge funds in return for large capital commitments. While established "star" managers may be immune from this fee pressure, it is all but certain that emerging managers will have to succumb to fee compression; thereby creating a trend toward a new and lower fee structure which those who follow will have to comply with. This was the trend in the "long only" institutional money management business, which saw fees decline precipitously over the past 15 years due to increased competition and consolidation. This was also the trend in the mutual fund business where high loads and high internal fees were the norm only ten years ago. The hedge fund business will follow this trend as it matures. It is not a question of "if" but "when" and "by how much?" Trend 6 pertaining to hedge fund replication is one response that addresses the desire on the part of investors for lower fees (Trend 1), increased liquidity (Trend 2), and increased transparency (Trend 3).

Trend 2: Increased Liquidity

Some private investment funds, such as those making venture capital investments in developmental stage firms, have a clear and valid need for long-term lockup arrangements. These funds have returns that typically exhibit a "J Curve" effect where returns are negative in early years as capital is put to work, but strongly positive in later years as the investments are harvested. However, most hedge funds have a one-year lockup provision and advance notice of ninety days prior to any capital withdrawal. Yet, the underlying instruments in most hedge funds are sufficient for thirty day or less liquidity. Other than the desire to earn fees for a longer period of time, it is hard for the average hedge fund to argue that it is absolutely necessary to hold client funds beyond thirty days.

All else being equal, from the investor's perspective, one does not want to be a year away from accessing their money. The investor wants to be able to withdraw their money in the event that they see something with the fund they do not like, or simply if they need the liquidity. Since most hedge funds do not "need" to have these lock up provisions, as the industry matures, this will be one easy way for managers to distinguish themselves and accommodate client needs. Indeed, we have seen the rapid growth in hedge fund trading platforms, such as Société Générale's Lyxor, that provide attractive liquidity terms and factor level transparency (see **Trend 3** below)[3]. Thus, we see increased liquidity becoming the norm of hedge fund investing, not the exception.

Trend 3: Increased Transparency

Investing on faith was once accepted as part of the "price of admission" into the hedge fund industry. Indeed, the cachet of an exclusive or closely guarded strategy may have been a positive thing. Then came Long-Term Capital Management — the most spectacular of all hedge fund blowups, where a "dream team" of traders and academics lost nearly all of their investors' capital and threatened to send the global financial markets into a tailspin. Clearly there has been a movement towards increased "factor transparency" since Long Term Capital, that is reflecting the macro characteristics of a fund at month end such as the percentages of long and short exposure. In our view, factor transparency does not meet the due diligence requirements of most sophisticated retail or institutional investors. Investors have a right to know exactly what they own and how returns are generated. More investors will make these demands on their hedge funds managers on the face of misleading, and in some cases, fraudulent activity, news of which finds its way into the popular press on a semi-regular basis. As such, many funds, especially those newer emerging funds, will be forced to deliver full transparency if they wish to raise substantial assets.

Institutional investors often demand that their hedge fund investments be located in a managed account vehicle (that by definition offers complete transparency) run *pari passu* with the hedge fund company's traditional partnership structure. To preserve strategy confidentiality, non-disclosure agreements with "teeth" may have to be signed and enforced in return for transparency. Hedge funds managing more than $100 million must list their long holdings on a quarterly basis via Form 13F. This data may be of value for deciphering the strategy of longer-term equity oriented hedge funds. However, for active hedge fund managers the stale data may give insight into the strategy, but little comfort with respect to a fund's current holdings. In addition, the 13F data do not adequately enable investors to get a good understanding of funds trading in swaps and other complex securities. Short sellers have come under pressure in light of the dramatic drops in shares of financial companies in 2008 and have had to temporarily disclose their holdings to the SEC. In our view, manager short and derivative positions will eventually be *required* to be disclosed in Form 13F or through some new regulation. To summarize, increased transparency is already occurring, but it may never be fully complete.

Trend 4: Focus on Emerging Managers

Several studies have found that emerging hedge fund managers generate the best performance. For example, a white paper by HFR Asset Management (2005) finds that funds managed by emerging managers, defined as funds with less than a two-year track record, outperform the overall hedge fund universe by a wide margin. The paper finds that the most significant outperformance occurs over the first twelve months of operation. However, over the entire ten year length of the study, the difference between the emerging managers and the most experienced ones, averages more than six percent per annum. Furthermore, they find that new managers outperform experienced managers who start new funds.

Size may be a disadvantage to certain hedge fund strategies at high levels of assets. In their later years, some of the top performing hedge funds, such as those run by George Soros and Julian Roberston, had difficulty in replicating the spectacular performance of their earlier years. Part of the reason for diminished performance may be due to the difficulty in putting large sums of capital to work profitably. For example, a $100 million fund needs to find only $30 million of market inefficiencies to generate a 30% rate of return. Conversely, a $10 billion fund would have to uncover $3 billion of inefficiencies in order to put up the same return — a far more difficult task. Other reasons are some managers' inability to build a scalable business. This occurs either due to limitations on their strategy, or the simple fact that some hedge fund managers are great investors, but poor business people who function more efficiently in smaller environments devoid of bureaucracy.

In other cases, successful funds attract competition and suffer from key staff defections, as star analysts who have been major contributors to performance, leave to create their own funds — often running a similar strategy. A certain size is necessary to ensure critical mass and organizational viability. But there is no free lunch, as smaller fund management firms require extra due diligence and monitoring. Hence, hedge fund investors in the future will have to carefully weigh the balance between confidence in delivering alpha and operational risk.

Many hedge fund management companies are registering as investment advisors (RIA) with the SEC not because it is required by law (anymore), but because it is demanded by many of their large institutional investors. Hedge funds that are also RIAs provide many investors with a fair amount of comfort (akin to investing in a non-household "name" mutual fund) due to the increased regulatory requirements and may tip the balance in favor of those firms that are able to deliver investment performance in highly competitive markets.

Where do you find attractive emerging managers? We discussed this issue in some detail in Chapter 13 on Hedge Fund Due Diligence, but to briefly recap the findings, one can find managers that spin out of well known funds (e.g. Tiger Cubs, SAC Capital alumni), Wall Street trading desks (e.g. Goldman Sachs), or "undiscovered gems" via industry databases and word of mouth.

Trend 5: Focus on Niche Strategies and Markets

Although this trend is clearly related to the prior trend on emerging managers, there are some subtle differences. For example, the bulk of the 15,000+ hedge funds are following traditional strategies such as long / short fundamental equity, event driven, statistical arbitrage, global macro, merger arbitrage and so forth. But how many funds trade carbon credits or use esoteric forms of technical analysis and combine them with option overwrites to earn extra income and reduce risk? Probably not too many.

In Chapters 3–6 we discussed the alpha opportunities in the BRIC countries. Currently, hedge fund assets in these countries constitute a relatively small portion of the hedge fund investment universe, but they are expected to grow rapidly over the next few decades. As the BRIC financial markets mature, new regions in Eastern Europe, Asia, and Africa may take their place as "the next big thing." The key takeaway is that as more managers flock to the hedge fund space, investors should seek out those funds that have a definable niche or sustainable edge. They should run a strategy that is not easy to replicate, as this superior performance will be more likely to persist.

Trend 6: Hedge Fund Replication — To A Limited Extent

Hedge fund replication, the method of attempting to mimic the fundamental strategy utilized in a specific hedge fund category by using liquid financial instruments such as equities, ETFs, and derivatives has grown rapidly over the past several years. Some observers prefer to use the term "synthetic hedge fund" in place of "replication." Although replication is closely related to the notion of a hedge fund index fund, there are some slight differences. Tracking error, or deviation in performance from a stated benchmark, is avoided at all costs for a traditional index strategy, but may be tolerated and even encouraged for a replication strategy. In addition, index funds are generally of a passive or buy and hold nature, while many replication strategies utilize an active trading program. Replication strategies may be more akin to enhanced index strategies, since some tracking error is tolerated and perhaps desirable in the search for alpha. However, it is unlikely that the net return to a replicator will deviate wildly from the average return of its appropriate hedge fund category. In many respects, replicators are similar to quantitative hedge funds without the high fees, lack of liquidity, and limited transparency.

Major Wall Street firms, such as Goldman Sachs, Morgan Stanley, J. P. Morgan, and Merrill Lynch offer replication products to their clients. Index IQ is launching a publicly available replicator fund (ticker symbol TBD as of August, 2008) designed to track a mix of the following hedge fund categories: Emerging Markets, Event Driven, Global Macro, Equity Market Neutral, Fixed Income Arbitrage, and Long / Short Equity. Since the concept is fairly new, investment performance evidence is not widely available. A recent *Business Week* article characterized the performance as mixed, citing two replicators earning slightly below the overall hedge fund index performance and one replicator underperforming by nearly 6% in 2007.[4]

Replication strategies attempt to find the primary factors that drive the returns for a particular hedge fund category and maintain a dynamic exposure to these factor betas, or sensitivities. For example, a merger arbitrage replication strategy would buy a basket of target firms for announced deals and sell short a basket of corresponding bidder firms. Leverage may also be utilized efficiently through the use of derivatives and / or via a carry trade. The major risk in a merger arbitrage strategy is the possibility of the deal being cancelled or renegotiated at unfavorable terms to the target. The performance of the aggregate stock market as a whole has a secondary or minimal effect on merger arbitrage fund performance, unless specific collars are placed on the deal.

As noted above, the most attractive features of the replicators are reduced fees, liquidity, and transparency. Most hedge fund replicators charge a flat 1% asset based fee and generally have a lockup on the order of thirty days or less. Transparency ranges from good to complete. Much of the interest in hedge fund replication is being driven by institutional clients that are accustomed to allocating material capital to index like strategies. Their due diligence procedures often require that an investment have reasonable fees and adequate transparency before investing.

What's not to like about replicators? The main issue is that dispersion among the best and worst performers within many hedge fund categories is wide, thereby rendering replication techniques unreliable at best, and way off the mark at worst. For example, consider a typical Long / Short equity hedge fund containing fifty to one hundred positions. There are more than twelve thousand stocks in the United States and fifty thousand globally. The degrees of freedom are simply too large to create a replication model that is representative of the average return of the entire Long / Short category. Additionally, many investors view the notion of a hedge fund index type product as an oxymoron, since they allocate funds to hedge funds in order to earn high nominal and risk adjusted rates of return. By definition, replicators may not be effective in illiquid hedge fund categories, such as Distressed Debt. In our view, hedge fund replicators and index funds will play a modest, but growing role in the alternative investment universe. Active hedge fund managers should be prepared to answer in detail how their strategy offers better value than a replicator in their category offering the advantages of low fees, high liquidity, and excellent transparency.

Trend 7: Convergence Between Hedge Funds and Private Equity

Hedge funds and private equity firms have several common characteristics. For example, both industries attract among the "best and brightest" newly minted MBAs and seasoned employees due to the high compensation potential and (slightly) better working hours than traditional sell side positions. Both industries have similar fee structures with an annual asset management fee and incentive fee common to most hedge fund and private equity vehicles. However, many private equity funds eventually rebate the asset management fee and often have to achieve a hurdle rate, on the order of seven or eight percent annually, before an incentive fee can be earned.

The most obvious signs of convergence are seen in the activities of traditional private equity firms, such as Blackstone and Carlyle, which are now also in the hedge fund business. In the same vein, traditional hedge fund firms, such as D. E. Shaw and SAC Capital, are active in private equity. Investment banks, such as Goldman Sachs, with large alternative investment divisions, have been active in hedge funds and private equity for many years. Famed investors such as Edward Lampert, Carl Icahn, and T. Boone Pickens could easily be characterized as private equity investors.

The dramatic slowdown in the leveraged buyout (LBO) market from mid-2007 throughout 2008 has forced traditional private equity firms to restructure their businesses. In many instances, this restructuring takes the form of allocating capital and talent to the hedge fund industry. For example, Blackstone purchased GSO Capital Partners in 2008 to profit from the opportunities in the leveraged finance and distressed segments of the hedge fund universe.

Despite the similarities, hedge funds and private equity funds are not perfect substitutes of each other. The most obvious difference is the longer lockup period (typically seven to ten years) of most private equity funds. The hedge fund industry is arguably more scalable than the private equity industry, since the latter requires management attention to running an actual business. However, a hedge fund is more likely to go out of business due to the elusive nature of sustainable alpha. Much of the financial magic in private equity funds is due to leverage, which is usually available, but occasionally may be hard to obtain. In short, there is likely to be further convergence between hedge funds and private equity, but not complete fusion due to some inherent uniqueness in each respective industry.

4. Summary

Hedge funds play a useful role in portfolios due to diversification and lack of correlation with traditional stock and bond portfolios. The industry is still evolving and as it matures there will be a fallout of managers, compression in fees, increased liquidity, and improved transparency. Competition, a difficult market environment, increased institutional participation and added regulatory scrutiny will ensure the evolution. Emerging managers with niche strategies are best positioned to deliver superior investment performance. However, such managers are hard to find and require extra due diligence and monitoring. Many of these trends have already begun to manifest themselves. They will become part of the normal evolutionary process as the hedge fund industry continues to mature.

Hedge Fund Alpha Tear Sheet — Chapter 15

- The hedge fund market has grown rapidly over the past decade for several reasons:
  o Cachet of exclusivity
  o Strong relative outperformance during the 2000–2002 bear market for U.S. stocks
  o Moderate historical correlation with standard equity and fixed income benchmarks
  o High levels of fund manager compensation
  o Fewer constraints on managers
- In our view, over the next decade, the seven trends below will emerge in the hedge fund industry:
  o Trend 1: Lower Fees
  o Trend 2: Increased Liquidity
  o Trend 3: Increased Transparency
  o Trend 4: Focus on Emerging Managers
  o Trend 5: Focus on Niche Strategies and Markets
  o Trend 6: Hedge Fund Replication – To A Limited Extent
  o Trend 7: Convergence Between Hedge Funds and Private Equity
- The following factors may act as catalysts to drive the evolutionary changes in the hedge fund market:
  o The current difficult investing environment
  o Increased competition
  o The prospect of new compliance regulations
  o Increased institutional investor participation in the hedge fund asset class
  o Fallout from the Bernard Madoff fraud scandal
- Despite the elusiveness of sustainable alpha, hedge funds still play a useful role in portfolios due to diversification and lack of correlation with traditional stock and bond portfolios.

End Notes

[1] This chapter is a revised and updated version of Eichen and Longo (2006). Reprinted with permission by the Financial Planning Association, *Journal of Financial Planning*.

[2] PerTrac identified 15,250 single manager hedge funds managing $2.1 trillion in assets at the end of 2007.

[3] Lyxor has approximately $110 billion under management as of mid 2008.

[4] For specific return information, please see Goldstein (2007 / 2008).

References

Eichen, Mitchell and John Longo, "The Future of Hedge Funds: Five Emerging Trends," *Journal of Financial Planning*, between the issues publication, January 2006.

Goldstein, Matthew, "Hedge Fund Wannabes: Replicators Mimic the High-Risk Portfolios at a Fraction of the Cost — But Results are Mixed So Far," *Business Week*, Dec 31, 2007 / January 7, 2008, p. 76.

HFR Research, "Emerging Managers Outperformance: Alpha Opportunities From The Industry's Newest Hedge Fund Managers," 2005.

PerTrac, "Results of 2007 PerTrac Hedge Fund Database Study Show 14.5% Increase in Hedge Fund Reporting, While Fund Launches Slow," Press Release, March 4, 2008.

APPENDICES

Appendix 1

BOOKMARKS FOR HEDGE FUND MANAGERS
(as of November 2008)

1. Firm Specific Information

1.1 Advanced Valuation Techniques

a. Professor Damodaran on Valuation,
http://pages.stern.nyu.edu/~adamodar/New_Home_Page/

b. Professor William F. Sharpe's eTextbook,
http://www.stanford.edu/~wfsharpe/

1.2 Basic Valuation Techniques

a. Moneychimp,
http://www.moneychimp.com/

b. MSN Stock Research Wizard Investor,
http://moneycentral.msn.com/investor/research/wizards/SRW.asp

1.3 Earnings Whispers

a. EarningWhispers.com,
http://www.earningswhispers.com/

b. WhisperNumber.com/Market Sentiment LLC,
http://www.whispernumber.com/

1.4 Earnings History

a. Stocks at Smartmoney.com,
http://www.smartmoney.com/investing/stocks/ (enter symbol + click
Earnings)

b. Yahoo! Finance,
http://finance.yahoo.com/ (enter symbol + click Analyst Estimates)

1.5 Conference Calls

a. Bestcalls — The Internet's Conference Call Directory,
http://www.bestcalls.com

1.6 Patent Information

a. Delphion Research Intellectual Property Network,
http://www.delphion.com

b. PatentCafe's Artificial Intelligence Based Patent Search Tecnology,
http://www.patentcafe.com/

1.7 Accounting Information

a. AlphaSeeker.com,
http://www.alphaseeker.com

b. EarningsTorpedo.com,
http://webuser.bus.umich.edu/tradingfloor/earningstorpedo/default.htm

c. Earning Quality Analytics,
http://www.earningsquality.com

d. SEC and the Freedom of Information Act,
http://www.sec.gov/foia.shtml

e. Stock Diagnostics,
http://www.stockdiagnostics.com

1.8 Message Boards

a. CNBC.com, Profit from it,
http://www.cnbc.com

b. Fool.com,
http://www.fool.com

c. Raging Bull,
   http://ragingbull.quote.com/cgi-bin/static.cgi/
   a=index.txt&d=mainpages

d. Silicon Investor,
   http://www.siliconinvestor.com

e. Yahoo! Finance,
   http://finance.yahoo.com

1.9 Technical Analysis

a. ClearStation,
   http://www.clearstation.com

b. Investools Investor Education,
   http://www.investools.com

1.10 Short Selling Ideas

a. Asensio.com,
   http://www.asensio.com

b. Hackett's Special Situation Report,
   www.hacketts.com

c. PrudentBear.com,
   http://prudentbear.com

d. Sharesleuth.com,
   http://www.sharesleuth.com/

e. Stock Gumshoe
   http://www.stockgumshoe.com/

1.11 Insider Trading

a. Stocks at SmartMoney.com,
   http://www.smartmoney.com/investing/stocks/ (enter symbol + click
   Insider)

1.12 Stock Buybacks

a. Stock Buybacks (The Online Investor)
http://www.theonlineinvestor.com/buybacks/

1.13 General Company Info

a. Hoover's Online,
http://www.hoovers.com

1.14 Financial Statements

a. FreeEDGAR: Free Real-Time SEC EDGAR Filings,
http://freeedgar.com

b. SEC Filings and Forms,
http://www.sec.gov/edgar.shtml

c. SPREDGAR – Stock Market Invesment Software,
http://www.sspredgar.com

2. Industry – Sector Information

2.1 Sector Tracker

Smartmoney.com Sector Tracker,
http://www.smartmoney.com/sectortracker/

2.2 Journals – Industry Specific

a. CNET.com (Technology / Media Portal)
http://www.cnet.com

b. Nature Science Journals,
http://www.nature.com/

c. The New England Journal of Medicine,
http://content.nejm.org/

2.3 Valuation of Sectors

a. StockVal,
   http://www.stockval.com/

2.4 IPO information

a. IPO Monitor,
   http://www.ipomonitor.com/

3. Port. Mgt. – Macro Info

3.1 Sell Side Research Ratings

a. ClearStation,
   http://www.clearstation.com (Select Analyst Info from dropdown box)
b. Yahoo! Finance Stock Research Center,
   http://biz.yahoo.com/r/

3.2 Amateur Analyzes

a. ChangeWave,
   http://www.changewave.com/ (grassroots research)
b. Fool.com,
   http://www.fool.com
c. Marketocracy,
   http://www.marketocracy.com (amateur mock mutual funds)

3.3 Testing Analyst Records

a. StarMine,
   http://www.starmine.com
b. ValideaHome,
   http://www.validea.com/

3.4 After Hours Information

a. Midnight Trader,
   http://www.midnighttrader.com/

3.5 Asset Allocation

a. Financial Engines,
   https://www.financialengines.com (partly developed by William
   Sharpe)

b. SmartMoney.com Asset Allocator,
   http://www.smartmoney.com/investing/basics/?topic=asset-allocation
   (select One Asset Allocation link)

3.6 Top Manager Holdings

a. FreeEDGAR Online,
   http://www.edgar-on;one.com (Search for Form 13F)

b. FactSet Global Ownership,
   http://www.factset.com

c. IPREO Bigdough,
   http://www.bigdough.com

d. Nasdaq Real-Time Institutional Holdings-Insider Ownership
   http://www.nasdaq.com/asp/ownership.asp

3.7 Interest Rates – Fixed Income

a. BankruptcyData.com,
   http://www.bankruptcydata.com

b. Bloomberg.com,
   http://bloomberg.com/markets/rates/index.html

c. BondsOnline,
   http://www.bondsonline.com

d. ConvertBond.com,
   http://www.convertbond.com

e. SmartMoney.com Bonds,
   http://www.smartmoney/com/investingbonds

f. Yahoo! Bond Center,
   http://finance.yahoo.com/bonds

3.8 Futures Quotes

a. Futuresweb,
   http://www.futuresweb.com/

3.9 Options

a. iVolatility.com,
   http://www.ivolatility.com

b. Schaeffers Investment Research,
   http://www.schaeffersresearch.com

c. Yahoo! Options Center,
   http://biz.yahoo.com/opt/

3.10 Stock Screeners

a. B4Utrade.com,
   http://www.b4utrade.com/

b. Yahoo! Finance Stock Screener
   http://screener.finance.yahoo.com/newscreener.html

3.11 Exchange Traded Funds

a. Holders
   http://www.holdrs.com/holdrs/main/index.asp

b. NYSE Euronext,
   http://www.amex.com/

3.12 Proxy Voting / Socially Responsible Investing

a. Corporate Governance,
   http://www.corpgov.net/

b. How Domini Votes for Change
   http://www.domini.com/shareholder-advocacy/Proxy-
   Voting/index.htm

c. Proxy Voting Decisions,
   http://www.calpers-governance.org/alert/proxy/

d. RiskMetrics Group,
   http://www.riskmetrics.com

e. SocialFunds.com,
   www.socialfunds.com

3.13 Investment Columnists / Blogs

a. Forbes.com,
   http://www.forbes.com

b. Seeking Alpha,
   http://seekingalpha.com/

c. TheStreet.com,
   www.TheStreet.com

4. Performance Evaluation – Benchmark Risk

4.1 Correlation Tracker

a. State Street Global Advisors,
   http://www.ssgafunds.com/resources/correlation_tracker.html

4.2 Benchmark Components – Risk

a. MSCI Barra,
   http://www.mscibarra.com/

b. RiskGrades Measure
   http://www.riskgrades.com/

c. Risk Metrics Group
   http://www.riskmetrics.com/

d. Russell Invesments
   http://www.russell.com/

4.3 Backtesting – Historical Data

a. Financial Data Finder — Ohio State,
   http://www.cob.ohio-state.edu/fin/osudata.htm

b. St. Louis Fed: Economic Data,
   http://research.stlouisfed.org/fred2/

c. TradeGames: Powerful Technology for the SuperTrader,
   http://www.tradegames.com

d. U.S. Bureau of Labor Statistics,
   http://www.bls.gov/

4.4 Compliance – Ethics

a. U.S. Securities and Exchange Commission,
   http://www.sec.gov/

b. Securities Lawyer's Deskbook,
   http://www.law.uc.edu/CCL/index.html

5. Education

5.1 Education (Introductory)

a. Berkshire Hathaway Shareholder Letters,
   http://www.berkshirehathaway.com/letters/letters.html

b. Fool.com,
   http://www.fool.com/

c. SmartMoney.com Personal Finance,
http://www.smartmoney.com/personal-finance/

5.2 Glossary (bus — finance)

a. InvestorWords.com,
http://www.investorwords.com/

b. Campbell R. Harvey's Hypertextual Finance Glossary,
http://www.duke.edu/~charvey/Classes/wpg/glossary.htm

6. Core Finance Websites

a. Google Finance,
http://finance.google.com/finance

b. MSN Money,
http://moneycentral.msn.com/home.asp

c. SmartMoney.com,
http://www.smartmoney.com/

d. SmartMoney.com Map of the Market,
http://www.smartmoney.com/map-of-the-market/

e. Yahoo! Finance,
http://finance.yahoo.com/

7. Other Relevant Websites

a. deepVertical,
http://deepvertical.com/home/homee/460 (Negibot search engine)

b. Markit,
http://www.markit.com/

c. indexArb,
http://www.indexarb.com/

Appendix 2

HEDGE FUND MANAGER READING LIST

Achelis, Steven, *Technical Analysis from A to Z*, Probus, 1995.
Comment: A concise book on technical analysis, a topic of primary importance to active hedge fund managers. Longer-term hedge fund managers can fine-tune their entry and exit points through knowledge of this topic.

Bodie, Zvi, Kane Alex, and Allan Marcus, *Investments*, McGraw-Hill Irwin, 8th Edition, 2008.
Comment: The most popular textbook on investment in America and a good reference.

Burton, Katherine, *Hedge Hunters*, Bloomberg, 2007.
Comment: Interviews with top hedge fund managers, such as Julian Robertson, Michael Steinhardt, T. Boone Pickens, and James Chanos.

Dreman, David, *Contrarian Investment Strategies: The Next Generation*, Simon & Schuster, 1998.
Comment: One of the best books ever written on Value Investing. Dreman makes a clear case explaining why Value strategies outperform the market over time. He is primarily known as a Value Investor and Forbes columnist, but is also a hedge fund manager.

English, James, *Applied Equity Analysis*, McGraw-Hill, 1st Edition, 2001.
Comment: A good book on Fundamental Analysis from the perspective of a professional securities analyst.

Graham, Benjamin, *The Intelligent Investor*, Collins Business, Revised Edition, 2003.

Comment: Warren Buffett claims it is the best book ever written on investing. It is easier to read and a bit more practical than the Graham and Dodd classic, "Security Analysis".

Klarman, Seth, *Margin of Safety*, Harper Collins, 1991.

Comment: The only book published by the highly successful and somewhat reclusive hedge fund manager, who primarily runs a long-only hedge fund shop, Baupost Group. Discusses equity as well as distressed investing. Since the book is out of print, used copies on Amazon.com are listed at $800 and above.

Lederman, Jess and Klein, Robert, *Hedge Funds: Investment and Portfolio Strategies for the Institutional Investor*, McGraw-Hill, 1995.

Comment: Part of the inspiration for this book. Chapters are written by experts in their respective fields.

Lefevre, Edwin, *Reminiscences of a Stock Trader*, Fraser Publishing Company, 1990.

Comment: This fictional work is largely based on the life and times of Jesse Livermore, one of the best traders of all time. It is widely believed that Livermore actually wrote the book, with assistance from Lefevre.

Link, Marcel, *High Probability Trading*, McGraw-Hill, 1st Edition, 2003.

Comment: Makes a strong case for swinging only at good pitches, or when the trade is strongly in your favor.

Lowenstein, Roger, *Buffett: The Making of American Capitalist*, Broadway Books, 1996.

Comment: Perhaps the best of the many books ever written on Warren Buffett, the greatest investor ever.

Lowenstein, Roger, *When Genius Failed*, Fourth Estate, 2002.

Comment: Riveting story of the rise and fall of the "dream team" hedge fund, Long Term Capital Management.

Lynch, Peter and Rothchild, John, *One Up On Wall Street — How To Use What You Already Know To Make Money In The Market*, Penguin Publishing, 1989.

Comment: Provides the classic advice of "investing in what you know" in order to make money in the stock market.

Penman, Stephen, *Financial Statement Analysis and Security Valuation*, McGraw Hill Irwin, 2nd Edition, 2004.

Comment: High quality textbook that combines financial statement analysis, corporate strategy, and valuation. One of the few textbooks that emphasizes an understanding of the business model of the firm.

Reverre, Stephane, *The Complete Arbitrage Deskbook*, McGraw-Hill, 1st Edition, 2001.

Comment: A good reference for many types of arbitrage trades that are core elements of most hedge fund strategies.

Rubenstein, Mark, *A History of the Theory of Investments*, Wiley, 2006.

Comment: A thoroughly researched history of the financial theories with valuable commentary.

Shefrin, Hersh, *Beyond Greed and Fear: Finance and the Psychology of Investing*, Oxford University Press, 2000.

Comment: Contains a nice discussion of psychological biases and their implications for investors. Hedge fund managers should self-diagnose and correct their biases, if possible.

Schilit, Howard, *Financial Shenanigans*, McGraw-Hill, 2nd Edition, 2002.

Comment: Provides some good insight for fundamental oriented hedge fund managers on impending earnings problems for companies.

Schwager, Jack, *Market Wizards*, Marketplace Books, Original Classic Edition, 2006.

Comment: One of the first books to conduct interviews with top hedge fund managers, such as Paul Tudor Jones, Richard Dennis, and Michael Steinhardt. It remains an inspirational work for new hedge fund managers and analysts.

Soros, George, *The Alchemy of Finance: Reading the Mind of the Market*, Wiley, 1994.

Comment: Soros' original book that explains his Reflexivity Theory. Reflexivity argues prices affect fundamentals through a feedback loop.

Soros, George, (with Krisztina Koenen and Bryon Wien), *Soros on Soros: Staying Ahead of the Curve*, Wiley, 1st Edition, 1995.

Comment: The book is conducted in an interview format and is easier to understand than "The Alchemy of Finance".

Staley, Kathryn, *The Art of Short Selling*, Wiley, 1996.

Comment: One of the few good books that exists on short selling. The book takes a fundamental, not technical, approach to finding shorts.

Stefanini, Filippo, *Investment Strategies of Hedge Funds*, John Wiley & Sons, 2006.

Comment: Does an excellent job introducing the core strategies of hedge fund managers.

Taleb, Nassim Nicholas, *The Black Swan: The Impact of the Highly Improbable*, Random House, 2007.

Comment: An informative discussion of the limits of effective risk management and forecasting. Taleb's points are illustrated using many insightful examples throughout history.

Tjia, John, *Financial Modeling,* McGraw-Hill, 1st Edition, 2003.

Comment: One of the few good books that exists on Financial Modeling, a skill that links historical and pro-forma financial statements in an integrated manner.

Appendix 3

SAMPLE MANAGER BACKGROUND REPORT

Below is an *abridged* sample background check from CheckFundManager.com. The complete report is approximately 34 pages.

□ **CheckFundManager.com**
Check Fund Manager LLC
365 Willard Ave #2C
Newington, CT 06111
Phone: +1 888.523.4483 x103
International: +1 860.666.9595 x103

November 24, 2008

....

Dear Sir/Madam,

As per your request we have conducted an investigative due diligence background check on the following individual and companies:

BRIAN N. JOHNSON, CFA

(This is a fictitious person, but the records found are derived from real cases on people we have researched)

JOHNSON INVESTMENTS, INC., New York,
NY MOONBRIGHT CAPITAL LTD, London

We performed the investigation on Mr. Johnson and the companies and funds with which he is associated. Utilizing the information you originally provided us about Brian N. Johnson, our research shows that he has lived in the following cities:

New York, London, Pennsylvania, California, and Ohio

We also researched his UK records, and that of his London based company, Moonbright Capital, Limited. The results of our investigation using of both public and non-public records is documented in the attached report. We hope you will find the information invaluable in your due diligence efforts and appreciate your consideration.

If you have any questions about this report, please contact me, or one of our fraud examiners for further clarification.

Sincerely,

Guy Simonian, BS, MS, IEEE, WAD
Check Fund Manager LLC
CheckFundManager.com

BRIAN N. JOHNSON

JOHNSON INVESTMENTS, INC., New York,
NY MOONBRIGHT CAPITAL LTD, London

Information provided in the *Comprehensive* report:

- Executive Overview
- Regulatory and Litigation Summary
- Biographies
- CheckFundManager.com "Watch List" Notification
- Media & Internet Summaries
- Personal Data Summary
- Investment Publications research
- Extensive Internet, Media, and news publications search
- State & Federal Regulatory Agency references network
- SEC & NASD Arbitration & Disciplinary action archives
- Stock Exchange Disciplinary Decisions
- Multiple Educational Verifications
- Employment Records Verifications
- Other Professional Credentials verification
- Corporate Affiliations research
- Business filings research
- SEC Cases & Proceedings
- SEC National Non-Public documents research
- NASD Disclosure Events research
- Investment Advisor registrations research
- U.S. Federal Denied Persons list research
- NFA/CFTC & NASD Regulatory Registrations
- Multiple Property records research
- Multiple State Criminal records
- Multiple State Dept. of Corrections Incarceration, Parole, and Probation
- Multiple County Level Criminal records research
- National Bankruptcies, Liens, and Judgments

- Federal Criminal, Civil, Appellate, Bankruptcy (subject and company)
- All 50 States Civil court records research (subject & company/fund names)
- Name, Social Security Number Validation, Relatives and Address history
- United Kingdom* directorships, Ltd company essentials financial report, UK regulatory, UK media, insolvencies, receiverships, liquidations, and county court judgment research

---

Executive Summary

Overview

Brian N. Johnson, 45, born in Ohio, is married to Joan Johnson. The Johnsons own property on E 77th Street in Manhattan that they purchased in 1999 for $5,000,985 currently valued at $8,361,000. The property was refinanced in 2002 for $7,000,000. Brian and Joan Johnson also own property in London, purchased in 1999. Brian Johnson is best known for managing Johnson Capital Management, but we also found affiliations with the Classica Group, and Moonbright Capital. We verified his educational credentials and business affiliations as reported. Mr. Johnson is a registered CPA and CFA Charter holder. We also found a directorship record and residential information in London, which caused us to examine the UK records on Mr. Johnson, and on his UK concern called Moonbright Capital.

We found civil actions against Mr. Johnson in both local and federal court, and a 4-week suspension of trading privileges enforced by the Commodity Futures Trading Commission. Also found was a weapons charge from 1993 that was dismissed, and a 1996 $36,000 tax lien by the state of California.

Also of note is that one of the funds he managed, Moonbright Capital, was charged in Illinois federal court with violations of the SEC Act of 1934. Moonbright later brought a slander suit against Mr. Johnson and his advisory company. Moonbright was liquidated in 2000 per an intervention order and action taken by the UK Securities and Futures Authority.

Regulatory and Litigation Summary

Company:

Moonbright Capital was charged with violations of the SEC Act in Illinois Federal court in a 2001 case brought by PRIME MARKETS GROUP, LLC. The demand was for $99,000,000.

No suits or disclosures were found against Johnson Capital Management, or Johnson Investments, however Moonbright Capital brought a Federal slander suit in 1999 against Johnson Institutional Investment Advisors in 1999 demanding $10,000,000. Mr. Johnson was also named in the suit.

In the UK, the Securities and Futures Authority said it has issued an intervention order against Moonbright Capital due to its failure to maintain adequate capital requirements. The SFA said it does not believe there is a reasonable prospect of Moonbright Capital rectifying its capital deficiency in the immediate future. The intervention requires it to cease all investment business and to close or transfer all positions, it said. According to SFA calculations, the company has a capital deficiency of £633,000.

The UK research also shows an unsatisfied county Court Judgment for £2,492 from 1999 for Moonbright Capital. Subsequent to that On 14/04/2000 a Meeting of Creditors was held at 24 Bevis Marks, London, EC3A 7NR and it was decided that the company be wound up (Dissolved).

Personal:

The Commodity Futures Trading Commission (CFTC) filing against him was for a "wash sale" for which he was fined $1500.00. He was also denied trading privileges for 4 weeks. He was found "reporting non bona-fide prices," being involved in "non-competitive trading," and dealing in "wash sales, cross trading, and fictitious sales."

Mr. Johnson is the defendant in a Federal lawsuit by Moonbright Capital for slander. This trial took place in the U.S. Northern California District Court from 1999-2001 (Case # 99-CV-9999). Johnson Institutional Investment Advisors was also named in the suit.

Brian Johnson was the also defendant in a NY civil trial in 1996. The plaintiff was United Protective Alar, who was suing for $3,355. The trial was held in the Manhattan Civil Court (Case # 37896).

A California state tax lien of $36,808 was issued against Brian Johnson in 1996.

Brian N. Johnson was charged with possession of a concealed weapon and possessing an illegal weapon during 1993 in Colorado. The case was dismissed in 1996 (Case # 1993CR000383)

Research performed	Result of Research
Social Security Number	SSN Found and verified
DOB, Marital Status, Address History	25 Year History documented
Property Records	Both US & UK records found
Educational Verification	NYU BS 1983 & Wharton MBA 1985 verified
CFA Charterholder	In good standing since 1994
Other Professional Certifications	NY CPA licensed in 1989
Past Employment Verifications	Two Employers Verified
Bankruptcy, liens and judgments	**1 CA Tax lien from 1996 found**
All 50 State Level Civil records	**1 record found from 1996**
Multiple County level criminal records	No records found
Multiple State level criminal records	**1 weapons charge from 1993, dismissed**
Federal Civil, Appellate & Criminal records	**2 civil cases found**
Internet & Media Research	**Numerous Articles including negative articles found**
Investment Advisor records	**1 registration record found**

SEC NASD records	No records found
SEC Confidential Contacts	No adverse records found beyond action already known
State/Local Regulatory Agency References	No adverse records found beyond action already known
National Futures Association	**1 action found from 1993**
NFA & NASD Arbitration & Disciplinary Action Archives	**CFTC fine & sanction from 1993**
OFAC Federal Denied Persons	No record found
UK Securities & Futures Association	**1 action found from 1999**
UK Director Disqualifications	No records found
UK Land Registry Records	**1 Registered Charge (Mortgage) found**
UK Civil Courts	**1 Judgment Found from 1999 (company)**
UK Liquidations	**Record of Liquidation found from 2000 (company)**
UK Receiverships	**Record of Receivership found from 2000 (company)**

Internet and Media Summary

Mr. Johnson founded Johnson's Institutional Research in 1993 and currently serves as the president. Before that he was a staff writer for FORBES magazine and an analyst at Intrinsic Value Management (where he dealt with biotechnology and pharmaceuticals). He is a graduate of the Wharton Business School. And he has been doing independent research on the medical industry since 1991.

Johnson's Institutional Research works to provide medical technology assessments of FDA Panel meetings, disclosure of clinical data, and industry news. Johnson's Research is comprised of a team of analysts, including Ph.D.s and M.D.s, along with over 600 contacts at academic centers, clinics, and healthcare companies.

Marring his record however is a great deal of negative press from the Federal slander suit brought by Moonbright Capital in 1999.

Research Summaries

US Manager Research Summary

On Brian Ned Johnson, we first examined our database of manager research to obtain the manager's date of birth, residential addresses, and SSN (not disclosed), or we utilized our People Search expertise to identify the same. We then compared past and current biographies and looked for any inconsistencies. The personal information found was then used to verify educational references. Corporate registration records maintained by the secretary of the state offices were examined to identify other possible corporate affiliations. In addition to incorporation records, regulatory reports were examined to find other company affiliations. A 15 year address history was then researched, any alias names were identified, possible spouses and property found. Regulatory research was conducted and we examined these records for any sanctions, suspensions or disciplinary actions. National liens, judgments, and bankruptcy files were researched. Extensive media research was conducted including an alternative investment community information services resource, then general Internet research and a search of several national and international news and business publications. SEC public documents were examined. The US Department of Commerce Denied Persons List was researched as well. A compilation of criminal histories from several states going back to the 1970's in some cases was examined for any offenses. Local jurisdictional county felony and misdemeanor records going back at least 7 years were also evaluated. Finally we conducted extensive federal civil, criminal, appellate, and state and local lawsuits, bankruptcies, judgments, and UCC filings research.

US Company Research Summary

First we verified the corporate identity of Johnson Investments and Johnson Capital Management through the office of the secretary of the state corporate filings and the various names under which they may be doing business. We then identified any securities registrations found for the firm, and examined these records for any sanctions, suspensions or disciplinary actions. We conducted extensive federal civil, criminal, appellate, and state and local lawsuits, bankruptcies, judgments, and UCC filings research on the firm. SEC public as well as unpublished non-public documents were examined. We also contacted one or more of our contacts inside each state regulatory offices to look for any irregularities in their internal files.

UK Manager Research Summary

On Brian N. Johnson, we first examined our database of manager research to obtain the manager's date of birth, residential addresses, and SSN where applicable (not disclosed), or we utilized our PeopleSearch expertise to identify the same. For UK based managers, we examined Directorship Directories and conducted a directorship trace to find past and present company affiliations. We examined records from the Register of Companies and Register of Disqualified Directors to find any record of the manager's name, address, length of disqualification status, and reason for disqualification. We examined regulatory filings through the Financial Services Authority reports for any company affiliations and looked for any disciplinary actions. We then looked in the UK for any Civil Court filings, Judgments, Bankruptcies, or Insolvencies on the manager. We then compared past and current biographies and looked for any inconsistencies. For the UK based managers, regulatory research was conducted and we examined these records for any sanctions, suspensions or disciplinary actions. SEC public documents were examined and the US Department of Commerce Denied Persons List was researched as well. Extensive media research was conducted including an alternative investment community information services resource, then general Internet research and a search of several national and international news and business publications.

UK Company Research Summary

First we verified the corporate identity of Moonbright Capital through financial registrations in the UK, and the various names under which they may be doing business. We then identified any securities registrations found for the firm through the Financial Services Authority, and examined these records for any sanctions, suspensions or disciplinary actions. SEC published documents were also examined. Finally we ran a Company Essentials Report on the firm, which shows the Company Identification, Company Capitalisation/Shareholders, Charges/Debentures Registered, Gazette or Detrimental Information, and County Court Judgments. It also list the Company Officers registered for the firm. We then examined Receivership records in the UK going back 7 years for any record of insolvency. For a US based firm, we conducted extensive federal civil, criminal, appellate, and state and local lawsuits, bankruptcies, judgments, and UCC filings research on the firm.

INDEX